The Bloody South Carolina
Election of 1876

ALSO BY JERRY L. WEST

The Reconstruction Ku Klux Klan in York County, South Carolina, 1865–1877 (2002; paperback 2010)

The Bloody South Carolina Election of 1876

Wade Hampton III, the Red Shirt Campaign for Governor and the End of Reconstruction

Jerry L. West

McFarland & Company, Inc., Publishers
Jefferson, North Carolina, and London

LIBRARY OF CONGRESS CATALOGUING-IN-PUBLICATION DATA

West, Jerry Lee.
　　The bloody South Carolina election of 1876 : Wade Hampton III, the red shirt campaign for governor and the end of reconstruction / Jerry L. West.
　　　　p.　　cm.
　　Includes bibliographical references and index.

　　ISBN 978-0-7864-4889-0

　　1. South Carolina — Politics and government —1865–1950.
2. Governors — South Carolina — Election — History —19th century.
3. Hampton, Wade, 1818–1902.　4. Chamberlain, Daniel Henry, 1835–1907.　5. Reconstruction (U.S. history, 1865–1877) — South Carolina.　I. Title.
F274.W46　2011
975.7'04 — dc22　　　　　　　　　　　　　　　　　　2010037136

British Library cataloguing data are available

© 2011 Jerry L. West. All rights reserved

No part of this book may be reproduced or transmitted in any form or by any means, electronic or mechanical, including photocopying or recording, or by any information storage and retrieval system, without permission in writing from the publisher.

Front cover: Wade Hampton III (courtesy of South Caroliniana Library, University of South Carolina, Columbia); background Congress Street, Yorkville, ca. 1905 (courtesy Culture & Heritage Museums); border Library of Congress

Manufactured in the United States of America

McFarland & Company, Inc., Publishers
　Box 611, Jefferson, North Carolina 28640
　　www.mcfarlandpub.com

Table of Contents

Preface   1
Introduction   3

One. Redemption's Nativity   11
Two. Satan's Rule   22
Three. The Redeemer Cometh   55
Four. All the Redeemer's Men   87
Five. Casting Out Satan   110
Six. Redeemed!   133

Epilogue   167
Appendix 1. The Making of South Carolina   175
Appendix 2. Asbury Coward   178
Appendix 3. Lewis Mason Grist   182
Appendix 4. General Evader McIver Law   184
Appendix 5. Isaac Donnom Witherspoon, Jr.   186
Appendix 6. Diary of Dr. James Rufus Bratton   189
Notes   197
Bibliography   207
Index   209

Preface

> The very fact that our state is passing through so terrible ordeal as at present, should cause her sons to cling more closely to her.
> — Wade Hampton III

When my work on *The Reconstruction Ku Klux Klan in York County, South Carolina* was published in 2002 (McFarland) I had already begun to see the need of a subsequent work. The story of the Klan in York County is but a half-told tale, and to end there would be like leaving Snow White asleep without the prince's kiss. South Carolina's prince is found in Wade Hampton and the kiss of life is in his Red Shirts. It was South Carolina's 1876 gubernatorial race that brought aristocrat Wade Hampton to the forefront along with his political machinery, commonly known as the Red Shirts.

Since a number of excellent books on Hampton's 1876 campaign and how he overthrew Radical Republican rule in South Carolina are available for research, I had originally hoped to focus mainly on York County as I had done with the Ku Klux Klan. Early in my research, however, I ran into a problem. When the state's political morass of 1876 centered on activities in Columbia, the York County Red Shirts were not on the scene. While thousands of angry Red Shirts were filling the streets of Columbia, ready to participate in a second bloody civil war, York County men were home by a warm hearth. When Hampton made his plea for a peaceful transition and asked the companies of Red Shirts still at home to "stay put" until he called for them, the York County men demonstrated an unusual willingness to comply and waited anxiously at home. Yet, I was determined to tell the story of York County's role in Hampton's campaign and decided to give a brief overview of the campaign with periodic glimpses of York County.

The Reconstruction Era (1865–1876) is a fascinating, but a very complex period in United States history. Those years were a defining period, and an important milestone in the development of the South. Reconstruction was so revolutionary that it demanded seven new amendments to the United States Constitution. Today, each and every American enjoys the rewards purchased through the hardships and disappointments of those who struggled through that era.

The era is complicated because so much was happening on the national, state, and county levels, all hinging on a struggle for supremacy between Conservative Democrats and Radicals of the Republican Party. The heart of the struggle was political, but its body was racial. For that reason I ask the readers to approach this work with as little prejudice as possible. As with any age, few living during the era of Reconstruction were able to rise above their times and places; yet, many men of both races did good and remarkable things for their times.

Without a doubt the reader will see a great similarity between the presidential elections of 1876 and 2000. Both held the nation in suspense through recount after recount. Both went through a legal process that was filled with suspicion and anger, with Washington giving the verdict on who — Democrat or Republican — would take the White House. Just as Florida was the key to the election of George W. Bush, three states — South Carolina, Florida and Mississippi — decided the election of Rutherford B. Hayes.

Introduction

> If there ever was an hour when the spirit of the Puritan, the spirit of the undying, unconquerable enmity and defiance to wrong ought to animate their sons, it is this hour, here, in South Carolina. The civilization of the Puritan and the Cavalier, of the Roundhead and Huguenot, is in peril. Courage, Determination, Union, Victory, must be our watchwords. The grim Puritans never quailed under threat or blow. Let their sons now imitate their example![1]

With these words, South Carolina's Republican governor, Daniel Henry Chamberlain, declined an invitation to speak before the New England Society in Charleston in 1875. The governor chose to use words that were part of a curious myth that had been magically spun and continues to distort the ethnic roots of the South. Although a high proportion of Southerners descended from Irish, Scots-Irish, German, Welsh and Scots settlers, the South adopted the romantic idea of a new England filled with lords and ladies. The antebellum South portrayed as a "cavalier society" is a myth springing from the fact that a few English settlers came first to America's shores. Jefferson Davis, president of the Confederacy, voiced this myth shortly after his inauguration address when he said Northern Roundheads were "bred in the bogs and fens of Ireland and northern England" and could never dominate the Southern people, who were "descendants of the bold and chivalrous cavaliers of old."

Through the years, the idea of Cavaliers and Roundheads made the transition to describe the continuing conflicts between the industrial North and the pastoral South. The antebellum South was well steeped in Walter Scott's *Ivanhoe* and other historical novels that romanticized old England and extolled the virtues of manhood and valor. By the time of the Civil War, Southerners were clinging to these virtues as to life itself— overdosed on the steroids of chivalry and honor. The idea of a romantic war between the Roundheads and the Cavaliers easily transferred to the Civil War and on into the Reconstruction Era with the appearance of the Ku Klux Klan and the 1876 campaign of Wade Hampton. That period between 1860 and 1876 was the South's final opportunity to display true cavaliered romance. The campaign of 1876 marked the end with thunderous applause from South Carolina.

When Governor Chamberlain declined to speak at the annual meeting of the New England Society in 1875, Radical Republicans had a stranglehold on the state that had begun ten years earlier. The state coffers were empty, corruption was rampant and justice was lost. It seemed the basic guarantees of the U.S. Declaration of Independence — "that they are endowed by their Creator with certain unalienable Rights, that among these are Life, Liberty and the pursuit of Happiness" — had begun to be empty words to white Democrats in South Carolina.

At the close of the Civil War everyone, both North and South, was tired of war and looking forward to a peaceful restoration of the Union. This was the dream of President Lincoln and his successor, Andrew Johnson, but no one had counted on the revenge some Republican congressmen were ready to wreak on the South. When the South seceded from the Union, it left the Republicans with the majority in Congress. The Republican Party had two factions, Conservatives, who were in the minority, and Radicals, who held the majority. The Radicals

Wade Hampton III (courtesy of South Caroliniana Library, University of South Carolina, Columbia).

were hell-bent for leather to punish the South and there was little to nothing that the Northern Democrats and the Conservative Republicans could do about it.

Sick of President Johnson's compassionate approach to the South, the Radicals in Congress overrode the president's veto and passed bills that placed a heavy yoke of bondage on the shoulders of the South. By 1875 a good number of southern states had regained control of their governments, beginning with Virginia in 1869. By the election of 1876, eight of the eleven southern states had thrown off the yoke of radical rule, but three — South Carolina, Florida and Louisiana — were still in the hands of Republicans. Two states, South Carolina and Louisiana, were still occupied by federal troops, and Republicans were desperately holding on to the last southern state governments, using any method that was handy.

Most whites were disenfranchised and heads of state government were appointed by Congress, which opened the doors to graft and corruption. It was not until the fall election of 1868 that South Carolina Democrats faced the fact that the overthrow of the Republicans was going to be slow, arduous work. That year Republicans made a clean sweep of the election ballots and ousted Democrats. Federal troops were garrisoned in a number of piedmont counties and Columbia. Though the people saw the handwriting on the wall in 1868, it is doubtful they believed it would take eight more years to break the Radical stranglehold.

The struggle for freedom from a corrupt government in South Carolina absorbed lives and fortunes. Romantically speaking, the drama, moving from disenfranchisement to "redemption," was easily explained by prevailing Christian thought as a struggle between good and evil. Church folk might have likened the process to a sinner's being delivered from the clutches of Satan and hell. Radical Republicans were the Satan of the South, Reconstruction was their hell, and Wade Hampton would be their savior.

It was particularly odious to white South Carolinians that their state government was reported to be more corrupt than any in the South. Those years of corrupt Republican rule in South Carolina might have defeated a lesser people, but those white Democrats remained undaunted in spite of disenfranchisement, martial law, military occupation, defeat at the election boxes, and political humiliation. Their determination and drive came from the resolution to regain political power and restore white supremacy in South Carolina — but the question was, how?

The road from political bondage to redemption was a long hard one for South Carolinians. Every level of society was faced with complex decisions—decisions that involved compromise, interpretation and adaptation, all filled with mistrust, disappointments and hatred. Emancipation demanded a redefinition of relationships; but there were two ideologies that stood in the way—white Democrats who refused to accept blacks as free and equal citizens, and Radical Republicans who had a driving determination to rule at the expense of freedmen. Though the South was defeated on the battlefields, it would not surrender to a punitive Reconstruction, nor would the people be convinced to surrender their racial attitudes and constitutional principals.

To fight fire with fire, the Ku Klux Klan appeared in the spring of 1868 and continued its nefarious work through 1872 until Federal troops were quartered in nine counties. Still, the people of South Carolina continued to look for the light at the end of the tunnel—self-rule by the Democratic Party. They needed a plan and a leader and a political machine that could not be stopped. Party leaders now knew that it would take more than words and threats to restore the old aristocracy and send every Republican and Scalawag packing. The plan would come later, but first appeared the most tangible and visible emblem of the campaign—the red shirt.

There are a number of ideas on the origin of the Red Shirts. Some claim they were derived from Garibaldi's Red Shirts of 1860 in Italy. Others debunk the Garibaldi theory as pure Southern romanticism. Without a doubt Garibaldi Red Shirts were widely known. At one time Governor Francis W. Parker referred to Garibaldi in justifying South Carolina's secession against tyranny, and during the war many in Hampton's Legion wore red shirts as part of their uniform while women wore Garibaldi hats.[2] Most experts, however, give credit for the origin of the red shirt to Indiana's United States senator, Oliver P. Morton, who was speaking in the Senate and accused the South of cruelty. He waved a blood-soaked shirt of a black victim before the senators in an effort to rally the North behind Reconstruction.[3] The bloody shirt was also waved during the presidential campaign of Ulysses S. Grant against Democrat Horatio Seymour in 1868, at which time Seymour and the Democrat Party were accused of treason for not supporting Reconstruction. Gradually the phrase "waving the bloody shirt" became political slang for grandstanding.

There are as many ideas about when the red shirts appeared as there are about their origin. One source claims they were seen in August 1876 when Charleston celebrated Hampton's nomination.⁴ The more likely account places their appearance a month later, in September, when the men charged for their activities in the Hamburg Riot appeared at their arraignment. Some days earlier, these men had met on the Kalmal Heights between Aiken and Graniteville to discuss their appearance in court. At that time George D. Tillman and A.P. Butler suggested the members of the Sweetwater Sabre Club wear red-stained shirts in derision of Morton's bloody shirts. The women of Aiken, led by Miss Ada Chafee, made long homespun shirts and dyed them in Venetian red and juice from pokeberries. The afternoon before the bail hearing the Sweetwater Sabre Club, in their new red shirts, paraded through the streets of Aiken to the horror of the black population.⁵

Clark Starnes, a citizen of Rock Hill, recalled the formation of the Red Shirts in York County shortly after the nomination of Wade Hampton, and put into words what was true across the state: "We went to work with all the energy we had in our bodies. We formed 'Red Shirt' companies all over the State and attended all the big meetings in a body. We rode almost day and night in that campaign and yelled for Wade Hampton until our throats were sore. We never let up till election time. That day we put in all the tickets we could fold conveniently."⁶

In a letter to the *Yorkville* (SC) *Enquirer*, printed in the fall of 1911, James A. Hogue of Hickory Grove called himself the "Father of the Red Shirts of York County." He claimed that shortly after Hampton's nomination in August, he and L.L. Smith had a conversation agreeing that if "every good citizen would put on a red shirt and go down to Yorkville on Hampton Day, we could redeem York County from radical misrule and oppression." This conversation, he said, took place near the first of September. So inspired was he by the idea that he said he immediately began to promote it with every man he met, "Democrat or Radical." According to Hogue, his work was so fruitful that on the morning of 13 October, 210 mounted Red Shirts under the command of Colonel Andrew Jackson assembled at John Watson's store in Kings Mountain Township. Then Hogue writes an account that is questionable: "These were the first and only mounted Red Shirts that were in Yorkville on October 13, 1876, and when the marshal of the day asked Gen. Hampton about the arrangement of the procession, Gen. Hampton told him 'to put those Red Shirt fellows in front.' We were put in front and we remained there all day." However, the newspaper account of the parade in Yorkville says nothing of a mounted company leading the parade but of Hampton and Coward leading the column of Red Shirts. Yet, Hogue said there were plenty of western York County men who would vouch for his account.[7]

The Red Shirts of the 1876 Democratic campaign was a colorful grassroots movement that included whites, blacks, rednecks and white-collar gentlemen, as well as many veterans of the Gray and their sons. Describing a typical rally held at Williamston in Anderson County, one up-country newspaper reported that "twenty odd clubs were represented. Blue jackets, red jackets, gray jackets, green jackets, and some without jackets."[8] Though there was a change of garb, the heart remained the same, as violence always lurked just below the surface; when intimidation failed, strong-arm tactics were not far behind.

William Watts Ball, in his *The State That Forgot*, examined the social and violent origins of the Red Shirts and concluded the organization had evolved from three types of "rough, desperate young men." The first were "well disposed men under thirty [who] chafed from a sense of having been cheated by being born a little too late for the war, they wanted to show their mettle." The second were well-born men who were "without fear at any time, when drinking they were dangerous to whites as well as blacks." The third consisted of "dull brute[s] who killed Negroes and shot one on the roadside to slake his blood thirst."[9] These same words might have been used earlier to describe the Ku Klux Klan.

Wade Hampton III was well known by South Carolina planters and yeoman farmers, having taken an interest in and participated in antebellum politics. After the Civil War, he resumed his interest in politics but faded from the scene, spending much of his time on his Mississippi plantation and his South Carolina mountain home near present-day Cashiers — his time had not yet come. Whenever a discussion on Wade Hampton occurs among historians, there are a lot of mixed feelings exhibited. There are those who think he could have done no wrong; on the opposite end are those who would say he was a true politician who would say and do anything to promote himself.

Whatever may be said of Hampton, we must admit he loved South Carolina and wanted its government redeemed from radical rule. He may not have been as pristine in his political dealings as we would wish, and

Introduction

he certainly may be accused of pushing policies that helped him to regain his fortune; still he demonstrated a genuine love for his home state and wanted to see it prosper and take its place in the overall scheme of things. In spite of his inconsistencies, Hampton was — and remains — South Carolina's hero and darling redeemer. Though the present generation knows little of Wade Hampton III or what he did for South Carolina, the number of streets and roads across the state named for the conquering hero testifies to the love and admiration for him instilled into the hearts of the people. During and after Reconstruction, no other man was so well respected and no other had the near-magical quality of being able to calm the hearts of malcontents. Over and over he led the state away from the brink of bloodshed and civil war when others were urging violent overthrow.

Today, 140 years after Hampton defeated Radical oppressors and restored the state to full statehood, we are left to read the historical record apart from the emotions of the times. Separate from ill will that motivated the radical controlled Congress to pass the punitive bills of the 1860s, one may wonder about the hullabaloo over Reconstruction. While the overt aim of the Reconstruction Acts was to equalize society and attempt to give "makeup time" to the black population, the covert design was to control the black vote and the federal government and to remove real power from the states.

One must admire the brilliance of each political party and especially that of Wade Hampton, who sought to forge a New South against the wishes of many of his constituents. Beginning with South Carolina's redemption from Radical rule in 1877, the mettle of a New South was forged in the heat of determination and hammered out on the anvils of initiative and ability. The aftermath of the Civil War — generally known as the Reconstruction Era — is now seen as a minor pothole in the road to the New South — a bump in history mainly lost between the saber and smoke of the war and the nation's booming industrialization and expansion.

Chapter One

Redemption's Nativity

Wade Hampton III, South Carolina's "redeemer and worshipful son," was born in Charleston on 28 March 1818, the eldest son of Wade II and Ann Hampton. Though he has been dead for more than one hundred years, Wade III stands comfortably among the greatest men in South Carolina history, and until recent times he resided in the memories of the people. However, most of today's generation travel streets and avenues across the state named Hampton without an inkling of how and why they got that name, but at one time it was not so.

To understand who Wade Hampton III was we must begin the Hampton genealogy with Anthony Hampton, Hampton's great-grandfather. Anthony and his wife, Elizabeth, lived on the Dan River in North Carolina from 1754 to about 1773, when they and their four sons — Preston, Wade, Edward and John — moved to South Carolina and settled in present day Laurens County. With them came Anthony's daughter and her husband, Richard Harrison. On the Carolina frontier the Hamptons settled in a community, enlarged their families and made a living as surveyors and by trading with settlers and Indians.

During an Indian uprising in 1776 instigated by the British, Preston Hampton was killed while serving in the militia. About fifteen days later, on June 30, the Cherokees raided the Hampton settlement and murdered Anthony and Elizabeth and the infant son of Elizabeth Harrison and two children of Preston Hampton.[1] Twenty-four-year-old Wade and his brothers, Edward, Henry and Richard, were away from home when the raid took place, and they escaped slaughter. After the massacre Richard Harrison moved to Cross Keys (Union County) and opened a store at the intersection of the Charleston and Augusta roads with his brother-in-law Wade I. The partnership lasted only about a year.[2]

General Wade Hampton I, son of Anthony Hampton, was past thirty when the Revolutionary War ended. He married a widow, Martha Epps, but within a very short time she died. In 1786 he married Harriet Flud and laid out a large plantation outside Columbia, the newly established capital of South Carolina. By 1790 he had substantially increased his holdings and in another four years he was a wealthy planter with eighty-six slaves. Wade I was one of the first men in the up-country to make his fortune from cotton. In 1799 he earned $75,000 ($920,000 in today's currency) and by 1810 was receiving a return of $150,000 ($1,840,000) from his cotton acreage.

This wilderness-born man created a large library, supported Trinity Episcopal Church, and was an endower and trustee of the newly created South Carolina College. He raised fine racehorses that won every first prize at the 1800 prestigious Charleston Jockey Club. He served in Congress two years. In 1801, following the death of Harriet, he took his third wife, Mary Cantey. He reentered the army as a peacetime officer and in 1809 received a brigadier general's commission and served in the War of 1812.[3] When he died in 1835, he was one of the wealthiest men in the south.[4]

His son, Wade Hampton II, was born in 1791 and was enrolled at the South Carolina College when the War of 1812 began. When Wade II decided to join the fight with Britain, Wade I secured a staff officer's position for him under Wade I's old friend, Andrew Jackson.[5] Some years after the war many in South Carolina took part in a great migration to the west, but the Hamptons chose to stay in South Carolina and invested in the rich lands of Louisiana, where an acre produced three times as much as South Carolina soil.[6] By 1817, Wade I was wealthy in his own right.

His son, Wade II, wealthy in his own right, married Ann Fitzsimmons, the only daughter of shipping magnate Christopher Fitzsimmons. Wade II and Ann moved into Millwood, an elaborate mansion he built on the Congaree River plantation. The house front exhibited six tall fluted columns with a two-story piazza across the width of the house. Inside was a ten thousand-volume library that filled two rooms, drawing rooms for men and women and a large dining room where the aristocracy from across the south was feted. Millwood was the center of social life for the state's elite and there was a constant flow of visitors attending parties and events for every season. The Negro butler who opened the doors of Millwood was adroit in attending to the needs of the guests. He would choose one

One. Redemption's Nativity

of the house servants to take care of the guest's every need, even making sure the selection of a horse suited the guest's temperament.

Millwood was modern for its day. Cool spring water was piped into the manor house and adjoining buildings. Surrounding the mansion were flowerbeds, lush shrubbery and five acres of gardens with a majestic view of the river. The plantation contained two thousand acres of fertile bottomland and orchards and vegetable gardens, all enough to support an army. To operate such a plantation, hundreds of slaves were housed in two villages of cabins. One village was located near the family home for house servants and skilled workers and the other was for field hands and was located near the fields for convenience. This village included a gristmill, cotton gins, sawmills, a blacksmith shop, a pig farm and a church for the slaves. Near the "big house" were stables for prize-winning horses, some purchased from the estate of England's William IV.

The Hamptons experienced the best life had to offer. In Charleston they enjoyed dinners, balls and horse races. They, like others of the South Carolina aristocracy, had their summer retreats. Many escaped the summer heat of the low county and the midlands to homes in the Carolina foothills and mountains. An enclave of the social elite formed at Flat Rock, North Carolina, not far from the Hamptons at Cashiers. The name of the Hampton estate had an odd genesis. Originally the plantation was known by the Hamptons as the "High Hamptons" until an untimely death of Caesar, one of the prize bulls maintained on the plantation. Caesar had a wide spread of horns which became entangled in a thicket and in an effort to free himself he broke his neck. In honor of the bovine the Hamptons called that section Caesar. Local residents corrupted the word and it became known as Cashiers.

Wade Hampton III was born 28 March 1818 in Charleston, but the happiest memories of South Carolina's "Redeemer" was at Millwood. One of the family's memories is so cute and full of prophecy that no biographer can resist telling it. The story goes this way. On the Millwood plantation there lived a large ill-tempered Muscovy drake. This patriarch of a large web-footed family never passed an opportunity to threaten and chase young Wade from his own land. Over and over again the drake intimidated the youngster with his warlike posture of a lowered neck, outstretched wings, and frightful hissing. Soon, however, the old drake would meet the fate of all tyrants.

One day while Wade was with his father and mother in Columbia on a shopping trip, his father told him he could pick out a toy. The boy surveyed all the wonderful toys before him, searching for the one thing that would bring him the most fun and satisfaction. Among all the choices, one toy caused his blue eyes to sparkle: a toy sword. He picked up the toy weapon and drew the blade from its tin sheath. He studied the blade like a seasoned warrior; it was iron, not too sharp or too dull, and fitted his hand comfortably. He envisioned the mock battles he might have on the lawn of Millwood, imagining himself to be a skilled soldier like this grandfather. Once more he scrutinized the saber, its sheath and leather belt, as any militia colonel might do. This was the prize!

Back home on the spacious lawn of Millwood young Wade thrust and jabbed in the air, pretending and practicing for war. Tired of pretending, and feeling well qualified for war, he recalled an old enemy. Off he marched to the pond, with a stiffened backbone, and confidently into the territory of the Muscovy drake. The great lord of the pond and patriarch of all those who sailed through its water and rested upon its shore waddled boldly to the young upstart, hissing and ruffling his feathers to look larger than he was. Little Wade was not intimidated but struck a stance and held his own at the approaching enemy. When the drake was in range, the conqueror unsheathed his iron sword and with a mighty blow whacked the feathered tyrant. The blow dazed and confused the Muscovy which quickly began to retreat from the battlefield for the safety of the pond waters. The young soldier outran the flustered drake and cut off his retreat. Now, the two faced each other and Wade closed in for the kill. With all his might, he slashed and thrust until the tyrant lay dead and bloody at his feet. In an overwhelming victory Wade had redeemed his homeland and he alone ruled the gardens and pond of Millwood. Taking the event as divination, neither his parents nor his grandfather scolded the boy; they silently agreed he was following in the footsteps of his predecessors that would ultimately lead to his destiny.

Wade grew into a six-foot tall man, with wide, square shoulders, large arms, and legs so powerful it was said "he could make a horse groan with pain." He was the picture of an athlete. Typical of the times, Wade's father saw to it that his son learned to manage a plantation and its various support industries. Wade and his father made numerous trips to their Mississippi and Louisiana plantations, where he learned the work and management of their large holdings and how to deal with the managers and slaves.

Wade gained his sense of responsibility toward the family's slaves from his predecessors. It was said he was kind to an extreme and had the respect of the hundreds who lived on the various plantations, who gave him their full loyalty, looking to him as a patriarch. Typical of the antebellum south, the Christmas season marked the end of the agricultural year and the beginning of another. At that time the Hamptons allowed a limited vacation of two weeks, during which time the slaves came before their master to present their new babies and receive gifts and supplies. In their 1850 Christmas visit to the Houmas plantation in Louisiana the Hamptons distributed to each of more than one thousand slaves a blanket, stockings, hat, handkerchief, and either a calico dress and a checked apron or a pair of fine bleached pants and fancy pants.[7]

Wade graduated from South Carolina College in 1836, a year after his beloved grandfather Hampton's death. Two years later, at the age of twenty, he married Margaret Preston of a notable Columbia family. Following his father's council that his position in life required him to serve his state through government, Wade took his place in politics in 1852 when he was elected to the South Carolina House of Representatives from Richland County. He served two terms in that body.

A year after Hampton began his political career tragedy struck the family through the death of their daughter, Harriet. Margaret Hampton was not well in the succeeding years and, after thirteen years of marriage, she died in 1855. Apart from Margaret's death, 1855 was a watershed year for the Hamptons. The legislature of South Carolina was proposing to repeal the anti slave-trade laws of 1807 and 1819 for the want of cheap labor. Hampton was not in favor of repealing the laws, knowing it would bring about wholesale trafficking in human beings and would bring the ire of northern abolitionists on the state. He offered a resolution against repeal, believing the act was "fraught with greater danger to the South."[8] The legislature ignored his resolution and later faced the fact that Hampton had been correct.

Also in 1855, Wade Hampton II and his sons Wade Hampton III and Christopher Fitzsimmons Hampton borrowed $345,370 (nearly $8 million today), mortgaging three Mississippi plantations — Wild Woods, Bayou and Walnut Ridge. These plantations totaled more than 4,500 acres and incorporated 420 slaves. Added to this loan was another $30,000 ($630,000) borrowed from the Bank of Charleston. Though the Hamptons were heavily in debt their estates were secure and the elder Wade was confident enough to sell Houmas for $1.5 million two years later. Wade II died in the early spring of 1858, leaving his sons to face heavy debt. With war only three years away, these loans would prove to be the bane of the Hampton family.

Hampton was elected to the state senate in 1856; and two years later, soon after his father's death in 1858, he married Mary Leighton McDuffie, who was eleven years his junior. Mary was the daughter of George McDuffie, a former South Carolina governor and senator who had died in 1851. The Hamptons and the McDuffies were longtime friends and often spent vacations together. At the death of her father, Mary, an only child, was saddled with the operation of a plantation and other businesses. It may have been that Mary turned to the Hamptons for guidance with Wade as her business manager.[9]

In 1860 Wade was elected to his third term in the senate. At that time he was probably the wealthiest man in the South. He owned 3,000 slaves, and in a good year he could expect $200,000 (more than $4 million) from his crops. The good life for the Hamptons was not to continue. The trouble

Congress Street, Yorkville (courtesy of Culture & Heritage Museums).

One. Redemption's Nativity

between the North and the South that had been gaining momentum for more than thirty years crested in 1860 and a wave of destruction never before seen fell upon the South. That year most South Carolina legislators were stricken with secession fever and the only coolant was states' rights. Wade agreed with his peers that the state had the right to hold slaves, but he believed it was not expedient to press the issue with the federal government.[10] Neither he nor the other Hamptons approved of the principle of slavery; in fact, they detested the system.[11] For those of us living in the twentieth-first century it may be difficult to understand how a person could despise a system and still remain a major participant in it. Hampton may have reasoned there was little good in freeing thousands of slaves into a state or nation that was not ready to defend their civil rights or provide for their well-being, leaving them at the mercy of state laws (both North and South) that would restrict their freedom or place them back into bondage.

For years the Wade Hamptons wintered habitually in Mississippi on the Wild Wood plantation, but in 1860 Wade delayed his family's departure while he was busy in the state legislature. Like Virginia's Robert E. Lee, Hampton opposed the states' rights movement, believing secession would bring no good to the South. However, Governor Pickens, an avid secessionist, was bent on secession and called for a special session of the legislature. Hampton, who had no respect for the governor and at one time called him a fool, refused to attend.[12] Without him South Carolina voted to secede; and though he opposed secession, he, like Lee, remained loyal to his beloved state and volunteered to protect the state and the developing Confederacy.

On 1 January 1861, just three months before the outbreak of the Civil War, the Hamptons defaulted on a payment of $47,500 on a mortgage secured by one hundred and eight acres of the Sand Hills plantation. The interest on the loans continued to accumulate throughout the war years and on 24 December 1868 the Hamptons were forced into voluntary bankruptcy with a confessed debt of $1,042,000—not including $11,970 in interest due to the Bank of Charleston and unknown amounts in private debts. Hampton entered the war as one of the wealthiest of men, but he would leave it as one of the poorest.

When war began in April 1861, Hampton was forty-three years old and had two sons, Preston and Wade, enrolled in South Carolina College.

Though Hampton and Lee were so much alike in politics and view of secession, Hampton did not agree with the general's strategy for war. Diametrically opposed to Lee's strategy, he went to Montgomery, Alabama, and virtually demanded President Jefferson Davis put him in command of a military unit bearing his name. He returned to South Carolina and, though his dislike of Governor Pickens was openly known, the governor gave him a colonel's commission.[13] Within a week eleven thousand men volunteered to serve in Hampton's Legion. Organized on 12 June, the legion consisted of six companies of infantry, four troops of cavalry and a battery of "flying" artillery.

Hampton threw his wealth into the Confederacy, contributing horses and money to supply his legion and making personal loans to field officers — in all, a huge amount. He presented fifty-two bales of cotton to the Confederacy that was estimated to be worth a million dollars and suggested to President Davis it be shipped to England, where it could be sold to fund the war. Due to Davis' hesitancy, the cotton was caught in the Union's blockade of ports and was burned on the dock. Judah Benjamin, the treasurer of the Confederacy, gave the same advice to Davis, but he, too, was ignored. Benjamin followed his own advice and sent his own cotton to England and after the war was able to begin life anew from the fortune saved.

Hampton's Legion served mainly in the Army of Northern Virginia in Stuart's Cavalry. After Stuart's death, Hampton distinguished himself in opposing Sheridan in the Shenandoah Valley and was made lieutenant general, commanding Lee's whole force of cavalry. The legion served gallantly in more than fifteen major battles, some imbedded in the nation's memory: first and second Bull Run, Seven Pines, Gaines' Mill and the Seven Days Battles. In May 1862 Hampton was promoted to brigadier general and later to lieutenant general, on the same day Sherman was burning Millwood.

In April 1865, as the final scenes of the Civil War were being played out, Lee, seeing the Union army was surrounding him, suggested President Davis flee Richmond. Just days before Lee's surrender on April 9, Davis withdrew from the Southern capital with a large escort and the Confederate treasury estimated at $12 million and headed for Mississippi in hopes of raising an army to continue the struggle. Less than three weeks later, General Joseph Johnston surrendered in Greensboro, North Carolina, as Davis raced by. At the time, Hampton was under special assignment by President Davis to prevent Sherman's advance through the Carolinas. Under orders of the president, Hampton believed he was not bound by either Lee's or Johnston's surrender and instead of going to Greensboro to sign a surrender and receiving a parole, Hampton and a few of his staff officers set out to find Davis, who was two days' travel ahead.

Davis arrived in Yorkville, York County, South Carolina, on 27 April and was promptly escorted to the home of Colonel J. Rufus Bratton, where crowds assembled to see their president. Bratton noted the following in his journal: "He appeared to be somewhat fatigued in body and depressed in spirits though easily aroused with his native fire. He caressed and spoke kindly to my four boys, Louis, John, Andrel and Moultrie." The president's fatigue did not disappear during the night, and the following morning as he prepared to leave, he declined making a speech in spite of the urging of the people of Yorkville. General John C. Breckenridge, the secretary of war, stood in for the president. Speaking from the balcony of Rose's Hotel next door to the Bratton home, he encouraged the people to keep the faith. The cavalry escorts led the president and his cabinet southward on the Pinckney Road toward the courthouse town of Union. Sometime before noon they reached the small community of Blairsville, where the escort cavalry was directed to turn off onto the Rutherfordton Road in order to cross the Broad River at Smith's Ford. Davis, his cabinet and his guards proceeded on toward the Pinckneyville ferry.

The entourage stopped at a tavern about a mile from the Pinckneyville ferry and waited while preparations were being made for their crossing. Many in the area who had gotten word that Davis would pass their way gathered at the tavern to get a glimpse of their president, who took time to visit with the crowd. He had no way of knowing that a large force of Stoneman's troops was drawing near Smith's Ford with orders to capture Davis and the Confederate treasury. Discovering that the fleeing entourage and their escort had crossed the river into Union County, the Union troops took time to raid farms along on the York County side and exchanged fire with local farmers.

Meanwhile, having heard that Davis had passed through North Carolina, Hampton and his comrades set out for Charlotte, North Carolina, in hopes of rendezvousing with him in Yorkville. Having fled Columbia, away from Sherman's advancing army, Mary Hampton had taken refuge

Top: Yorkville. Circa 1905 view of North Congress Street, looking toward the business district, showing early utility poles supporting an overhanging streetlight. *Above:* The Bratton House, built sometime before 1830 by Robert Clendenin, a Yorkville lawyer and South Carolina senator from York District (1816–1830). Dr. James Rufus Bratton purchased the house in 1847. The Confederate president, Jefferson Davis, spent the night here as he fled the Union troops. The house passed to Bratton's son, Dr. R. Andral Bratton and was razed in 1956 (both courtesy of Culture & Heritage Museums).

in the small village. After fording a flooding Catawba River in York County, a wet, saddle weary Hampton arrived in Yorkville two hours after midnight. After a warm exchange between Wade and Mary, the general found that his president had left Yorkville two days earlier and was probably forty miles away. Wade told his wife that he had no plans to surrender and would continue the war; but Mary was of a different mind. She labored to make her husband see the futility of continuing, reminding him they not only had lost their home and fortune, they had also lost their son Preston on a Virginia battlefield. She pleaded for him to see that their way of life had vanished and how futile it was to continue. When he would not abandon the struggle, she sent for General Joe Wheeler, who was staying nearby. Wheeler and Mrs. Hampton together were eventually able to dissuade the general, appealing to his obligation to a defenseless family and state. Wheeler informed him that Davis had narrowly escaped capture by Stoneman's troops on the Broad. Finally, Hampton penned a letter to the president and gave it to Wheeler, saying, "Tell the President that if in the future there should appear any way in which I can serve him, I will do so to the last." Wheeler took the message and rode southward in pursuit of Davis. Hampton turned northward to North Carolina to seek out one of Sherman's patrol officers and surrender.

With the war over, the Hamptons returned to Columbia with others to survey their damages and losses, and figure how they and their family could begin anew. The Hamptons, though their fortune was devastated, were luckier than many of their peers. After a short stay in the ashes of Columbia, the Hamptons retreated to High Hamptons. For several years Wade retained his permanent address in South Carolina but eventually he changed his residency to Mississippi and his plantation on the Yazoo Delta. Other than short visits he would not permanently return to South Carolina until 1876, on the eve of his nomination.

CHAPTER TWO

Satan's Rule

From the fall of the Confederacy in 1865 to the summer of 1867, South Carolina landowners endeavored to rebuild their society, naively believing that life would resume as before. While they tended to their farms, Democrats trusted President Andrew Johnson to implement Lincoln's plan for a gracious reconstruction. This plan, slightly amended by Johnson, considered the Southern states never to have left the Union and called for them to be restored to full power with minimum reconstruction. In the North, the populace had grown weary of war and when Lee surrendered at Appomattox they considered the argument with the South ended and wanted only peace. One northern newspaper posed this question:

> Considering their present admirable bearing, ought we to treat them as friends or as enemies? When we separated from Great Britain, we proclaimed to the world ... *"enemies in war, in peace friends."* Shall we treat our own repentant brethren with less magnanimity than foreign nations practice toward each other? ... Why should our newspapers teem with calumnies on their character? When they so frankly accept the new order of things, and the mighty revolution in their social system, what sense, what magnanimity, what decency even, is there in subjecting them to needless humiliation and indignities? Nobody fears a new rebellion; nobody believes that the frank submission of the South is feigned; and it is unworthy to the character of a great nation to practice a mean, suspicious, and irritating surveillance over a proud and spirited community.[1]

Before radical Republicans stirred the emotions of the northern press, the *Washington Intelligencer* lauded the South's contrite attitude and announced that its "admirable temper is attracting general attention and sympathy.... [T]he Federal Government is, on all hands, acknowledged by them as the superior and sovereign power; and Southern men crowd under the excepted clauses in the Amnesty Act to ask its forgiveness."[2] As though

Two. Satan's Rule

President Andrew Johnson, the 17th President of the United States and the first president to be impeached. He was the only Southern senator who did not leave his congressional desk when the South seceded. Historians have consistently chosen him as one of the worst to serve as United States president.

the reporter had a premonition of things to come, he hoped "no side issues, involving technicalities and parchment questions, can be made to divert the hearts of the sections from coming together, so strong in consent and love for a common country as to defy danger from all future party combinations and machinations." Though a general benevolent feeling seemed to have been expressed in the North, the radicals of Congress would soon begin to transform those feelings into ones of vengeance.

The drama of Reconstruction actually began with Congress nearly six months before the close of the Civil War and the assassination of President Lincoln. In the fall of 1864, five months before the war ended, the Union elected the 39th Congress, with a three-fourths Republican majority. By the time of Lee's surrender in April 1865, the 38th Congress had adjourned and the 39th was not scheduled to convene until the following December. President Lincoln's assassination a few days after Lee's surrender brought Vice President Andrew Johnson to the presidency. Johnson, a Southern Democrat and one-time slaveholder, had remained loyal to the Union, and though he was bitter toward the "Rebels" for their secession, he retained a strong sympathy for the South. Johnson had the confidence of Republicans, who believed the country was in good hands. That confidence, however, would be short lived.

Johnson's heritage and sympathy prompted him to carry through with Lincoln's plan for a gracious restoration. During the interval between the 38th Congress and the 39th Congress, Johnson began dealing with reconstruction of the South through executive powers rather than calling a special session of Congress. On 29 May 1865, he issued two proclamations. The first of these, the Amnesty Proclamation, laid out terms for Southern men to obtain pardons (by taking a loyalty or amnesty oath), and the second provided for provisional governors for each of the Southern states.

The Amnesty Proclamation pardoned all Southern men who had participated in the war, with two exceptions that disqualified much of the South's governing elite from participating in framing a new state constitution. The first disqualified any who had served in the Confederate army above the rank of colonel and lieutenant in the Confederate navy. The second excluded those who had participated in any way in the rebellion and had a taxable property value over $20,000.[3] While the exceptions excluded a wide range of people, the old ruling class felt the greatest impact.

Within President Johnson's Executive Order was a provision that the states were to hold an election of at least one-tenth of qualified voters to call a Constitutional Convention to "amend the state's organic law in conformity with the results of the late conflict," i.e., to comply with the federal agenda to (1) declare the prewar ordinance of secession null and void, (2) ratify the Thirteenth Amendment, (3) renounce any share in the war debt, and (4) adopt a new state constitution. Voters could be qualified through the provisions of the 1860 South Carolina constitution, which was still in effect, and the loyalty oath.[4]

On 30 June 1865, Johnson appointed Benjamin F. Perry provisional governor of South Carolina and charged him with the duty of reorganizing the state government and establishing a date for a constitutional convention to frame "a new republican government."[5] Perry was passionately opposed to any form of reconstruction, and shortly after his appointment he pressed all citizens to "abandon at once and forever all notions of Secession, Nullification and Disunion, determined to live, and to teach your children to live, as true American citizens."[6] Upon taking office Governor Perry issued a proclamation that all men were to take the oath of allegiance to the United States and proceed quickly with the business of electing delegates to a state constitutional convention.

In compliance with Perry's proclamation, public meetings were held throughout the state to nominate delegates. The York County meeting took place in August, at which time William C. Black, Colonel Cadwalder

Jones, the Reverend Robert A. Ross and Major James W. Avery were nominated.⁷ Their names were published in the local newspaper resolving "That we approve of the call made by His Excellency B.F. Perry, for a Convention of the State, with authority to alter or amend the Constitution thereof, to restore civil authority, and to exercise all powers necessary and proper to restore the State to its constitutional relations to the Federal Government."⁸

With county nominees duly elected, the constitutional convention met in September at Columbia's First Baptist Church — the same place where the secession convention had met nearly five years earlier. President Johnson's order was cut-and-dry, but South Carolina delegates found it difficult to comply and squabbled over its

Benjamin F. Perry. Appointed provisional governor of South Carolina in 1865, it was Perry's duty to reorganize the state government. Perry opposed any form of Reconstruction and challenged South Carolina citizens to abandon all notions of secession and strive to become loyal Americans.

wording. Instead of declaring the Order of Secession null and void, they *repealed* the ordinance, and played the same word game with Johnson's request to acknowledge that slavery no longer existed. Beating around the bush, they declared "that because the slaves had been emancipated by the action of the United States authorities, it would never be reestablished in South Carolina."⁹ The South Carolina convention, like its counterpart in Mississippi, failed to renounce the Confederate debt. In spite of the state constitution's lack of political weight, Johnson approved the constitution. Having completed their business in Columbia, the state began to prepare for the October election of governor, members of the legislature and United States senator.

On 25 September a garrison of about thirty federal troops arrived in Yorkville, similar to those placed in other areas of the state as a peacekeeping force to ensure the continuance of civil order.[10] White South Carolinians went to the polls on 18 October 1865. Due to the exceptions of the loyalty oath, and perhaps widespread complacency, only 1,271 votes were cast for United States senator and members of the house of representatives. On the state level, James L. Orr[11] was elected governor (narrowly defeating Wade Hampton III), with W.D. Porter as lieutenant governor. Provisional Governor Perry was elected to the United States Senate.

With James Orr, a member of the old aristocracy, in the governor's office and another aristocrat headed to the United States Senate, Radical Republicans concluded South Carolina was attempting to rebuild its old power structure. Earlier, these congressmen had been troubled that so many disqualified men were being chosen as delegates to the constitutional convention, and now they saw the election as being indicative of South Carolina's no-compromise attitude.

Governor Perry was well aware of the uneasiness among the Radicals; hoping to head off any interference from Congress, he rushed two to three thousand applications for pardons to the president and received them just in time to seat the forty-eight representatives. Other state offi-

James L. Orr. With the election of James L. Orr, a member of the old magistracy, as South Carolina governor in 1865, congressional Radicals feared the state was attempting to rebuild its old power structure. One step ahead of Congress, Orr was successful in getting two to three thousand presidential pardons and authorized 48 representatives to sit.

cials who had not received their pardons were allowed to stay in office provided they took the amnesty oath at some undefined time. Among the pardons granted to South Carolinians, 650 of the men had property valued in excess of $20,000, a definite violation of the Amnesty Proclamation.

The South Carolina general assembly met in October 1865 to comply with President Johnson's stipulation for readmission to the Union, that is, to ratify the Thirteenth Amendment; but franchising black ex-slaves stuck in the craws of white South Carolinians. This was not the first time Democrats had gagged over its passage. In June 1864, during President Lincoln's administration, the amendment had come before the United States House but was defeated by Northern Democrats. Although the bill was not scheduled to come again before that body until the following January, President Lincoln urged Democrats to put aside their partisan ways and unite with the Republicans to pass the historic bill. He made little headway, but the bill passed 119 to 56 with only sixteen of the eighty Democrats voting with the Republicans. Within three months all but one Northern state had ratified the amendment.[12]

When the amendment was presented to the Southern states Johnson advised the governments to franchise only those who could pass an education test.[13] Congressional Radicals were alarmed that the president had not made specific provisions for Negro suffrage. If the Radicals had any doubts, South Carolina proved their fears to be valid. Ignoring the president's advice, the general assembly prepared a ridiculously biased voter's qualification that piqued Radical fears that blacks might be disenfranchised and the old order fully reestablished. Just reading the voter qualifications sent cold shivers up the collective spine of the Radicals:

> He shall be a free white man who has attained the age of twenty-one years, and is not a pauper, nor a noncommissioned officer or private soldier of the army nor a seaman or marine of the navy of the United States. He shall, for the two years next preceding the day of election, have been a citizen of this State; or for the same period an emigrant from Europe, who has declared his intention to become a citizen of the United States, according to the Constitution and laws of the United States. He shall have resided in this State for at least two years next preceding the day of election, and for the last six months of that time in the district in which he offers to vote.

At the same time, the general assembly formed a set of "Black Codes" that redefined slavery and used such terms as master and servant. The codes forbade interracial marriages; limited travel; forbade trading without a license that had exorbitant fees attached; limited freedmen use of certain courts; denied social and political equality with whites; and forbade possessing a hunting weapon without permission of a court judge. Under the Black Code blacks were allowed to bring lawsuits but denied any opportunity to testify against a white person. Furthermore, any black who was not employed could be arrested under the laws of vagrancy and forced into a contract to a white employer.[14]

Democrats claimed these codes were an honest effort to create order out of chaos, and to protect freedmen by making whites their guardians. Governor Perry justified their existence, saying it was not necessary for the general assembly to comply with Johnson's orders to spell out the freedmen's rights. Republicans, however, saw this as an attempt to re-enslave the freedmen. Although these codes were never activated because of intervention of the federal government, they would come back to haunt the Democrats during the 1876 campaign.

To see that Reconstruction was carried out, the U.S. Senate prepared a bill calling for dividing the ten "rebellious states" into five military districts, declaring their governments to be provisional and subject to be overridden by occupying forces. At the end of summer 1865 Secretary of War Edwin M. Stanton nominated Major General Daniel E. Sickles for military governorship of South Carolina. Governor Orr was content to share the power with his old friend.

Sickles' political career is illustrative of the corruption that was rampant in the government. As a young New York lawyer, Sickles made his political appearance in 1853 when President Franklin Pierce appointed him secretary to James Buchanan, minister to England. Pierce's secretary of state, William Marcy of New York, refused to sign the commission, citing Sickles as a Tammany Hall brawler who had flouted his prostitute in the halls of the State House. Buchanan insisted on the young lawyer's appointment and thirty-four-year-old Sickles sailed to England that same year. He lived up to his reputation, leaving behind a young wife and infant and taking along Fanny White, a woman of dubious character who had run a whorehouse in New York.

Four years later, when Buchanan became president in 1857, Sickles came to Washington as a congressman and became one of the president's closest confidants and one of the more powerful men in government. The congressman and his wife, Teresa, moved into an elegant neighborhood

Major Daniel E. Sickles (1819–1914). Sickles was involved in a number of public scandals as a New York politician, the most notable the killing of his wife's lover. He was eventually acquitted on the first ever use of temporary insanity as a defense. His military career ended when he was struck in the leg by cannon fire at Gettysburg. As a congressman he made important legislative contributions for the preservation of Gettysburg Battlefield.

near the White House where many prominent Southern leaders lived. Among them were Attorney General Philip Barton Key, the son of Francis Scott Key and who had been described as "the handsomest man in all Washington society." Key became friends with the Sickles and was a constant escort of Teresa. This relationship turned into a love affair that became the talk of Washington. To accommodate the affair Key rented a brick house at 383 Fifteenth Street, just two blocks from the Sickles' home. The Fifteenth Street neighborhood consisted of white craftsmen and somewhat better-off freed slaves. Common knowledge had it that Key would hang a string from a window in his home to signal Teresa that he was available and that the front door was unlocked.[15] On 24 February 1859, at a dance in Washington, Dan Sickles was handed a note from "R.P.G." informing him of the affair between Barton and Teresa.

Dan, brokenhearted and betrayed, required Teresa to write a full, detailed account of the affair, even describing their undressing. Attorney-like, he required her to write that she had not been coerced or threatened to write her confession. When the confession was complete, a visitor, Octavia Ridgely, and a servant, Bridget Duffy, witnessed the document. After taking Teresa's wedding ring Sickles spent the night sobbing in his bedroom. Teresa slept in the room with Octavia but, as was the custom of repentant Catholics, on the floor.[16]

The following day Sickles invited his closest friends, Sam Butterworth and George Wooldridge, to his home to decide what he should do. He feared his career was over, since the affair was known by all his Washington friends, party leaders, President Buchanan and even the "Negroes in the neighborhood."[17] While the men studied the situation, Barton Key strolled down the street toward the Sickles' home with a pair of opera glasses in his coat pocket. He was so determined to see Teresa and know of her condition that he threw all caution to the wind and lingered outside the Stockton Mansion where the Sickles lived. Everyone in the house, including Bridget and the family greyhound, Dandy, saw Barton. Dandy ran to meet Barton, who petted the dog and then wiped his pants with a white handkerchief. From the house the voyeurs saw Key waving the handkerchief over his head as if signaling.[18] In a fit of rage Sickles rushed outside and confronted his wife's lover: "Key, you scoundrel, you have dishonored my house — you must die!" Dan pulled his pistol, the men locked into a scuffle and Barton was shot in the hand. The gun went off again and Barton was wounded just below the groin. As he lay on the ground, Dan stepped over him to deliver the coup de grace. Barton cried out, "Don't shoot me! Murder! Murder!" Coldly Dan placed his pistol near Barton's body and fired; the pistol misfired. Again he cocked the weapon and fired. This time the bullet entered Barton's left side just under his heart. Barton died within minutes.[19]

J.H.W. Baritz, a young White House page from North Carolina, witnessed the shooting and rushed back to inform the president. Buchanan told Baritz he had better get back to North Carolina and gave him a razor as a memento and money to pay his train trip to Wilmington. Thus the president of the United States obstructed justice by advising a witness — the only witness as far as Buchanan knew — to flee without notifying the law.[20] Sickles was arrested and placed in a deplorable jail cell, but his old friend, the Speaker of the House, James L. Orr, pulled strings and got him moved to the jailer's quarters. During a speedy trial, eight prominent attorneys led by Edwin Stanton, who would be appointed attorney general by President Buchanan the next year, represented the defendant. Throughout the trial prosecutor Robert Ould, who had been appointed to replace Sickles, seemed to show little interest in the case. The defense swept away Ould's disinterested arguments on the grounds that Sickles had suffered from temporary insanity, making it the first time this plea was used in the American judicial system.

When Sickles' acquittal was announced, Stanton danced a jig in the courtroom and led the crowd in three cheers. A tremendous party followed the trial, where Sickles was congratulated and praised. Three and a half months later these same people turned their backs on him when he reconciled with his fallen wife. Enmity between Sickles and the Tammany Democrats continued for several years, but in time they forgave their old friend and reelected him to Congress.

Prior to the outbreak of the Civil War, Sickles supported the South's complaints until South Carolina fired on Fort Sumter. Though he vowed he would never send New York City troops against the Confederacy, he delivered the necessary soldiers when he was commissioned a general. During the war he was serving under Commander Meade at Gettysburg where Sickles' right leg was shattered by a twelve-pound cannonball. He was sent to Washington to recuperate. Always able to make the best of a bad situation, Sickles became closely acquainted with the Lincolns, even attending the séances held by Mrs. Lincoln. President Lincoln sent him as an emissary to Panama and Colombia. After the war he was appointed and served as the military commander of North Carolina and South Carolina during the first years of Reconstruction. He retuned to New York and was appointed ambassador to Spain

John L. Rainey (dressed in the cadet uniform of the Kings Mountain Military Academy in Yorkville, South Carolina). Rainey served in the Confederate army and was discharged at Greensboro, North Carolina, when Lee surrendered at Appomattox. Without transportation he walked home to York County, a distance of about 150 miles. Rainey became a successful planter, banker and merchant, and is known as the "Father of the Town of Sharon, South Carolina" (courtesy of the Museum of Western York County, Sharon).

by President Grant. There, the one-legged general met Caroline de Creagh and began to court her. On a trip to Paris he met the deposed queen of Spain, Isabella II, and continued an affair with her while courting Caroline. He and Caroline were married in the fall of 1871 (Teresa had died in 1867), but it was rumored he soon began an affair with Senora Domeriquy, a Cuban conspirator. In 1879 Dan and Caroline said their mutual goodbyes and he returned to New York. He continued his involvement with politics until he died of a cerebral hemorrhage in 1914 at the ripe old age of ninety-five.[21]

Sickles, now the new military commander of North Carolina and South Carolina, arrived in Charleston by steamer in late summer of 1865 and promptly established his headquarters at the Citadel. Commissioned to protect freedmen and whites loyal to the Union, General Sickles was in charge of a force of three hundred and fifty officers and more than seven thousand soldiers scattered across the state. The general soon became aware of violence being used against freedmen and Republicans by a pre–Ku Klux Klan organization known as the Regulators. This paramilitary group roamed the state and dealt with what they called the "Negro menace."[22]

A few months after Sickles arrived in South Carolina he nullified the Black Codes in January 1866 and declared Negroes to have the same rights and judicial recourse as whites. President Johnson was unhappy with Congress' appointment of Sickles and in the summer of 1866 he tried to lure the general away from the Carolinas by offering him the post of minister to the Netherlands. Sickles declined the offer. Then the president declared rebellion no longer existed in the South and reduced Sickles' forces to just over two thousand.[23] Although the general's jurisdiction had been expanded, the reduction of his peacekeeping force gave the Regulators the upper hand. During that fall and winter, threats on blacks in Edgefield, Laurens and Newberry counties increased, and Sickles told the whites in those counties that unless the threats ceased, the freedmen's ration, housing and protection would be at their expense.[24]

Sickles continued to provoke Johnson with his absolutist style. In the spring of 1867 Sickles issued General Order Number 10, imposing a twelve-month moratorium on foreclosures. Though the order saved small farmers from court process and allowed them to raise their crops, the president was highly irritated with the general's high-handedness and dismissed him.[25]

Two. Satan's Rule

Nearly two years before Sickles' dismissal, and as 1865 came to a close, South Carolina lawmakers were still taunting Radicals by stalling the ratification of the Thirteenth Amendment until just three days before the legislature adjourned on 21 December. The general assembly congratulated themselves on their work and had no doubts they had met the demands of Reconstruction and would be fully represented in the next Congress. The *Yorkville Enquirer* happily announced that South Carolina was "the first of the States ... to accede to that cardinal prerequisite of President Johnson's to the restoration of Union fellowship contained in the adoptions of the amendment to the National Constitution abolishing and forever prohibiting slavery throughout the country."[26]

Congressional Radicals, however, were not pleased. In addition to ratification, the Radicals in Congress expected a repentant and contrite spirit from the "Mother of Secession." The state had done itself no favor by delaying and playing word games with Congress. The advantage was on the side of the Radicals and they were more than happy to grind their axes slowly. The state's delay and out-right refusal to open the door for civil rights eventually led to the undoing of President Johnson's plan for a simple Reconstruction. With Johnson's plan out of the way, Congress was free to devise their own plan, a plan that would satisfy their thirst for revenge and vent their outrage over South Carolina's cavalier attitude and high-handedness.

The driving ambition of Republicans to politically rule the South stemmed from earlier years when Southern Democrats had control of the national government. Due to segmented politics in the North the "Solid South" had enjoyed having things its way for years. With its ever-growing slave population and the 1787 passage of the three-fifths clause of Article I of the Constitution, the South increased its representation in Congress and the electoral college. With this majority it was easy to promote slavery and its advance across the North American continent.

Until the election of Lincoln, southern presidents had governed from the White House for fifty of the nation's seventy-two years, and a southerner had been Speaker of the House for half that time. On the eve of the Civil War, nineteen Southerners sat on the Supreme Court in opposition to fifteen Northerners. In spite of the industrial power of the North and a growing Southern population, divisive legislation by Southerners that promoted slavery was constantly forced upon the North. When the

South seceded from the Union, Republicans gained the White House and control of Congress. After so many years of having mere fringes of power, Republicans were in no mood to relinquish their power and relished the opportunity to punish the South for the years of forcing slavery on the nation.

During the same time the South Carolina general assembly was developing the Black Codes, the 39th Congress met for their first session. All the Southern states except Texas had operating governments and sent their representatives to Washington. At the opening of Congress these men waited with confidence to answer the roll call, but eventually realized the House clerk was deliberately omitting Southern members from the roll call.

Without notification Republicans lodged a complaint that Southern Democrats did not meet the proper qualifications to be seated. To further stall the process a fifteen member joint committee was formed to determine their eligibility. In the meantime Republicans busied themselves seeking a way to derail the presidential reconstruction and permanently deny Southern representation. First, a constitutional theory had to be developed. This task fell to Pennsylvania representative and House leader Thaddeus Stevens, a Radical Republican. Stevens theorized that the war and ultimate surrender of the former Confederate states had turned them into "conquered provinces" without constitutional rights. Joining him was another Radical, Senator Charles Sumner of Massachusetts. Sumner had no love for the South and particularly South Carolina, having received a severe cane-whipping from South Carolina's Senator Preston Brooks following a mean-spirited speech by Sumner in 1856. Still suffering from the crippling effects of that prewar attack, Sumner was more than willing to wreak vengeance on South Carolina. Sumner added to Stevens' theory that secession was unconstitutional and when the South seceded they had committed "state suicide" and politically ceased to exist. Two months later, in February, Congress heard the committee's report and adopted a resolution "that no representative from the Southern States would be seated in either the House or the Senate until both houses declared the state entitled to representation."[27]

It was no surprise to Congress when President Johnson rejected Stevens' theory and the congressional plan for a punitive reconstruction. The ensuing dispute developed into a long-term argument that led Stevens into proposing impeachment in 1868. When Stevens' theory was made public, the Northern states gave him the dubious title "Father of Reconstruction." In the South, however, he was referred to as "the Devil camped outside the Constitution."

Having carefully developed Stevens' theory, Congress passed several bills. One nullified Southern governments and reduced them to territorial status under military rule. A second bill was the "Freedmen's Bill," designed to strengthen the Freedmen's Bureau that had been established to protect the interest of the freedmen and refugee whites. A civil rights bill was passed, but there was doubt as to its constitutionality, so Congress, on 13 June 1866, passed the Fourteenth Amendment granting all males (except Indians), twenty-one years of age and native born, full citizenship and equal rights. Having pushed these bills into passage before adjournment, the Thirty-ninth Congress paved the way for the Fortieth Congress to proceed with more punitive practices and rebuild the South into a mirror image of the North.

The Fourteenth Amendment was sent to the states for ratification, with attached instructions that restoration to the Union depended on ratification. Of course, the amendment was particularly odious to Southern governments. Eric McKitrick, in his *Andrew Johnson and Reconstruction*, simplifies the situation: "This amendment — a long step toward Negro suffrage — designated Negroes as citizens entitled to security of life, liberty, and property; it specified penalties of reduced representation for former slave states who withheld the franchise from such citizens; it denied state and federal office holding privileges to persons who had broken oaths of loyalty to the Constitution in order to support the rebellion; and it forbade any state to invalidate the federal debt or to validate the Confederate debt. It thus represented a major definition of emergent congressional policy on reconstruction."[28] The third section of the amendment was just as loathsome, as it disenfranchised many Southern legislators then serving:

> No person shall be a Senator or Representative in Congress, or elector of President and Vice President, or hold any office, civil or military, under the United States, or under any State, who, having previously taken an oath, as a member of Congress, or as an officer of the United States, or as a member of any State legislature, or as an executive or judicial officer of any State, to support the Constitution of the United States, shall have engaged in insurrection or rebellion against the same, or given aid or comfort to the enemies thereof. But Congress may by a vote of two-thirds of each House, remove such disability.[29]

Like other Southern governments, the South Carolina general assembly was loath to ratify the Fourteenth Amendment. When Governor Orr made it clear the federal government would not allow black men to be singled out under the law, the assembly decided "all special provisions as to persons of color were repealed, and the statute was made applicable to all persons, without regard to race or color."[30] South Carolina, like all Southern legislatures with the exception of Tennessee, refused to ratify the amendment because of the section that completely disenfranchised the state's representatives. Johnson's struggle with Congress continued through the fall elections of 1866 and beyond.[31] During this time two thoughts were abroad in South Carolina: some believed a peaceful compliance with Congress' demands would appease the radicals; but others warned that "a wolf is not to be cured of his taste for sheep, by feeding him on mutton; nor can the radical party reasonably be expected to become less grasping, by the undisputed possession of the South as a prey."[32]

While the newly elected Fortieth Congress would not convene until March 1867, the Thirty-ninth began its second and final session in December. Since this session would run only until March, it was known as the "Short Session." By this time Congress had growing apprehensions over reports that Republicans were being abused in the Southern states, thus Radicals proceeded to accomplish two goals: destroy President Johnson and deal with the South in such a way as to obtain "security and repentance."[33] In spite of the moderate Republicans and Democrats who did their best to derail any attempt to punish the South, the Radicals succeeded in getting a number of punitive acts passed.

With the end of their work in view, Congress enacted a bill on 22 January calling the Fortieth Congress into special session on 4 March, immediately after the expiration of the Thirty-ninth. This was done so there would be no break between the sessions and Congress could continue their reconstruction labors. Johnson continued to defy the Radicals. Fearing the president might dismiss secretary of war Edwin Stanton, on whom the Radicals depended for execution of the Reconstruction Acts, they introduced a bill entitled the Tenure of Office Act. This bill was designed to limit presidential powers in dismissing an officeholder of the executive branch without approval of the Senate. Johnson vetoed the bill, but Congress overrode the president and the bill passed into law.

On the same day the Tenure of Office Act was passed, the Army Appropriations Act (officially termed Command of the Army Act) became law. Not only did it make appropriations available to the army for the year ending 30 June 1868, it severely diminished presidential control of the United States Army. With rising threats to Freedmen throughout the South, the military was placed at the disposal of the Freedmen's Bureau. To further decrease the possibility of violence, and to keep an iron hand on the South, the state militias of these states, excepting Tennessee, were disbanded.[34]

The Tenure of Office Act did not deter Johnson; he promptly dismissed the secretary of war. Radical Republicans were sure the president had violated the Tenure of Office Act and they set into motion the process to impeach him for "high crimes and misdemeanors." Chief justice Salmon Chase presided over the Senate trial, but it soon became evident the president had broken no law. When the Senate went to vote, seven Republicans defied party pressure and voted with Democrats for his acquittal. By one vote Johnson escaped impeachment and removal from office. Stanton, knowing he was done for, resigned.

Johnson remained in office for the remainder of his term as a lame duck. His gracious "Presidential Reconstruction" officially came to an end in March 1867. That month Congress overrode President Johnson's veto and passed into law the first of three Reconstruction Acts. The first, "An act to provide for the more efficient government of the rebel States," laid out the process in which the Southern states might gain readmittance into the Union.

> Sect. 1— Whereas, no legal State governments or adequate protection for life or property now exists in the rebel states of Virginia, North Carolina, South Carolina, Georgia, Mississippi, Alabama, Louisiana, Florida, Texas and Arkansas; and whereas, it is necessary that peace and good order should be enforced in said States until loyal and republican state governments can be legally established: Therefore: Be it enacted, that the said rebel States shall be divided into military districts and made subject to the military authority of the United States....

Sections 2, 3 and 4 continue to deal with the military control in the rebel states by the United States Army.

> Sect. 5 — That when the people of one of the said rebel States shall have formed a constitution of government in conformity with the Constitution of the United States in all respects, framed by a convention of delegates elected by the male citizens of said State, twenty-one years old and upward, of whatever race, color, or previous condition, who have been resident in the said State for one year

previous to the day of such election; except such as may be disfranchised for participation in the rebellion or for felony at common law, and when such convention shall provide that the elective franchise shall be enjoyed by all such persons as have the qualifications herein stated for electors of delegates, and when such constitution shall be ratified by a majority of the persons voting on the question of ratification who are qualified as electors for delegates, and when such constitution shall have been submitted to Congress for examination and approval and Congress shall have adopted the same, and when said State by a vote of its Legislature elected under said constitution shall have adopted the amendment to the Constitution of the United States, known as Article Fourteen, and when said article shall have become a part of the Constitution of the United States, said State shall be declared entitled to representation in Congress, and Senators and Representatives shall be admitted there from on their taking the oath prescribed by law [meaning the "test oath"], thereupon and thereafter the preceding sections of this act shall be inoperative in said State: provided, that no person excluded from the privilege of holding office by said proposed amendment to the Constitution of the United States shall be eligible as a member of the convention to frame a constitution for any of the said rebel States, nor shall any such person vote for members of such convention.

Section 6 declared that the existing civil governments of the states subject to the action were "provisional only and in all respects subject to the paramount authority of the United States at any time to abolish, modify, control, or supersede the same...."

When the Fortieth Congress convened, it continued the labors of its predecessors. A bill entitled "An Act Supplementary to the Act to provide for the more efficient government of the rebel states" was put before President Johnson. The president's veto was ignored and the Second Reconstruction Act was put into force. The act dictated: "Before Sept. 1, 1867, the Commanding General in each district shall cause a registration to be made of the male citizens of the United States, twenty-one years of age and upward." When registration was complete, the commanding general was to call for an election to vote for or against holding a convention for the purpose of framing a state constitution and to elect delegates to the convention. Should the constitution meet with congressional approval, the state would then be entitled to representation on the national level.[35]

From his headquarters in Charleston, military governor Sickles issued an order in May setting into motion a registration of all qualified voters in North and South Carolina, beginning in July. This registration would be a landmark event as it was the first in which the black population would participate.

Two. Satan's Rule

A few days before the registration began Congress overrode another presidential veto and enacted the Third Reconstruction Act, entitled "An Act supplementary to an Act entitled 'An Act to provide for the more efficient Government of the Rebel States,' passed [2 March 1867], and the 'Act supplementary thereto,' passed [23 March 1867]." This act declared the existing governments of the "rebel states" illegal and subject to military commanders. Providing assurance that the old aristocracy order would not be reestablished, it disenfranchised any man who had served in the state government, stipulating that "no person who has been a member of the legislature of any State government, whether he has taken an oath to support the Constitution of the United States or not ... is entitled to be registered to vote."[36]

In preparation for statewide registration, military post commanders designated boards of registration, with three members on each.[37] In York County, three such boards were appointed; and while blacks were eligible to serve on these and others throughout the state, none were appointed in York County. Returning boards were also established in every Southern state capital. The function of these boards was to review election ballots with the power to throw out any ballot deemed "illegal." While the purpose of these boards was to insure fair elections, corrupt men found ways to revise elections and guarantee their party's position.

During the month of August, while the state was preparing for the voter registration, Republicans assembled in Columbia to form the Union Republican Party of South Carolina. Local clubs or chapters known as Union Leagues were developed and became the first new political organization formed since the end of the war. These leagues were the Republican Party's version of the Democratic Clubs, with their main objective to educate the black population regarding their civil rights. All too often, however, they were used to manipulate freedmen into believing they must vote the Republican ticket. In October the editor of the *Yorkville Enquirer* gave his opinion of these leagues and the following warning:

> I deem it my duty to caution the public against it. It is gotten up chiefly by aspirants for political advancement, who see no other chance to get office. These men seek to create the impression that to be truly patriotic; everybody ought to join the Union Leagues. Those who are so confiding as to take this advice are immediately bound by solemn oaths to vote for none but loyal men; but they are not left at liberty to judge for themselves, as to who are loyal. The heads of the League assume this duty.... Strange as it may seem, this trap for

votes is meeting with considerable success throughout the country, and is catching not a few victims in our District. Quite a number of voters have bit at the bait of extra patriotism which the League offers as an inducement to its dupes, and have pledged themselves, blindfold, to it requirements.[38]

Four black ministers from York County were among the delegates to the Republican meeting in Columbia. Their presence created a stir among white Democrats who were unaccustomed to seeing blacks exercise constitutional rights or assemble with whites in a social setting. They worried that these "self appointed delegates to the black and tan convention" would create political unrest among the black population.

Though the derogatory title "black and tan" was little more than racial rhetoric in the postwar South, by the early 1880s it represented a viable faction within the Republican National Party. As blacks across the South formed a coalition to guarantee seats at the national convention, an all-white wing known as the "Lily Whites" opposed them. Though the black faction was decimated by registration laws designed to disenfranchise the black population it continued with some validity in South Carolina until the late 1930s.[39]

Joseph W. Tolbert of Ninety-Six, South Carolina, led the Black and Tans of the Union Republican Party for many years. "Tieless Joe" Tolbert was a prominent figure in the party and wielded power throughout the state and Washington. Over the years he had been successful in seating both black and white delegates at the national convention, until Rock Hill's Carl Hambright fractured the party when he organized the Republican Party of South Carolina. Hambright had hopes of luring whites from the Democratic Party by offering a "Lily White" party. A showdown between the "Hambrighters" and the Black and Tans was inevitable.[40]

On 26 April 1930 the Lily Whites met in convention in Columbia with nearly a thousand delegates attending the meeting. The *Clover Herald* touted: "[N]o Negroes appeared ... in contrast with the recent meeting of a rival state Republican group led by J.W. Tolbert." The maxim of the Lily White convention was "In the year 1932 we will march to victory with that peerless leader, the Honorable Herbert Hoover!"

Desiring the heads of Tolbert and Perry Howard, a black leader from Mississippi, President Hoover, who was pressing for "purification" of the party throughout the south, supported the Lily Whites. The party's national committee, however, refused to oust the two old-line southern bosses. The *Yorkville Enquirer* fumed: "Both Tolbert and Howard stand out as shining symbols of the old 'black and tan' regime which built up little dynasties by virtue of control of the Southern Negroes — a residue of reconstruction 'carpet bag' days — and 'delivered' delegations at national conventions to the candidate who had most to offer."[41]

Leaders of the National Republican Party instructed state committees that every delegation had to have black representation or it would not be received at the national convention. "Personally," said one Rock Hill Hambrighter, "I don't like it a bit, and I know that it has beaten any chance we might have had to build up a Republican Party in South Carolina. And I'm telling you," he continued, "I am not for sure that the Hambright crowd is going to be seated at Chicago as delegates. Joseph W. is going to have his checker-board bunch there too and a battle royal is in sight. It may be settled by the Hambright crowd seating half the state's delegates; and the Tolbert tallymen making up the balance."

When the South Carolina Republican Party was told their delegation must have black representation, the editor of the *Yorkville Enquirer* labeled Hambright and his party as the "tinged lily white" wing of the Republican Party. Yet, Editor Grist acknowledged that just because the National Executive Committee, of which "Uncle Joe Tolbert of this state is the dean ... doesn't necessarily mean that the Hambrighters, with the administration forces behind them, will also lose out when the matter comes before the convention credentials committee."

As Grist had suggested, Hambright's delegation was seated at the convention and the "black and tans" faded from the political scene. Yet, it took nearly fifty years for the Republican Party to reinvent itself into a conservative platform, shuck off its radicalism, distance itself from its Reconstruction history and become a force in South Carolina to be reckoned with.

In 1867, however, the "black and tans" were rapidly developing. One of the four black delegates from York County to the convention was John W. Mead. Mead took a major role in discussions, favoring free schools and colleges, improvement of railroads, and a fair distribution of labor contracts. With other delegates he proposed legislation to divide or sell unoccupied lands to benefit the poor and encourage immigration to South Carolina. W. Wright, a black lawyer from the Low Country, introduced a subject none of the party's leadership was eager to consider. Wright proposed the party spend its energies on placing blacks in leadership roles and suggested a black man should be on the next presidential ticket. Boldly he resolved that "the colored race shall not shrink from pushing the movement on, until they are allowed to sit in the councils of the nation." Robert Delarge, a powerful black legislator from Charleston, disapproved of Wright's proposal, saying he would not allow color to dictate how he voted. Other Republicans, however, feared this might lead to crossover voting and forced the position that any candidate who failed to support the Union Republican Party would not be nominated.[42]

Voter registration in York County began Thursday morning, 17 August 1867, and continued till 5 o'clock P.M. the following Saturday. Before registering, each man had to "solemnly swear in the presence of Almighty God" his loyalty to the United States, vowing he had never been a state or national officeholder, had not participated in the war or aided anyone who did, and promised to support the United States Constitution. The *Yorkville Enquirer* reported that the county's registration ran smoothly, without any disturbing incident, and related a story of one well-known black man by the name of "Jink" who listened attentively to the reading of the oath until he heard the phrase "support the Constitution of the United States." At this point Jink interrupted with "Stop, sar! Stop, sar! I can't do dat; it's all I can do to supoort my own family, and I'm not going to supoort anybody else!" After an explanation, Jink signed the oath.[43]

Not all newspaper accounts of the registration made light of blacks. One gives a poignant picture of those men who knew they were participating in a history-making event. When the Board of Registration was scheduled to arrive at the small agricultural community of McConnellsville, area blacks began to gather early in the morning. A *Yorkville Enquirer* reporter on the scene noted that the board's arrival "was anxiously expected by a large crowd of Freedmen, who had gathered in the vicinity at an early hour in the morning, and whose eyes, beaming with anxiety, were constantly turned in the direction whence the gentlemen were expected to come."[44]

Neighboring Chester County began its registration two days earlier and, like York County's Democratic leaders, complained of the apathy among the whites: "The white population of this District is for the most part, passive and indifferent." Unable to lay complete responsibility on whites, the writer suggested they were "prevented by the crowds of blacks, who surrounded the registers 'from morn till dewy eve,' and from their indisposition to encounter the odors exhaled in this hot August weather, in the thronged Courtroom. When another opportunity is afforded, and the weather becomes cooler, it is hoped that the records will show a larger increase of white voters."[45]

By September 24, all York County registration returns had been reported except for the Bethel Precinct that was expected to show a black majority. County wide tallies showed 1,870 white men and 1,908 black men had registered.[46] Just prior to the election, the registration books were opened again, and new registrations brought the tallies to 2,203 whites and 2,130 blacks. Throughout the Reconstruction Era the racial ratio for York County generally remained fifty-fifty, with the majority of whites voting the Democratic ticket while blacks consistently preferred the Republican Party.

Freedmen were not as ignorant as the South portrayed them, nor as brilliant as the North expounded. Although the mass of freedmen were uneducated, clearly they were able to learn. William Beverly Nash, an uneducated freedman and delegate to South Carolina's 1868 constitutional convention, declared, "We are not prepared for the suffrage. But we can learn. Give a man tools and let him commence to use them, and in time he will learn a trade. So it is with voting. We may not understand it at the start, but in time we can learn to do our duty."[47] Of the fourteen black congressmen and two black senators elected in the South from 1868 to 1872, all but three had some secondary education and four had attended college. Francis L. Cardozo, who had served South Carolina as state secretary for four years and state treasurer for another four, had attended the University of Glasgow and theological schools in Edinburgh and London.[48] Regardless of the tremendous learning strides blacks made in the first few years of their freedom, as a whole, the white Southern Democrat was unable to concede his abilities.

A meeting of white conservatives took place in Columbia on 6 November to "deliberate upon the present condition of our political affairs." Twenty districts (counties) were represented. Delegates from York County were James F. Hart, General Evander McIver Law and Robert G. McCaw.[49] After some discussion the assembly prepared a resolution that expressed in no uncertain terms the heart and mind of the white population. It equated white conservatism with all that was right and "Christian," and claimed that its members promoted peace, equality and the true advancement of civilization:

> We desire peace ... for its holy Christian influence, and for the civilization and refinement, which spring up in its path. They [the Reconstruction acts of Congress] sow the seeds of discord ... and place the best interests of society into the hands of an ignorant mob. They disfranchise the white citizen and enfranchise the newly emancipated slave. The slave of yesterday, who knew no law but the will of the master, is today about to be invested with the control of the government.
>
> We are not unfriendly to the Negro; on the contrary, we know that we are his best friends. In his property, in his life and in his person we are willing that the black man and the white man shall stand together upon the same platform and be shielded by the same equal laws.... We, therefore, feeling the responsibility of the subject and the occasion, enter most solemn protest against the policy of investing the Negro with political rights. The black man is what God and nature and circumstance have made him.... [H]e is not fit to be invested with these important rights.... The government of the country should not be permitted to pass from the hands of the white man into the hands of the Negro.... As citizens of the United States we should not consent to live under Negro supremacy, nor should we acquiesce in Negro equality. Not for ourselves only, but on behalf of the Anglo-Saxon race and blood in this country, do we protest against this subversion of the great social law?
>
> We have shown that free Negro labor, under the emancipation policy of the Government is a disaster from which ... it will require years to recover. Add to this the policy which the Reconstruction acts propose to enforce, and you place the South politically and socially under the hell of the Negro. These influences combined would drag to hopeless ruin the most prosperous community in the world.
>
> In the name of humanity to both races — in the name of cit-

Major James F. Hart commanded Hart's Battery of Hampton's Legion and was wounded at Burgess Mill 28 October 1864, losing his right leg (courtesy of John Wine, York).

izenship under the Constitution—in the name of a common history in the past—in the name of our Anglo-Saxon race and blood—in the name of the civilization of the nineteenth century—in the name of magnanimity and the noble instincts of manhood—in the name of God and nature—we protest against these Reconstruction acts as destruction to the peace of society, the prosperity of the country and the greatness and grandeur of our common future.

The people of the South are powerless to avert the impending ruin. We have been overborne; and the responsibility to posterity and to the world has passed into our hands.

Not only did this resolution put into words the feeling and thinking of the white population, if taken at face value it might also be used to jus-

Home of Major James F. Hart. Located on Cleveland Avenue, this home was built c. 1815 for Judge William Smith and later sold to Robert McCaw, in 1852, Major James F. Hart—a Citadel graduate, attorney, senator and Confederate officer—purchased the house in 1870. After a fire in 1881, Hart redesigned the house in Victorian style. After Hart's death in 1905, his son, John R. Hart, inherited the property. John practiced law in Yorkville and later became mayor of the town (courtesy of Culture & Heritage Museums).

tify any action against an opposing view in the name of peace, prosperity and the general good. This document may be seen as a pronouncement of impassioned fury and violence.

Now that voters were registered and certified, the election was scheduled for Tuesday and Wednesday, 19 and 20 of November.[50] During those two days the state's voters were to cast ballots "For a Convention" or "Against a Convention" to draft a new state constitution and for delegates to that convention.

When the November election day arrived, there was an obvious absence of white voters. Statewide, registered voters numbered over 125,000 (46,346 whites and 78,982 blacks), but only 71,807 cast their vote (2,211 whites and 68,876 blacks). This same lack of participation was reflected in York County; out of a total of 4,084 registered voters only 1,773 cast ballots. The *Yorkville Enquirer* reported: "very few of the whites voted, not exceeding sixty!"[51]

At one of the county's polls the lack of white people caused a black voter to become suspicious. "No sir, there's something wrong about dis election," he said. "I don't see any white people voting, like they used to do, and I ain't gwine to have nothing to do wid it."[52] One black voter thought the occasion of casting his first ballot was such a memorable event that he refused to put it in the ballot box, preferring to take it home for a souvenir. He finally agreed to cast his ballot after he was given a blank one for remembrance.

Statewide, the black vote decided the election in favor of a constitutional convention that would open in Charleston on 14 January 1868.[53] Delegates from York County, all Republicans, were John L. Neagle (white), William E. Rose[54] (white), John W. Mead (black), and J. Hannibal White (black).[55] Convention delegates had their work cut out for them and they would labor more than fifty days before a new state constitution was ready for submission to the voters.

That election was scheduled for 14–16 April. Voters in this election would decide on the state constitution as well as congressional candidates, a senator and four representatives to the state legislature, governor, and lieutenant governor, secretary of state, and comptroller general. A lot was riding on the outcome of this election, since it would elect a legislature that would determine the future rights of everyone in South Carolina. Even more intriguing was that the tallies of this election would be counted differently from those in previous elections. The old state constitution had required a percentage of registered voters to participate in an election before it was valid, and voters could invalidate an election by simply refusing to vote. This was known as the "do-nothing" policy. The Reconstruction acts, however, required an election to be decided by a majority of voters.[56]

In preparation for the election, the Boards of Registration across the state were ordered to open their books for a final revision. At the same time, Democratic Conservative Clubs were being organized statewide to plan their strategy. The number one aim of these clubs was to sponsor mass meetings or rallies in hope of generating excitement among white voters. One such rally held in York County on 6 April was reported to have a crowd as large "as any political exigency ever brought here before."[57]

Three days later Yorkville awakened to find its "streets filled with blue coats."[58] During the night, a peacekeeping company of about thirty soldiers arrived under the command of Lieutenant Wells to oversee the upcoming elections. As the federal government had done in 1865, similar units were dispatched to other select parts of the state. When these troops arrived in Yorkville that night, few county residents were aware another troop — the Ku Klux Klan — had arrived a month earlier. Membership in the Klan was rapidly enlarging across twelve piedmont counties, and as they enlarged violence increased.[59]

The tally of ballots brought white conservatives face-to-face with their worst fears. The state constitution had been ratified and Radical Republicans had won every position on the ballot. It should not have been a surprise to Democrats as nearly a third of the state's registered voters had opted to ignore the election.[60] This time the editor of the *Yorkville Enquirer* placed blame squarely on the shoulders of the Democrats:

> [F]ailure resulted partly from the indifference manifested by some of our citizens in regard to the issue before them; and partly from the heavy rains prevailing during the three days of election.... The Negroes did as they were instructed — voted *en masse* on Tuesday; and it had been well if the Conservatives had adopted their example. It was not until after Tuesday, that the streams became too much swollen for crossing. But our failure is nevertheless inexcusable. The contest for District officers is soon to come off and we will have then an opportunity to wipe out the disgrace of our late defeat. Therefore let every man to work at once. Organize Conservative Union clubs throughout the District, put these organizations in communication with a central organization at this place, and then strive to perfect and enlarge in every possible way these organizations. By these we can succeed. If we neglect them, we may

fail again. We all acknowledge that success in the coming election is a matter much more important than that which engaged our attention last week. It will be criminal in us to sleep over our fortunes now.[61]

Within days of the devastating defeat, York County Democrats met and adopted a resolution to permit black conservatives into its membership. Without a doubt, this sudden change in policy suggests the party had awakened to the power of the black vote and was hoping to siphon power from the Republicans. The resolution read as follows:

> *Whereas*, we desire, for the future as in the past, that kindly relations should be cherished towards the colored people; and that we will afford them every opportunity and privilege in our power whereby they may become instructed in the duties of citizenship, and in furtherance of these views, be it
>
> *Resolved*, That the colored people be invited to attend the meetings of this Club, and that such as choose to do so, be invited to enroll their names as members of the same.
>
> *Resolved*, That we, the members of this Club, do cherish, patronize, and otherwise uphold and sustain those colored persons who have patriotically and intelligently decided that the interests of all classes in this State are identified with each other, and who have voted to sustain this principle; and we do further pledge ourselves to prefer those persons who are members of this Club, in the matter of employment and wages, over and above all other persons whosoever.[62]

When an all black Democratic Club was formed in Rock Hill a month later, the *Yorkville Enquirer* boasted how the "colored people" were "awaking to their true interests and cutting themselves loose from oath bound societies, and the influence of persons who are luring them on to destruction."[63]

A week or so after the York County Democrats adopted their resolution, a large number of white and black conservatives gathered in Yorkville to select a nominating committee for various offices in an upcoming county election. Doubt and suspicion between the races seemed to have been put aside when a sixteen member committee consisting of equal numbers of black and white was formed.[64] However, when the nominating committee retired to private chambers to decide upon candidates and remained in session for an extended period, old fears and suspicions began to rise. Some whites began to speculate that the black committee members had previously come to an agreement to reject a ticket that had only white men on it. Someone suggested that blacks had joined the clubs only to influence the election; after all, they had read that Lucius Windbush, "a mulatto grog-seller, [had been] brought up from Columbia for that purpose."[65] Gradually the white members began agreeing among themselves that they had been "sold out." Just before the situation got out of hand the committee returned with their choice of candidates. White tempers cooled when it was announced that an all white ticket had been formed without one dissenting vote.[66]

With ratification of a new state constitution behind them and subsequent establishment of the state government, whites believed that strengthening of the Democratic Party would give the Radicals a good thrashing in the November election. Feeling their political oats, Democrats openly denounced the Reconstruction acts and Republican policies. Five days before the National Democratic Convention opened in New York on July 4, General Wade Hampton publicly berated Congress for their punitive Reconstruction Acts of 1867. Throughout the convention, the hall echoed with denunciations of Reconstruction and the policies of the Republican Party.

Democrats nominated Horatio Seymour of New York for President and General Frank P. Blair, Jr., of Missouri for vice president. Blair was the third and youngest son of Francis P. Blair, Sr., who had been a member of Andrew Jackson's "Kitchen Cabinet." Frank Blair was a veteran of the U.S. House of Representatives and Senate and had served in the military during the Mexican War. Typical of those living in the border states, the Blairs were Unionist Democrats and staunch supporters of Lincoln before the Civil War. Blair was convinced slavery was an insult to the Union flag and when the South seceded, he believed those states needed to be taught respect and submission. Blair served the Union during the war as a brigadier general; but after the war he worked diligently to readmit the South without retribution.

During the Civil War Horatio Seymour, as governor of New York, denounced Lincoln's Proclamation of Emancipation, supported the theory of states' rights and protested the national conscription as unconstitutional.[67] Both Seymour and Blair were Southern sympathizers and agreed wholeheartedly on Reconstruction. Several days before the convention, Blair wrote a letter denouncing the Reconstruction Acts and proposed that the new president should nullify the laws. South Carolina's Wade Hampton completely supported Blair's idea and unsuccessfully attempted to get it included in the Democratic platform. After the convention Hampton continued berating the Republican Congress in his campaign speeches for Seymour and Blair and soon became known to Northerners as a Southern fire-eater, eventually having to bear the ire of both Republicans and Democrats. His party leaders began to see him as a liability and called for Seymour to quieten him and repair damages. Hampton's outspokenness garnered the loathing of one of his party's most powerful leaders — New York governor Samuel Tilden. The governor's loathing turned to hatred when the Democrats lost the 1868 presidential election, believing Hampton was personally responsible. The party's loss of 1868 solidly stuck in Tilden's craw and it remained there for years.

Following the 1868 National Democratic Convention enthusiasm, electrified Democrats across the state held mass rallies in every county. The Yorkville streets on 29 August overflowed with two thousand white men and women, as well as two hundred blacks who ignored "the slavish orders of the League [and] had come out to hear the other side of the question."[68] Colonel J.P. Thomas, a South Carolina presidential elector, arrived from Columbia by train and was met by a crowd led by Colonel W.H. McCorkle, marshal of the day. Theodore Parrish was there to greet the party leader with a salute from an artillery piece.

McCorkle led Thomas to the public square, where a Seymour and Blair campaign flag was raised followed by a thundering salute from Parrish's cannon and shouts and huzzahs. The Chester Brass Band[69] led a parade up Congress Street to a park where a platform had been built. Following an opening prayer by the Rev. Robert Lathan, Thomas addressed the crowd, tracing the party's history to 1787 and pointing out how the Jeffersonian theory of states' rights and limited federal powers had always been the party's policy. He cited the issues of constitutional invasion and despotism presented in the form of the Fourteenth Amendment:

> What was the substance of that Amendment? It was that all who had taken an oath of office prior to the war, and afterwards engaged in it, should be deprived of holding office. That is, you were called upon to put the brand of infamy upon those who led us in the war and in the councils of the State. It was to make us lose our self-respect.... History records the atrocities of Genghis Khan, the Great Conqueror, and of Attila, the Scourge of the World, but it has been reserved for modern radicalism to improve upon these barbarities, and subject a conquered people to the dominion of their former slaves. Nowhere will you find perpetrated, such acts of despotism as have been accomplished in this land.[70]

General Evander Law denounced the Republican Party and its punitive acts, arguing the Reconstruction Acts were unconstitutional. Turning his attention to the freedmen, he exhorted them to realize they were mere tools of the Radicals who used them for their own selfish ends. Throughout the day, cheers resounded and it seemed as though "Parrish and his gun were almost ubiquitous — thundering in the streets in the morning — banging away at the depot on the arrival of the train — back in town saluting the flag when it was raised — and finally stationed near the platform bellowing its applause to the speakers — it played the part of 'flying artillery' to perfection."[71]

Sometime during the festivities, fourteen delegates from the various county clubs met to schedule two other mass meetings. The first was to be held in Yorkville on 18 September and the second in Rock Hill the following day. Later both events would be deemed successful and proof that the people of York County were "keenly alive to the issues to be determined in the coming election, that proof is afforded in the frequency of political gatherings and the attentive interest and large outpourings of the people that characterize them."[72] A rally in the village of Clover in the northwest section of the county was spoken of as the place where the white people of York County "quit foolin'" and the work of "rousing the county was started."[73]

Though political in design, these rallies were festive social affairs involving barbeques, picnics or covered dish dinners. One of the best-described took place on 7 October at Whiteside's Mill on Clark's Fork Creek. According to the *Yorkville Enquirer* a speaker's stand, three long tables and benches had been built and decorated in preparation for the meeting. People from the area, party leaders and guests began arriving early in the morning by wagon, horseback, buggy and on foot — most with an armload of homemade foods. The Chester Brass Band was seated under a U.S. flag while black and white leaders took their places under a Seymour-Blair banner. The Yorkville Colored Club, which had been formed in September, took their places under their symbol of a mighty mule.[74]

A self-described "satisfied Democrat since 1832," the Rev. Robert A. Ross of the Sharon Associate Reformed Presbyterian Church opened the meeting with prayer. He was followed by Representative William D. Simpson, who spoke for more than two hours comparing the platforms of both parties and policies on state and federal levels. After the morning had passed, more than fifteen hundred people gathered at the three long dinner tables — one for the ladies, one for the gentlemen and a third one for freedmen. A *Yorkville Enquirer* correspondent reported that all three of the tables were "trembling under the mighty weight of well-prepared homemade eatables; the half of which was not consumed."[75]

At a meeting in Yorkville a month earlier, the question of debts incurred during the war and the hardships they created was discussed.[76] This discussion may have resulted from an order issued by Commander Sickles in the spring of 1867 imposing a twelve month moratorium on debts. J. Newman McElwee, a Yorkville businessman and creditor of more than $30,000, was seated as chairman. He described the financial condition of the county, noting that property within the county would not pay fifty cents on the dollar. McElwee suggested that since white people had no representation in Washington or Columbia there was no other option but make a compromise between the debtor and creditor. "Yes, fellow citizens," he said, "a liberal, just and equitable compromise will restore harmony; unite the white people; exhume morality and social feeling; pay more debts and bury Radicalism in York District in an infamy so deep and so profound, that nothing short of resurrection will ever reach it."[77] To demonstrate his sincerity, McElwee said he was prepared to commit his debts to flames for the betterment of the county. Before the meeting ended a committee of eleven men was appointed to prepare a report on a compromise of debt and present it at an October meeting.[78]

Amid all the Democrats' rallies, picnics and meetings in York County, the Republicans attempted a mass meeting of their own. Compared to the Democrats, the October Republican turnout was puny. The *Yorkville Enquirer* reported "a number of local Mogols of the party could be seen on the wing, hurrying to and fro, trying to produce a moderate degree of enthusiasm among their deluded followers, but with little success, as was afterwards demonstrated." If the pro–Democratic paper can be believed, a head count of Republicans taken as they marched along Congress Street revealed only one hundred and eight freedmen present. The newspaper boasted, "The indications are that Radicalism in York District is on its last legs, and before many months have elapsed, it will, doubtless, only be remembered as a thing of the past. Rumors are current that many of the freemen who have heretofore acted with the Radical party are deserting it, having become satisfied that their true interest is identical with that of the respectable white man of the country."⁷⁹ Democrats probably comforted themselves with the report and could not believe it would be another eight years before freedmen would defect from the Republican Party.

Always expecting riots during elections, a company of forty men of the Eighth U.S. Infantry disembarked at the Yorkville depot on the evening of Thursday, 21 October. These men were under the command of Brevet Major W.S. Worth. Units of similar size and orders were also arriving in Chester, Union, Laurens, Abbeville, Newberry, Edgefield, Beaufort, Georgetown and Darlington.⁸⁰

As election day drew near, newspapers encouraged voters to support the Democratic ticket and reminded them that votes must be cast at the precinct where they registered or their ballot would be disqualified: "The issue is plain and simple. Every one has an equal interest in the result. See to it that every man is at his place on Tuesday next. We are all tired of the abomination of radicalism"⁸¹; "If radicalism is to be voted down in York District, every man must be at his own box or precinct. There will be no exception made in any case. You must vote at home or lose your vote. Remember you cannot vote at Yorkville unless you have registered at Yorkville. Explain to your neighbors, that all may understand."⁸² Another pleaded, "We desire that the full vote of the District be polled on Tuesday next. Had our people all voted in June last, we would now be represented and not misrepresented. See to it that all of your neighbors are out. If they cannot walk, haul them to the polls. If every man turns out, radicalism will go up in York District. If we do not turn out, strife and contest will be secured in the next election. Success will secure us peace and quiet in York District"⁸³; "We may or may not be able to elect a President at the approaching election. We certainly can elect the Hon. W.D. Simpson for Congress. We certainly can give [him] a large majority in York District. We can satisfy our colored people that they live among Democrats. Success in this District will diminish the evil influence of carpetbaggers. Our people, white and colored, can agree and understand each other better. Such will be some of the fruits of success and a general vote. Let us have peace."⁸⁴

Election day in Yorkville was especially merry. At two o'clock in the afternoon the Stone and Murray Circus opened, announcing itself as "the best in the world," unsurpassed by any circus in Europe and fifty years ahead of any other in America. For the admission price of seventy-five cents (fifty cents for those under ten years old) the circus-goer could be entertained by Madam Jeanette, "a most brilliant and daring Lady Diver ever seen," and Great John Henry, "the superb defiance champion, equestrian and Thaumaturgic Artiste." It was no coincidence that the circus opened on election day. This tactic was inspired by the Mississippi Plan in hopes of tempting the poor to exchange ballots for tickets.

Long before the polls opened at six o'clock on the morning of 3 November many freedmen assembled at the precincts. To insure their safety, Republican leaders had instructed them to arrive at the polls early before white Democrats arrived and tried to block the polls. By 11 o'clock all freedmen had voted and cleared the area.

Democratic presidential candidate Seymour became seriously ill before the election and was replaced with Republican Lucius Robinson. Though Democrats did not win as many positions as they would have liked, they were satisfied that William D. Simpson won the Fourth Congressional District seat over Republican W.A. Wallace. Nationwide, Ulysses S. Grant won the popular election by a close margin, but received two hundred and fourteen electoral votes. Grant carried twenty-four states, six of them in the South.

CHAPTER THREE

The Redeemer Cometh

Nearly simultaneous with the ratification of the state constitution in 1868, both the federal and state governments became aware the Ku Klux Klan was being organized across the state. By October the Klan was well ensconced in twelve piedmont counties and Governor Robert Scott was constantly receiving reports that Republicans were being intimidated and threatened by hooded terrorists. Not all terrorist acts, however, could be laid at the feet of Klansmen. On 19 November, black Democrat James Minor was killed at the Columbia Depot by black Republican Radicals who denounced Minor a traitor to his people and the Republican Party. The following day, Governor Scott charged the counties of Abbeville, Anderson, Edgefield, Lexington, Newberry, Chester, Laurens, Union, York and Darlington "with violating the laws, and the officers of the law set at defiance; that the peaceful citizens are murdered in cold blood, and the murderers not only permitted but assisted to escape from justice; that families have been forced to abandon their homes from fear of violence, and the utterance of political opinions stifled by threats of violence, &c; and that to carry out these principles, large quantities of firearms, of the most improved patterns have been secretly brought into the State and distributed."[1]

As a leader of the state Democratic Party and a member of the Democratic State Committee, Wade Hampton was warned by Governor Scott that violence would beget violence and that unless Hampton publicly tried to stem the tide of violence, Scott would allow freedmen to retaliate. Knowing that a clash of races would be fruitless and would certainly bring federal intervention, Hampton addressed Democrats through the newspapers, urging an end to violence. The moratorium he advocated lasted for nearly a year and a half.[2]

In the fall of 1870, terrorism and violence such as South Carolina had never seen exploded across the state and continued through the next year. The Klan was bold and their "justice" was brutal. In January 1871 black militiamen in Union County murdered a white wagoner when he refused to surrender his load of whiskey. The militiamen were arrested but Klansmen broke into the Union County jail and killed two of the suspects. Six weeks later five hundred Klansmen stormed the jail and killed the others. Their calling card read: "We want and will have Justice and this cannot be till a bleeding fight for freedom is fought. Until then the Moloch of Iniquity will have his victims, even if the Michael of Justice must have his martyrs."[3]

That same month Governor Scott requested military support from President Grant. But that support did not arrive until March, and then it was such a weak response both Democrats and Republicans recognized their presence was no real threat. Overall there were little more than nine hundred troops in a state that was about to explode in violence.[4]

The following month Congress passed the Ku Klux Klan Act, and in May President Grant threatened further federal intervention if violence continued. On 12 October Grant issued another proclamation demanding all armed groups surrender their arms within five days. On the deadline day he suspended the writ of habeas corpus and declared martial law in Chester, Chesterfield, Fairfield, Lancaster, Laurens, Newberry, Spartanburg, Union and York counties.

In most of these counties a large percentage of the male population were Democrats and members of the Klan. In York County, labeled as the hotbed of rebellion in the South, 80 percent of the men were estimated to be members.[5] Through violence and intimidation robe-clad Democrats were affecting every level of the social order. Numbers of Republican officeholders resigned out of fear and the Union Leagues were quaking. When Colonel Lewis Merrill was sent to South Carolina to investigate the insurgent movement in 1871 he reported that more than three hundred violent instances and at least seven murders had occurred in York County alone.

One hundred and thirty arrests by federal troops in York County had taken place by November 1871, and the numbers continued to rise. Less than one year later the number of indicted Klansmen across the state numbered about 1,300; of these only one hundred and fifty-eight cases had been disposed of.[6] These figures are indicative of the ineffectiveness of federal intervention. The Reconstruction Ku Klux Klan was the most powerful and effective grassroots movement the state had experienced up to that time. It accomplished what four years of civil war could not and helped to bring Reconstruction in South Carolina to an end.[7] Democrats were controlling the government on the county level by 1872, but the state level was a different matter. In November 1872, upon hearing that Franklin Moses had been elected governor, Hampton said it was time for white Southerners to "dedicate themselves to the redemption of the South."[8] Redemption, however, was four years away.

By 1875 an unprecedented and strange situation had developed between the South Carolina Republicans and Democrats. The government's reins were in the hands of Republican governor Daniel H. Chamberlain, who had been elected in November 1874; and though there was no love between the two parties, many Democrats found themselves having some real appreciation for the Republican carpetbagger.

John Thomas Scoggins. In April 1864, at the age of sixteen, Scoggins ran away from home, lied about his age, and enlisted in the Fifth South Carolina Regiment. After participating in the battles of the Wilderness, Spotsylvania and Cold Harbor, it was discovered he was underage and he was sent home. Within a few months he turned seventeen and was so determined to fight the Yankees he immediately enlisted in the Third Battalion of the South Carolina Reserves (courtesy of the Museum of Western York County, Sharon).

Chamberlain was born in Massachusetts and a graduate of Yale. He became an avid abolitionist and after a year of law school at Harvard, he joined the United States Army during the Civil War and was put in command of an all-black company. He had come to South Carolina in 1866 with visions of becoming a wealthy cotton planter and paying himself out of the debt incurred during his education. After two years of labor problems that enveloped the whole South, he admitted his defeat as a cotton farmer and began cultivating the fields of politics.[9] Chamberlain took an active role in the 1868 state constitutional convention and was later elected South Carolina attorney general, serving in this capacity during both terms of Governor Scott and one term of Governor Moses. Chamberlain participated in the "Printing Ring," which bilked the state out of a huge amount of money, and along with Senator "Honest" John Patterson relieved the state of the Greenville and Columbia Railroad. He was one of four carpetbaggers who drained the state's credit though the use of state bonds and was a member of a five-man land commission that spent nearly one million dollars of public money to buy land worth a quarter of a million.[10]

Speaking at a Yorkville reunion of Red Shirts in 1911, Colonel Asbury Coward, without calling Senator J. Hannibal White by name, spoke of one way the carpetbagger-scalawag legislature drained the government. He said, "It became an established custom that a member of the legislature must at least bring back a suit of furniture, and it is told that the Negro senator from York County brought back a bureau or a bedstead that was so large, that he had to tear off the side of his house so he could get it inside."[11]

Later in the month, at a reunion in Columbia of Red Shirts from all over the state, Governor Blease, before a thousand men, many of them in red shirts, announced that "a full, free and unlimited pardon for every Red Shirt

Hugh Hicklin Sherer. When Hugh Hicklin "Dock" Sherer passed away in October 1940, he was the last Confederate veteran living in western York County. After serving admirably in the war effort, he was caught up in the times and participated in the Ku Klux Klan, for which he spent eighteen months in a New York penitentiary. Sherer, a conservative Democrat, rode with the Red Shirts (courtesy of the Museum of Western York County, Sharon).

veteran in South Carolina" was on his desk.[12] A message from Mississippi Senator John Sharp Williams was read to the audience:

> I believe that the Red Shirt movement, beginning in Mississippi and South Carolina, and constituting the most nearly bloodless revolution in its magnitude that ever occurred in the world, saved the white man's civilization and his racial integrity in our southern states. I don't believe that the heroism of the Confederate soldier during the war had a parallel except in his patience, in his organization, in his decision and action, in bearing with and finally overthrowing Reconstruction regime. The white people of the South during that long period of wicked and oppressive saturnalia, exhibited solidarity unparallel in its results. They were unarmed by power and unsought by patronage.[13]

Although Chamberlain aligned himself with the most corrupt elements of the Republican Party, morally he stood head and shoulders above his political peers. Compared to his predecessors, Scott and Moses, he was a breath of fresh air in the State House.[14] Colonel Asbury Coward of Yorkville described him as a "shrewd, smart man, who understood the real situation and came near getting the support of the decent white people of the state on a plea of trying to save Anglo-Saxon civilization."[15] Two weeks before his inauguration Chamberlain made an effort to reform the Republican government by opposing the seating of two corrupt Republican judges: William J. Whipper and Franklin J. Moses, Jr. Whipper, a black man with little learning and no knowledge of law, was a confessed thief who passed his time

William B. Smith. It was said that William B. Smith of Clover sported the longest beard in York County. Supposedly he swore, as he went off to war, that he would not shave again until the Yankees were whipped. During the week, his beard was neatly plaited but on Sundays his wife would brush it to its fullest glory (courtesy of the Museum of Western York County, Sharon).

gambling. Moses was the former governor who earned the title "Robber Governor" after looting the state treasury during his administration.

When South Carolina entered the Civil War, the state was still paying on an "Old Debt" that existed in the form of bonds and stocks running down from the 3 percent stock issued in 1794 ($38,000 plus) in payment of Revolutionary War claims. Following the Civil War, on 31 October 1868, just three months after the Republicans took the reins of the state, the total public debt and interest was $5,842,697. The debt increased from $6,667,793 on 31 October 1869 to $7,665,908 on 31 October 1870 and to a whopping $15,851,327 by 31 October 1871.[16]

A financial deadlock existed in 1873. No interest on the debt had been paid since July 1871. The government knew that it could not levy another tax on the people as the limit had long before been reached. On 22 December the Consolidation Act became law and reduced the debt to about two-fifths of its amount by giving the state treasurer power to issue 50 percent of the full value of bonds and stocks, and no interest paid on bonds and stocks so long as they remain unconsolidated. Nearly six million dollars was repudiated in the Consolation Act. The bonds repudiated were conversion bonds that consisted of state securities and passed when the Republicans had a majority of the general assembly. Democrats opposed the act considering it unjust to place the Old Debt on equal footing with the Reconstruction Debt, when the state was receiving dollar for dollar in gold from the former. The Republican leaders, state financial agent Hiram Kimpton, state treasurer Niles G. Parker, Governor R.K. Scott and attorney general Daniel Chamberlain chuckled at their smartness as they issued nearly six million in bonds of the Greenville and Columbia Railroad owned by the state, without authority of the law, then repudiated them as illegal, and made large sums of money for themselves.[17]

Before the Republican administration multiplied South Carolina's funded debt, the state had a high rating as a borrower. Even before the Civil War South Carolina could obtain money from banks in the north or Europe as easily as any other state in the Union. Trust in the state's reputation continued into 1871, evidenced by the fact that when Governor Scott issued bonds they found a ready market, selling for a time at a high rate. Even the bonds issued in 1875 and 1876 were considered a good buy and easily found a market; that trust was enhanced when the canvass of votes in 1876 favored the election of Hampton.[18]

Three. The Redeemer Cometh

America was still a divided nation when 1876 began. The Civil War and Reconstruction had done nothing toward creating a true union. Republicans, Democrats, blacks and whites were actively devoting themselves to group identity rather than coming together as one people. They saw themselves as Republican Americans, Democrat Americans, black Americans or white Americans; beyond their origin of birth, few understood the concept of being American. South Carolina was even more fragmented. Not only was the state divided by race and party, the Democratic party was also divided by "Straight-outers" and "Fusionists," and the Republicans were either Radical or Independent. The Straight-outers strived for a clear definition on party lines and demanded the state Democratic party to nominate a full ticket of Democrats, while the Fusionists believed the only way to change the politics of the state was by cooperating with the Republican Party and sharing the ticket. The state and the Democratic party needed one man who could breech all rifts. For a while it seemed Governor Chamberlain was the man.

In spite of the great animosity between the two parties, Chamberlain's efforts to reform the Republican Party and his opposition to Moses and Whipper resulted in Democrats and Republicans finding themselves in bed with each other and participating in a willing but unlikely affair. In hopes of cleansing the government of corruption, Democrats supported Chamberlain in his fight with the general assembly for judicial purity and throughout the winter of 1875 stood with the governor and sustained his veto nineteen times. For the first time since the beginning of Reconstruction, Democrats and Republicans were aligning themselves and seeking common ground.

The Democratic State Central Committee, composed entirely of Fusionists, set its aim to affect the Democratic Executive Committee to support Chamberlain's reform policies and his second bid for governor. The committee consisted of Thomas Y. Simons (Charleston), M.P. O'Connor (Charleston), Francis W. Dawson (Charleston), Martin W. Gary (Edgefield), Matthew C. Butler (Edgefield), Wade Hampton (Richland), John S. Richardson (Sumter), S.P. Hamilton (Chester), Johnson Hagood (Barnwell), W.W. Sellers (Marion), Samuel McGowan (Abbeville), Henry McIver (Chesterfield), William H. Wallace (Union) and W.D. Simpson (Laurens). General Martin W. Gary was on the committee in name only. He fought tooth and nail against any association with the Republican

Party, yet he agreed to cooperate for the sake of the Democratic party. His zeal and impatience, however, drove him toward extreme measures to reestablish the old regime and more than anyone else he would be responsible for directing the Democratic party toward a Straight-Out ticket.

Upon the opening of the Civil War in 1861, Gary entered the Confederate army with the rank of captain and rose to the rank of brigadier general. He was one of the last Confederates to be captured, having been part of Jefferson Davis' entourage in his flight from Virginia to South Carolina. Until Gary's death, he proved himself to be an extremist and an agent of white supremacy. As long as Hampton remained in the governor's office extremists and advocates of white supremacy like Gary would be deterred in advancing their program. During Hampton's tenure as governor he was able to put into place a number of mid-stream policies and lay out a suffrage plan for African Americans. During Hampton's 1878 gubernatorial campaign, Martin Gary would try to use race as an issue to create a furor against Hampton. Hampton's prestige and the state's newspapers steadfastly took a stand for its hero and thwarted Gary's efforts. Gary's dogmatism and racial prejudice would plague the party's moderate policies and would eventually drive him to undermine Hampton after his election, as he hated Hampton's cooperation with black and conservative Republicans.

Martin W. Gary. General Gary was successful in convincing Wade Hampton to run for governor of South Carolina in 1876, but he constantly remained a thorn in Hampton's side. So clearly prone to violence, on several occasions he brought the state to the verge of civil war.

While serving on the Democratic State Central Committee in 1876, Gary was hammering out his own plan for the election; as expected his outline was dogmatic and simple:

1. Enroll every Democrat in every township on the Democratic Club roll.
2. Prepare a roll of every white and black voter in every township and return it immediately to the central executive committee.
3. Arm every Democratic Military Club and supply all members with thirty rounds of ammunition; stock a baggage wagon with three days' rations a day before the election in order to move on a moment's notice.

Though the central committee's efforts were spent on leading their party into Chamberlain's camp and forming one great party,[19] many Democrats shared Gary's sentiments and were unhappy with blurring party lines. Some Republicans were equally uneasy with Chamberlain's bipartisanship approach and suppression of Moses and Whipper. He drew their heaviest ire over a statement he made during an interview by Francis W. Dawson,[20] the Democratic publisher of the *News and Courier.* Hoping to get the bid for the Democratic nomination for governor, he made overtures to Democrats that appeared to his fellow Republicans that he had somersaulted into the lap of the Democrats.[21]

As Martin Gary continued to work on his campaign plan in January 1876 he must have been pleased with Republican reaction to the Chamberlain interview, but Fusionists saw Chamberlain's request for Democratic support in a positive light. York County Fusionists assembled in Yorkville on 3 January to draft a letter of appreciation to the governor for maintaining good government. Major James F. Hart delivered lofty praise of Chamberlain's actions, after which the Democrats agreed to deliver a resolution to the governor commending his actions and pledging their support for any such future acts. At that meeting black Republican senator J. Hannibal White of York brought other black Republicans to the meeting.[22] The proposal was accepted by all but one white Democrat. When the resolution was presented to the black men for their approval and signatures, not one would have anything to do with the resolution, fearing an ulterior motive in the budding alliance.[23]

Three days later, the members of the State Central Committee met in Columbia on January 6 to endorse a recommendation requesting Democrats to respond positively to Governor Chamberlain's appeal for the support. Eleven of the fourteen committee members endorsed the recommendation, but as expected, Martin Gary refused to have anything to do with it.[24] It seemed certain then that a strong alliance between the two parties was in the making.

Two events, however, would derail any possibility of an alliance between the two parties. The first was word that Mississippi had dragged itself from under Republican domination through elections and had restored white citizens to power. This news renewed the hopes of many Democrats in South Carolina that they too might cast the Republicans out of their midst. The second blow to a Republican-Democratic union came when the Republican controlled general assembly seated Moses and Whipper over Chamberlain's objections. It was bad news for Chamberlain as well. He said to Francis Dawson, "The reorganization of the Democratic party within the state is the only means left ... for opposing a solid and reliable front to this terrible crevasse of misgovernment and public debauchery."[25]

As the Republican Party began to prepare for its state nomination convention in April, the tide against Chamberlain rose to a high-water mark. The governor was hoping to be elected a delegate to the national convention, but with opposition on the rise he knew it would be the toughest fight of his political career. Chamberlain was right. His struggle for the nomination lasted through the night and demanded his finest oratory abilities. During the night, as Chamberlain's bid was weighing in the balance, C.E. Edwards, a black man from York County, wrote a note to the governor informing him of the situation that was developing among the county Democrats: "The Democratic party has concluded to put a man against you.... [T]he white people says this [is] the year to perish out the collard [sic] people to make them vote against you and President Grant." As a footnote Edwards made a request: "You will please help me a little bit with as much as five dollars."[26] At seven o'clock, as the sun was rising on 13 April, an exhausted convention granted Chamberlain his prize.

Three weeks after the adjournment of the Republican convention, the Democrats opened their convention to elect delegates to their national convention. Martin Gary was prepared to get his Straight-Out ticket in resolution, and though he expected opposition, he did not expect it to come so early in the convention. In his opening address, convention president Joseph B. Kershaw gave notice to the delegates that the party must take a wait-and-see position regarding whether Chamberlain would get the nod from his party for a second term as governor. Kershaw believed the best route for his party was to throw in their support of Chamberlain for a second term. The very thought sickened Gary, but it was to get worse.

Immediately following Kershaw's opening address he appointed former governors John L. Manning and Benjamin Perry and James S. Cothran as a committee on resolutions to form the party's platform. None of the committee members were friendly to Gary's Straight-Out ticket. Manning did not like Gary at all, Perry was an avid advocate of supporting Chamberlain, and Cothran always followed the lead of Francis Dawson, a hardened Fusionist. John C. Sheppard of Edgefield County presented Gary's argument for a Straight-Out ticket, but as expected, the committee quickly swept it aside and resolved to support Chamberlain.

Gary was not finished. He took his fight for an "undefiled" ticket to the floor and pressed the delegates to adopt the same platform as the national party and put forth a full Democratic ticket. Anything less, he said, would reveal a wishy-washy character in the party.[27] Committee member James Cothran hotly argued the point at length and when Kershaw called for a vote, the committee's plan to support Chamberlain passed easily with seventy votes while Gary's plan received only forty-two.[28]

In the middle of these political battles, others were making preparations to celebrate the centennial of Fort Moultrie. In Chester, Charles S. Brice, president of the Chester Rifle Club, made a daring request of the governor—to use public arms in the town parade and drill on Memorial Day.[29] The arms he wanted to use had been collected several years earlier when a black militia unit was disarmed following a bloody battle with the Ku Klux Klan. Considering the wave of violence the state had experienced four years earlier and the ever-present threat of a resurgence of violence, the governor was understandably hesitant to put arms into the hands of white Democrats. Before Brice heard from the governor, he wrote a second letter citing the poor condition of the arms in hopes of swaying the governor: "These arms have been much neglected and I fear much abused." He assured Chamberlain the arms would be taken care of "and returned at a moment's notice when called for," promising the firearms would not be used "for any improper or indecent purposes."[30] Chester County Sheriff John Walker, who had possession of the rifles, supported Brice's request and would see to it that the governor would not be embarrassed by some misuse. Perhaps Walker was a Fusionist and was giving signals that he and other upstate Democrats were willing to work with the Republican Party. Chamberlain granted Brice's petition.

During June, Charleston was filled with festivities as the Fort Moultrie centennial was being celebrated. A banquet was held in Hibernian Hall, where the elite hobnobbed and discussed politics over dinner and glasses of wine. Among the dinner guests was Wade Hampton, who had arrived from Wild Woods, his Mississippi home, and was seated at the main table to the right of Governor Chamberlain. With uplifted glasses, Chamberlain assured everyone that unity and peace were his aim for South Carolina. This toast was for the benefit of Northern guests, who had grown accustomed to reports of violence from the state. Hampton stood and asked the Northern guests to "Go back and tell your people what you have seen, not what you may have heard."[31]

Martin Gary was at the Charleston banquet, but he did not have celebrating on his mind. All he could think about was completing a Straight-Out ticket before the convention began. During the celebration Gary was busy garnering support for Matthew Butler, his personal preference for governor. Butler was not as radical as Gary, but agreed with him that a Fusionist ticket would not give South Carolina the solution she so badly needed.

Butler, like Hampton and Gary, was well connected with the aristocracy of South Carolina. His uncle was a U.S. senator and his cousin was none other than Congressman Preston S. Brooks, who nearly caned to death Massachusetts Senator Charles Sumner. Also, Butler's wife was the daughter of governor Andrew Pickens. Unlike other sons of wealthy planters, Butler had joined a cavalry regiment at the start of the Civil War as a captain and worked himself through the ranks to major general. He was severely wounded at the Battle of Brandy Station, Virginia, when a Yankee cannonball took off his foot.

Gary's zeal would allow him little time for celebration, but that did not bother him because he had work to do and, after all, he detested sitting with Republicans. By the end of the celebration Gary had worked out his Straight-Out ticket complete with men who had won fame during the Civil War. Surely this ticket would bother Radical Republicans who labored diligently to exclude aristocrats who had served as an officer in the Confederate Army. Gary's Straight-Out ticket proposed the following: governor — General Matthew C. Butler; lieutenant governor — General

Three. The Redeemer Cometh

John A. Wagner; comptroller general — General Johnson Hagood; attorney general — Colonel Beaufort W. Ball; treasurer — Colonel James N. Lipscomb; secretary of state — Colonel D. Wyatt; adjutant insp. general — General E.B.C. Cash.

As the centennial celebration came to an end, guests began making plans to return to their respective homes. As fate would have it, Gary found himself on the same Columbia-bound train with Hampton. Since the war, these two Confederate generals had little to do with each other. As early as 1865 Gary had become scornful of Hampton's conciliatory approach to Reconstruction of supporting moderate policies and voting rights for blacks.[32] Gary believed Hampton had been disloyal to the state and the party when he would not consider the governor's seat in 1865 and allowed the reins of government slip into the hands of James Orr. Though Gary and Hampton were separated by their personalities and antagonism, one thing they shared was a love for South Carolina.

Gary was traveling back to Columbia with Johnson Hagood and Joseph Kershaw when he noticed Hampton sitting a few seats away. He excused himself and joined Hampton. Politics was a natural subject for both men, and during their discussion Hampton

Matthew C. Butler. Born in 1838 at Eagle's Craig near Greenville, S.C., to a large, prominent family, Butler's father was a U.S. congressman. An uncle was a U.S. Senator and another uncle, Pierce Mason Butler, was a governor of S.C. Butler was the nephew of Commodore Perry, son-in-law of S.C. governor Francis Wilkinson Pickins, and cousin to Congressman Preston Brooks who cane whipped Senator Sumner. After the war Butler returned to Edgefield County to practice law and then practiced later in Washington, D.C. He was appointed major general of U.S. Volunteers during the Spanish-American War, one of the few Confederate officers to serve during that war.

confided that in spite of the courtesies he had extended to Chamberlain the night before, he was in favor of Democrats taking a stand apart from the Republican Party. When Gary realized they were in full agreement, the coolness that had existed for years began to dissipate. Gary urged Hampton to join him in the fight to free South Carolina with a Straight-Out ticket. Throwing all caution to the wind, Gary offered Hampton the gubernatorial nomination. At first Hampton was as humble as a young man trying to show his intended how unfit he was for marriage. He told Gary he had lost his fortune and had nothing to give but his time and some talent.[33] Gary was even more delighted to learn that Hampton had decided to change his permanent residency back to South Carolina. And even more delightful to Gary's ears than that, Hampton said if he were nominated for governor, he would run only on a Straight-Out ticket.[34]

Elated, Gary moved back to his fellow travelers with his joyful news. Both Kershaw and Hagood supported the fusion policy, but after listening to Gary's exciting news Kershaw responded, "Well, if the general is nominated, I will fall into line and support him." Hagood, however, was less receptive. After many miles and dinner in the dining car, Hagood relented and looked Gary in the eye, saying, "Gary, you are an extraordinary man. This is another one of your offhand moves or sudden inspirations ... that has knocked up in a minute all the plans in Charleston to run Chamberlain for governor with a mixed ticket."[35] That late June train ride from Charleston to Columbia changed the course of history in South Carolina and the nation. Within weeks, factions within the Democratic party began forging themselves into a single political force that would change the political, financial and social scene in South Carolina. After a nighttime layover in Columbia Hampton departed for Cashier's, North Carolina, where he spent the summer with his family.

Until July it appeared Chamberlain would easily be reelected with a solid number of Democrats casting their ballots for him. Not one of the Democratic party leaders had any idea that Wade Hampton would step out of his self-imposed exile and return to the political scene. Neither did anyone expect the Fourth of July fireworks that were about to light up the political sky over South Carolina. That day the whole political scene in South Carolina changed in favor of an undivided Democratic party and its champion, Wade Hampton.

The Hamburg Riot, which President Grant would later label as a "barbarous massacre of innocent men,"[36] exploded from a small incident similar to those that had occurred many times across the state. The situation began on the afternoon of 4 July when two young white men, Thomas Butler and his brother-in-law Henry Getzen, were on their way home to Edgefield County from Augusta, Georgia. After crossing the Savannah River bridge at the village of Hamburg, the two men ran headlong into a crowd of celebrating blacks and a parading black militia company. The buggy halted and was immediately surrounded by a crowd ready to have fun at the expense of the two young men. The militia's captain, Doc Adams, shouted, "Charge bayonets!" The white men pulled their pistols and threatened to shoot the first man who moved. The militiamen suddenly realized the game had turned deadly and began to fall back. When Adams' orders to advance were ignored, he flew into a rage and ordered the white men to be detained while he got a warrant from Prince R. Rivers.[37] Shortly Adams returned with a warrant charging Butler and Getzen with disrupting a militia drill. The two young men issued a cross warrant against the militia company for obstructing the highway. As soon as they were released they went directly to the home of Robert Butler, Thomas' father. Robert Butler was thoroughly outraged and promptly took out a warrant on Adams.[38] He also hired Matthew Butler to defend his son and son-in-law.

The trial was set for 8 July, only four days after the incident. General Butler arrived in Hamburg leading the Sweetwater Sabre Company. Seeing such a large and menacing force come into the village, Captain Adams issued a call for his militia and they promptly barricaded themselves in the brick armory. Willing to meet the challenge, Butler demanded the militia to disarm and surrender, but when Adams and his men ignored his demands Butler rode across the bridge into Augusta to get additional men.[39]

Late in the evening, seventy-five mounted men approached the armory, dismounted and formed a line. Momentarily gunfire came from the armory and one of Butler's men fell. The line held while a piece of artillery was brought forward and loaded with scrap metal. Before the order to fire was given, the militiamen hastily abandoned the armory through rear windows and fled into the night with a mob of furious men in hot pursuit. When the fracas was finally over, four black militiamen were dead and more than twenty-five had been taken captive. Fearing the violence would spread and envelope him, Jim Cook, the hated town marshal, made an attempt to flee from the town and was shot down near the railroad bridge. With his mission accomplished, Butler returned home during the night, leaving the captives in the hands of the posse. Still thirsty for blood, the posse led five chosen prisoners away, set them free and shot them down as they ran.[40]

The next day a letter from Matthew Butler appeared in the *Columbia Register* recommending Hampton as the Democratic party's nominee for governor. Butler and Gary decided it would insure Hampton's nomination if Butler would remove his name as a nominee. In a public letter, Butler assured Hampton that he was more than willing to yield to his old friend. Some time later when Hampton referred to Butler's letter, Hampton wrote Gary: "Butler has got me into a scrape, but I shall try to do as Runy [sic] Lee used to say, & 'pull out.' I am satisfied that the convn. will be straight out & we must be gentle with our Charleston friends, appealing to them to go in with us. The *News and Courier* must either be made to sustain our policy or to quit the party, which it is defeating & disgracing."[41]

On July 29 an inquest into what was being called the Hamburg Riot brought in its verdict charging seven with murder: John Butler, R.J. Butler, Harrison Butler, Thomas Butler, Henry Getzen, John Lamar and John Swearingin. Others, including sixty from Georgia, were charged as accessories before the fact. Governor Chamberlain issued warrants for several hundred white men and charged attorney general William Stone and district attorney David T. Corbin with the work of arresting them, but the Radicals were afraid to take this many into custody. On the day of the hearing, several hundred men rode into Aiken, led by Martin Gary, D.S. Henderson and G.W. Crofts, and they virtually swamped the courthouse. Corbin did not want them released on bail, but Judge John J. Maher granted them all bail.[42]

Both Democratic and Republican newspapers were united in denunciation of the Hamburg Riot, chewing the accused into mincemeat, labeling them as brutes, butchers and cowardly assassins. The papers went so far as to accuse all residents of Edgefield County as an unthinking mass that relished bludgeoning Southern Democrats. The *News and Courier*, a Democratic paper with Republican leanings, labeled Gary as an advocate of a "shotgun policy." The *New York Daily Times* raved that "the nomination of Wade Hampton in South Carolina, the shotgun policy in Mississippi, Louisiana, South Carolina and Florida, were inaugurating a new rebellion and the first step toward a new establishment of human slavery."[43]

While Democrats easily reasoned the Hamburg Riot was a logical result of armed black men in a white man's society, Republicans agreed with the *Times* as proof Democrats had instituted the Mississippi Plan of violence in South Carolina. For both black and white Republicans the riot was too reminiscent of the earlier days of the nefarious Ku Klux Klan. Some, like black carpetbagger Richard "Daddy" Cain, were prone to meet violence with violence. He threatened whites in South Carolina: "Remember that there are 80,000 black men in this state who can bear Winchester rifles and know how to use them and that there are 200,000 [black] women who can light a torch and use the knife."[44]

Any ground of cooperation gained between the two parties before the Hamburg Riot was lost and from that point on the two parties would continue to experience greater polarization.[45] The Hamburg Riots and subsequent events drove Democrat Fusionists back into the fold of the Straight-Outers and the party became more solid and had fewer divisions than any time since 1868. Alexander Haskell and Martin Gary seized the opportunity to grasp the party reins and begin running its machinery like a well-oiled military organization.

In 1926, fifty years after the riot, Alfred B. Williams would recall the ensuing political situation in his writing: "South Carolina was comparatively safe the day after the Straight-Out uprising, following the disturbance at Hamburg, forced the nomination of Hampton for governor and the straight state ticket. Nobody realized the safety then and nobody foresaw what was to follow the action of the Democratic state convention, natural and inevitable as it all looks now. As subsequent developments proved, Chamberlain's professions of desire for clean government were sincere. When Hampton was nominated, opposition to Chamberlain within the Republican Party vanished. The Republicans hastened to huddle together like so many sheep with a powerful and deadly foe in sight. They knew a real war was on. Orders from Republican national headquarters sent every federal office holder in the state scuttling to Chamberlain."[46]

Though the more militant elements of the party looked to Gary, his leadership was made sporadic and mostly defused by the wise stewardship of Hampton and Haskell. It was obvious from the adjournment of the Democratic convention in August to the following spring that Haskell "was ruler of South Carolina more absolutely than any czar Russia ever knew."[47]

As the political firestorm over the Hamburg Riot continued to rage, the Democratic State Executive Committee met in Columbia to decide the date for their convention. Across the state many Democrats were tenaciously holding to their support of Chamberlain with hopes that the executive committee would delay the convention until after the Republicans had nominated their ticket. Gary, however, seeing the time was right to activate his plan for a full Democrat ticket, convinced the executive committee to push ahead. Alfred B. Williams reflected on the situation in 1926:

> Conservative white men who had favored watching and waiting and trying for combination and compromise with Chamberlain and the more decent Republicans found they had been whipped into a wonderfully good position of which they never dreamed. Instead of taking doubtful chances with Chamberlain against Whipper and Elliott, and even more villainous white men, the state now had to choose between Chamberlain, very best of the Republicans and Hampton. This brought at the middle of August a situation infinitely better than anybody would have dared hope for at the first of July. The splendid frenzy of the people had forced in six weeks results which the ripest and coolest wisdom did not foresee and never could have devised nor effected.[48]

The executive committee, led by chairman James Conner,[49] ordered the party to convene in Columbia on the evening of 15 August "to announce a platform of principals, nominate state officers and Electors for President and Vice President [of the United States], and to consider such business as may be brought before it."[50]

In the meantime, hoping to keep the black vote well secured within the Republican Party, Chamberlain toured the state making strong appeals to the black population. He declared the Republican Party was the party of freedom, equal rights and good government, and gave the party sole credit for destroying slavery and that, if allowed, it would certainly "cure the evils of the present hour."[51] Yet, all was not well between the Republicans and their governor. The schism that resulted from Chamberlain's flirtation with the Democrats was unhealed, especially among the black leaders. Black Republican R.B. Elliott doubted the governor could be trusted because his only appointees to the Board of Centennial Commissions were white. Chamberlain's association with the Charlestonian New England Society was considered an insult to black voters because the society was racially prejudiced. Too, it was elitist, accepting members only from the Low Country white aristocracy that shared profound convictions that the up-country whites would never produce a gentleman or have any political impact in South Carolina. Blacks concluded that if the society's ideology doubted the worthiness of whites, then what must they think of the black population.[52]

A second rift centered on the governor's reputation as a reformer. In general, the Republican Party was reluctant to admit to the most blatant acts of corruption; since Chamberlain had become known as a reformer, admitting to party corruption and promising to end the corruption within the party, he had his enemies. Chamberlain hoped party members would support reform, but because that would require admitting to corruption Chamberlain knew most would have nothing to do with reform. Not only did Republicans deny any charge of corruption, they denounced anyone who made such charges. Yet, in spite of the rift, the party nominated Chamberlain eighty-eight to thirty-five.

On the national level, the country had been shaken by one scandal after another and both parties were seeking presidential candidates that might be seen as reformers. President Grant's two terms had become one of the most corrupt and scandal-ridden

Robert Smalls. Born in 1839 in Beaufort, South Carolina, as a slave, after Emancipation he served in the South Carolina legislature and later the U.S. House of Representatives. Smalls authorized the first free and compulsory public school system in the U.S., in South Carolina. He is noted to be the last Republican to represent the South Carolina 5th Congressional District.

administrations in the history of the United States. Grant, trained only in military tactics, had come to the White House without any political experience, made terrible appointments and took advice from corrupt politicians who swarmed around the new president. He was persuaded by an immoral council to make decisions that permitted Jay Gould and Jim Fisk to obtain a monopoly on the country's gold, and though Grant eventually destroyed the monopoly, hundreds were ruined in the speculation.

The nation had also reeled under the scandal of the Credit Mobilier, a construction company organized to build the Union Pacific Railroad. Stockholders in the company looted the organization and, to head off an investigation by Congress, gave its stock to select members of Congress and to the vice president. In another financial scandal, a group of whiskey manufacturers known as the "Whiskey Ring" cheated the government out of more than a million dollars in revenues. In yet another scandal, secretary of war William W. Belknap was found to have taken bribes for appointments to the department of Indian Affairs year after year, and these appointees had enriched themselves by cheating and robbing Native Americans. Although Grant was not involved in the racket, he allowed Belknap to resign to escape punishment.

By 1872 a division had developed within the Republican Party as many party leaders grew weary of Reconstruction and wanted to remove the military watchdogs from the South, leaving it to solve its own problems. In that year's campaign a faction of the Republican Party nominated Horace Greeley for president; but as it turned out Greeley was a weak candidate. While Grant's administration was fraught with corruption and scandals, no one charged the president personally and he was reelected.

During Grant's second term, popularity began to swing away from Republicans, as Americans grew weary of scandals and corruption. The financial panic of 1873, caused by overinvesting in the Union Pacific Railroad, resulted in many of the working class suffering. Blame fell heavily on Grant's administration and the Democratic party began to swell in numbers. In the following year's election Democrats won control of several important states in the North, increasing their power in the Senate and gaining control of the House of Representatives for the first time since 1860.

The Republican leadership had a difficult time finding the right presidential candidate for the 1876 election. A number of Republicans with strong personalities were available but each of them had made too many internal enemies. Finally, the party settled on Rutherford Birchard Hayes, governor of Ohio, with William A. Wheeler as vice president.

Hayes was born in Delaware, Ohio, on 4 October 1822, the son of Rutherford and Sophia Birchard Hayes. Two months before he was born, his father died and an uncle, Sardis Birchard, took on the oversight of the family and paid for his nephew's education. After graduating at the head of his class at Kenyon College in 1842 Hayes spent two years in a Columbus law office and completed his studies at Harvard Law School in 1845.

When the Civil War began Hayes was elected captain of a militia and served in several battles, including the Battle at South Mountain, where he was wounded. In 1865 he was promoted to brevet major general and was still serving in the army when he was nominated and elected congressman from Ohio. Hayes was elected for a second term; but before taking his seat, he was nominated for governor. He served his home state for two years with plans to retire, but was asked to run for Congress again in 1872. He lost that election to a Democrat, as he had expected, but was persuaded to run again for governor in 1875 and won that election.

Luckily Hayes did not have to worry about his television appearance. Today, he would have paled in the camera's eye as studious and bookish with little humor or charm. One reporter described him as "robust and muscular; quick

President Rutherford B. Hayes (1822–1893). Hayes was elected president of the U.S. by one electoral vote as a dark horse candidate in 1876. His father having died ten weeks before he was born, he became the ward of his uncle. He graduated from Kenyon College in 1842 at the top of his class and graduated in 2 years from Harvard Law School. He was appointed major of the Twenty-Third Ohio Volunteer Infantry and rose to the rank of Brigadier general in 1862 and served in both the Thirty-Ninth and Fortieth congresses.

but not nervous of movement and speech. His voice is deep, strong, musical bass. His eyes are large, blue and kindly of expression. He wears his sandy beard full and carefully trimmed, and here and there in it you see a gray hair, as you also do in his ... closely cut shorn hair. His form is full, but not corpulent; his teeth are as white as ivory, and his features strong and well defined." His private life was "so pure and reproachless that all good men and women respect him. He never used tobacco or intoxicating liquors ... [or] profane language. He is candid, open, affable, and has no secrets; nothing to explain, nothing to refute. His character is above question, even after such bitter political campaigns in Ohio."

The Democrats found their reformer in the person of sixty-two-year-old Samuel J. Tilden, governor of New York, with Thomas A. Hendricks of Indiana as his running mate. Tilden exemplified the qualities of a reformer by breaking up corruption in his state, and he was confident he would be elected to the White House since the nation was sick of the corruption in Grant's administration. Tilden's confidence was fortified by his belief that he had more public appeal than Hayes, who was seen as a colorless wet blanket, as well as believing he had the South in his back pocket.

Tilden was an immensely wealthy lawyer and wielded tremendous political power that was not limited by party lines. During the campaign of 1868, when the Democratic presidential candidate Horatio Seymour of New York became too ill to run, Tilden was instrumental in replacing him with a Republican, Lucius Robinson. Tilden was no one to toy with, and he had no love for Wade Hampton. His loathing for Hampton sprang from the campaign of 1868 when Hampton drew the ire of both Republicans and Democrats by his open denunciation of Reconstruction. Tilden blamed Hampton personally for the defeat of the Democratic party that year.

The 1876 national campaign was extremely nasty and negative. Each side hurled insults and lies at the other. Hayes was accused of stealing the pay of dead soldiers and shooting his mother in a fit of insanity. Tilden was called a drunkard, thief, syphilitic liar and swindler. Radical Republicans labored to irritate the wounds left by the Civil War and pointed to Democrats as a treasonous party. "Every enemy this great republic has had for twenty years has been a Democrat," proclaimed Colonel Robert B. Ingersoll. "Every man that shot Union soldiers ... was a Democrat. Every man that loved slavery better than liberty was a Democrat. The man that assassinated Abraham Lincoln was a Democrat.... Every scar you have got on your heroic bodies was given to you by a Democrat.... Every arm that is lacking, every limb that is gone ... is a souvenir of a Democrat!"[53]

On the state level, Chamberlain took his campaign to Edgefield on 12 August 1876, planning to play up the Democrat's involvement in the Hamburg Riot. Gary wanted Hampton to attend, but he declined, thinking it would be presumptuous on his part since he had not yet received the party's nomination. Party leaders John Sheppard, Matthew Butler and Martin Gary attended the Republican rally on behalf of the Democratic party. When Chamberlain arrived, along with his friend and supporter Judge Thomas J. Mackey, Sheppard went to the governor requesting a share of time. When Chamberlain flatly refused, Sheppard told him in no uncertain terms that unless he shared the time there would be no meeting. Chamberlain conceded.

Toward the time for the speakers to proceed from town to Academy Grove where a shoddy platform had been constructed, a long column of parading blacks entered the town, led by a black band from Aiken. Passing down Main Street they suddenly came face to face with eight hundred mounted horsemen.[54] From that point on, the Democrats had complete control of the meeting.

When Chamberlain came to the speaker's stand he was obviously shaken by Sheppard's threat and the huge number of mounted Democrats standing by. For twenty minutes of his thirty-minute time limit he tried to put sentences together, but hecklers shouted him down. When Matthew Butler rose to speak, the governor decided it was time to retreat, but Gary told him to sit down and threatened to place a guard over him. Butler accused Chamberlain of smearing his name by accusing him of being a member of the Ku Klux Klan. When Gary came to the speaker's stand, he mustered all the hatred he had for Republicans and charged Chamberlain with being a cheat and a fraud who was involved in corruption and lied every time he promised reform. Gary delivered such stinging charges against Chamberlain that when he paused, Butler whispered, "For God's sake, Gary, hold up on him!" Gary ignored the advice and continued to bludgeon the governor and Republican leaders. In conclusion, Gary advised the governor that he "had better begin to pack his carpet bag for he will soon have to quit eating South Carolina rice and return to Massachusetts where he can enjoy codfish."

Several times the flimsy speaker's platform had threatened to collapse. The moment Gary made his last pronouncement, it completely collapsed, sending everyone sprawling. The Democrats laughed and cheered and later said it was a sign from heaven. Chamberlain slipped away in the confusion.[55] As he and other Republicans deserted the grounds Democrats began to assemble in the public square where John Sheppard was speaking to the masses. While he was speaking Judge Thomas Mackey came limping into the square asking to speak privately with him. The judge told Sheppard he had been impressed with Gary's convincing exposé of the Republican Party and assured him he would be supporting the Democratic campaign for honest government.[56] True to his word, Mackey later resigned from the Republican Party, saying he no longer wanted to be part of that "body of robbers, polygamists, perjurers and forgers."[57]

In a 1940 interview, Dr. Samuel B. Latham of Yorkville had this to say about Mackey:

> One of the most interesting political characters evolved in this cesspool of iniquitous politics was Judge T.J. Mackey. Born in Lancaster County of poor parents, he went with them at an early age to Charleston, S.C. By native ability, he won a beneficiary scholarship to the Citadel, the military College of South Carolina. He was a member of the Palmetto Regiment, and fought through the Mexican War. In the War Between the States, he was a commissioned officer on the staff of General Sterling Price toward the close of the war. When the carpetbaggers and Negroes got possession of the State government, he became a scalawag. Bright, witty, forceful, and with a veneer of good breeding, he was rewarded with the position of Judge of the 6th Circuit, and he resided right here in Chester. He was a conspicuous figure on the streets for years. Solomon in all his glory was no better arrayed. He wore broadcloth, Prince Albert coats, silk vests, checked trousers, and tall, silk top hats and carried gold-headed canes. During court week, he would have the sheriffs attend him with cocked hat and drawn sword, preceded by the bailiffs crying stentoriously, "Give way! Give way! The Honorable Court is approaching!" He conducted the court proceedings with great pomp, magnificence, and dignity.[58]

The South Carolina Democratic State Convention convened in the State House at eight o'clock in the evening of 15 August. Among those attending was Martin Gary, weary from a week of campaigning against Chamberlain and promoting the Straight-Out ticket, and John F. Coyle, of the Democratic National Committee, who was probably sent by Tilden to dissuade the delegates from nominating Hampton.

The first fight between Straight-Outers and Fusionists took place over the election of a convention chairman. The names of five nominees were placed before the convention; four of the committeemen were Fusionists, with W.W. Harllee of Marion County the only Straight-Outer. The convention looked good for the Straight-Outers, but midway of voting it looked as if they losing the fight: Charles H. Simonton of Charleston was leading Harllee forty to twenty-seven. When the final tally was announced, Straight-Outer Harllee won the chair by only seven votes. Gary was ecstatic and Hampton was revitalized by the vote. Though Harllee had won the chair, it was by a small majority and Hampton's opponents — John D. Kennedy, James H. Rion and General John Bratton — would continue their warfare.[59]

The next morning the convention went into a secret session to find a nominee for governor; the press, curious Radicals and observers were excluded from the house chambers. It took five and a half hours to come to a decision. As committee members argued for Hampton, John Coyle was asked what he had to say. Believed to be at the convention to prevent Hampton's nomination, Coyle reported that neither presidential nominee Tilden nor the members of the national executive committee had any faith in the Straight-Out ticket and little hope of South Carolina Democrats gaining control of the state. Coyle maintained Northern Democrats would not rally behind Hampton because he was an ex–Confederate general and was liable to embarrass the party as he had done before. Gary, as fiery and outspoken as he could be, argued that South Carolina was dedicated in its support of Tilden and Hendricks, but it was under no obligation to listen to anyone else other than its own people in selecting a nominee for governor. Other party members voiced their opposition to Hampton and it was no surprise when Rion and Bratton announced they would not support Hampton's nomination. Hampton saw a bleak future and was ready to withdraw.

On Wednesday morning, following the convention's routine business, Fusionists and Straight-Outers faced off on the convention floor. Again the convention went into closed session. For seven hours in the stifling heat of August the two factions argued their points. Though the battle surged back and forth like the tide, when the roll call was made it was the Straight-Outers who succeeded; but Hampton's fight for the nomination was just beginning. When the doors of the house chambers were opened around five in the afternoon, a wave of reporters and Radicals rushed in with questioning eyes. Gary leaned into Butler's ear and said, "Now is the time for you to nominate Hampton."[60] Butler hesitated, saying he believed it was Gary's place to do the nominating, but Gary insisted. Reluctantly Butler stood and with a strong voice placed Hampton's name into nomination. Robert Aldrich of Barnwell quickly seconded the nomination. Hampton was called to the dais. Tall and lean, he rose from his seat and majestically strolled to the podium to accept the nomination. Referring to Trinity Episcopal Church across the street where his family's burial plot was located, he said, "I have claimed nothing from South Carolina but a grave in yonder church yard. But I have always said that if I could ever serve her by word or deed her men had only to call me and I would devote all my life to her service."[61]

Hampton thanked the convention for the nomination and expressed his commitment to the party and said he was sure South Carolina would be redeemed from the rule of the Radicals when Tilden won the national election. He spoke openly of the argument that he might be an embarrassment to the party and said if that were so, he would not hesitate to withdraw. After encouraging the assembly to consider his worth to the party, he left the hall to allow them to discuss his nomination. The general was just passing through the doors when Rion placed Bratton into nomination. Following in short order, J.W. Stuckey of Sumter proposed former Governor Manning. Both refused to serve and Hampton was given the nomination by acclamation. The Democratic party of South Carolina formed an all white, Straight-Out ticket: governor — Wade Hampton; lieutenant governor — W.D. Simpson; secretary of state — R.M. Sims; state treasurer — S.L. Leaphart; attorney general — James Conner; comptroller general — Johnson Hagood; adjutant general — E.W. Moise.

The Democratic platform was easily constructed. The delegates knew that reform was being demanded from every segment of society. They were convinced reform could come only through the Democratic party and not the Republican Party, which was filled with fraud, corruption and mismanagement.[62] After the platform was completed, Hampton returned to the podium and made a short speech warning the party of difficult days ahead: "You are struggling for the highest stake for which a people ever contended, for you are striving to bring back to your prostrate State the inestimable blessings which can only follow orderly and regulated liberty under free and good government.... For myself, should I be elevated to the high position for which you have nominated me.... I shall be Governor of the whole people, knowing no party, making no vindictive discriminations, hold the scales of justice with firm and impartial hand, seeing, as far as in me lies, that the laws are enforced in justice tempered with mercy, protecting all classes alike."

Hampton's nomination united the South Carolina Democratic Party into a solidarity not known since 1868. Almost immediately vacillation and division came to an end. Following the violent days of the Ku Klux Klan, the state needed a moderate, peace-loving man; and after years of corruption the government needed a man who had remained aloof from fraud and vice. The state and the party needed a hero, and the black community needed a paternal figure. Hampton was the right man for every need, but victory had to be won.

At a 1911 Red Shirts reunion in Yorkville, Colonel Asbury Coward recalled the 1876 convention. Coward, like most Southerners, was prone to use Christian scriptures to describe contemporary events, and on this occasion he likened the unity of the party to the Jewish Passover. Pointing out how the feast united a people into a great nation and how it was still commemorated, he declared the convention "should be commemorated as the culmination of the long struggle for maintenance of Anglo-Saxon civilization."[63]

Shortly after Hampton's nomination, the *Charleston (SC) News and Courier* was of the opinion that if the Democrats won the election, it would only be through violence — not that it would be entirely the Democrats' fault, but the odds they faced were too overwhelming to be won without it. Democrats had to face a solid Republican vote as well as Chamberlain's power to obtain federal troops. Already troops were entrenched in the senate and the house, and the Republicans controlled the Board of Canvassers. The *News and Courier* was sure violence would erupt since both parties were so prone to violence and bloodshed. Hampton and the state executive committee, however, were convinced victory would be won by a solid white vote and an appeal to black voters.[64]

Early in the campaign the Democratic party adopted a nonviolent plan to deal with their opposition. This plan, though it spoke of nonviolence, had clear instructions as to how the election was to be won. The plan called for party nominees and leaders to invite themselves to Republican rallies, to go "and remain perfectly quiet, but ask for a division of time, and if rejected, to remain perfectly quiet, to keep order, listening to the speakers, and use any means at their command, by the ordinary rules of mass meetings, to indicate their pleasure or displeasure — but by no means to make any demonstration or threaten force or use it."[65] State chairman Alexander Haskell understood that any demonstration of force would unnerve the freedmen, reminding them of slavery and the Ku Klux Klan, which would certainly evoke a negative response. He believed that when Democrats made their appearance at Republican meetings and requested a division of time it would deliver a quiet message of their need to yield to white rule and the danger in resisting. Haskell also hoped this tactic would impress black voters with the power behind their campaign, defuse the power the Radicals had over their black supporters, and provide a method to reach the masses with Democratic policies that could not be done through the newspapers.[66]

Certainly the Democratic state executive committee publicly advocated a nonviolent campaign, and on at least one occasion called for all county chairmen to support Hampton's desire for a peaceful campaign. Yet, while the words sound right, we must wonder if the committee really expected serious compliance: "That they should not resort to any violence — to any illegal means whatsoever — no threats, no intimidation ... that they should develop the strength of the state, that they should exhibit it that it might have its moral and legitimate influence on our adversaries: that we must show our strength, but that no force should be used." The committee's choice of "should" over "shall" might be a reason to doubt their sincerity.

Hampton himself remained aloof from intimidation and violence, advocating his campaign to be forceful without violence. Yet, there are reasons to question his sincerity. Regardless of the benign tone to his instructions, we must remember that Hampton was a man of the times, and the times were rough and violent. Too, we know of cases, then and now, how men might advocate one thing and justify actions to the contrary. There is some difficulty in justifying certain remarks of his, such as the time he was expressing his feelings on departures from the Democratic Party and snapped, "If any sheep attempts to bite, shoot him on the spot."

Immediately after Hampton's nomination, Gary, always accompanied by force and violence, set about developing a statewide Carolina version of the Mississippi Plan. Rifle and Saber Clubs similar to those in Aiken County were organized across the state. Like the Ku Klux Klan before them, these clubs were nothing more than a paramilitary wing of the Democratic Party. Their primary goal was to lure the black population away from the influence of Republicans by use of various tools that included threats, physical assaults, coercion and chicanery. One tactic called for bands of mounted white men to arrive at the polls on election day just as they opened. Astride horses and mules, with ropes dangling from their saddles, these men might make an intimidating remark such as "The hanging will begin in fifteen minutes" while patting coiled ropes.

Behind the Red Shirt beat a heart of malevolence; many had ridden as Klansmen and their sons had been reared in a climate of turmoil and violence. Though the Red Shirts cannot be directly accused of instigating violence, they created an atmosphere where it thrived, and they were ever ready to meet force with force. Simply said, they were their father's sons. It is likely that some of the younger men who had been too young to participate in the Civil War may have seen the Red Shirt companies as their opportunity to share in "the glory of battle" and were happy to join their fathers and older brothers.[67]

To complete the Democrats façade of nonviolence, a number of high-ranking Democrats came forward to deny any knowledge of violence being used to oppress the voting rights of black voters. One of these was Judge Mackey, a converted Democrat who contended that "peace and order" prevailed throughout the Sixth Circuit, which included Chester, Fairfield, Lancaster and York counties. He assured his listeners that he had no knowledge of any armed organization that was obstructing judicial proceedings or violating voting rights.[68]

While Mackey vouched for peace in his circuit, Republican trial justice James L. Strain, who lived in Union County just across the Broad River from York County, was aware of trouble in that area. On 4 September he informed Chamberlain that a local Republican meeting had been disrupted by "an armed band of ruffians" and asked for help in preventing any such recurrence since the mob had promised to be on hand at all future meetings. "Nothing but enforcement on the part of the military will prevent troubles," he wrote, saying the mob contained "Cowardly Minute Men" who either never went to war, evaded the draft as long as they could, deserters, "and a very few who did their duty." Having personal friends and family among local Democrats, Strain was careful not to include all Democrats in his report and added, "The better class of Democrats denounce all such dastardly conduct!"[69]

Not only were some whites slow to abandon their violent and intimidating ways, black South Carolinians were prone to keep the fires burning as well. During the campaign a black state senator from Beaufort advised his constituents "that the torch at night was their safest and surest weapon." As late as March 1877, black arsonists were randomly at work. A correspondent from Chester reported to the *Yorkville Enquirer* that fires had almost ceased in the county since January, but "before that time they were of frequent occurrence.[70]

As the *News and Courier* had cited, Chamberlain was depending on a solid black Republican vote. But Hampton had an "ace in the hole." His former slaves numbered nearly a thousand and most remained fond of and loyal to their former master. Many still came to him for advice, for assistance in healthcare and other support from "Marse Wade" and his family. Most of Hampton's ex-slaves were delighted and proud their former master was running for governor and making a name for himself. The Rev. Francis Davie, a former slave living in York County, wrote as follows:

James L. Strain. While a member of the Republican Party, James L. Strain was appointed magistrate for parts of Union and York counties. During this time he informed Governor Chamberlain of an "armed band of ruffians" that was disrupting area party meetings. When Hampton came to the governor's office South Carolina Democrats petitioned him to remove Strain from office and replace him with a Democrat. Sometime later, Strain changed his party affiliation to Democrat and was reappointed magistrate (courtesy of the Museum of Western York County, Sharon).

Dear Marse Wade:

Seeing you are nominated for governor by the white people and hearing you have promised the black man all the rights he now has, and knowing you were always a good and kind man who will do what he promises I write to say that I will vote for you and will get all the black men I can to do the same. I have bought a piece of land in York County and am trying to make a support for my family, which I can do if we had good laws and taxes. My wife, Flora, is still living and we have but one child whom we wish to educate. Please write to me, care of Dr. T.C. Robertson,[71] Rock Hill, S.C.

Your friend and former slave,
Rev. Francis Davie[72]

In an effort to promote the "new" Democratic party, Hampton had to convince black voters that Democrats were a changed lot, but he had two liabilities that had the potential of tearing down the house of cards: Generals Matthew Butler and Martin Gary. Both had a history of advocating white supremacy. Butler was considered to have bloody hands from the Hamburg Riot and Martin Gary advocated that the United States was a white man's country and must remain that way. Nevertheless, Hampton assured his black listeners that the Democratic Party fully accepted the changes in the state constitution and had pledged to support it. He guaranteed justice and respect for all, knowing "no party, no race, nor color or condition."[73]

Throughout his campaign, Hampton was aware of South Carolinians' need for a paternalistic figure. Using this need to his advantage, Hampton had great success among the up-country black voters. The freedmen and their families soon began viewing him paternalistically, much as African Americans would see Franklin D. Roosevelt in the 1930s. Coming from planter stock, Hampton was easily seen as a friend who had the wit, knowledge and experience to provide for their needs. The idea appealed not only to blacks, but just as equally to many whites.[74]

Martin R. Delaney was the first black leader of some notoriety to respond favorably to Hampton. A descendent of African chiefs, Delaney had been educated at Harvard and came to South Carolina as an official of the Freedmen's Bureau. He soon grew unhappy with the trend of the bureau and left his post to practice medicine. Delaney had an eloquent speaking style and would later be credited with convincing thousands of his own race to cast Democrat ballots. As a reward for his invaluable help during the campaign one of Hampton's first official acts after his inauguration was to appoint Delaney as a trial justice.

Soon after Hampton's nomination was made public a reported eight thousand blacks had organized Democratic Clubs. Exactly how many freedmen defected to the Democratic Party we may never know; but their departure struck a severe blow to Chamberlain, who was counting on the black vote to furnish him a majority of twenty thousand. In the upper regions of the piedmont, two hundred mounted blacks clad in red shirts demonstrated for the party in a Rock Hill parade on 12 October 1876.[75] Other black Red Shirts were reported to have appeared in demonstrations in the town of Spartanburg and Union and other piedmont counties.

Black Democrats had little need to fear white Democrats; reprisals too often came from members of their own race. Promoted by Radical Republicans, black henchmen formed clubs with names such as to Loyal Leaguers, Hunkidories[76] and Live Oaks. As benign as the names may sound they were as brutal as any Ku Klux Klan. Many black Democrats suffered beatings and even murder at the hand of their own race; others were shunned by their neighbors, and wives and sweethearts threatened to withhold sexual favors from husband and boyfriends if they voted for Hampton.[77] There were some reports of black women accompanying their husbands to the polls to ensure they voted the Republican ticket, even "threatening them with assassination if they did not vote as [the women] wished."[78]

At Yorkville, in a case tried just two days before Hampton was to arrive for a rally, Henry Lowry, a black Democrat, accused Edward McDonald, a black Republican, of "assault and political intimidation because of his political principles."[79] Another account of reprisal occurred when black Democrat William Black went to Chester for a meeting and left his horse in Yorkville. Upon returning he found the horse had been strangled to death by a rope. While no one was charged, Black was sure it was done by a Republican because he had supported the Democratic ticket.[80]

Chapter Four

All the Redeemer's Men

During the first week of September 1876, just seven days after Hampton's nomination, he began his whirlwind campaign through the South Carolina piedmont. Anderson County, the first stop on the campaign trail, set the tone for every other stop. At least fifteen hundred Red Shirts led a mile long parade through the business district amid shouts and cannon booms. When Hampton rose to deliver his speech on "Reconciliation, Retrenchment, and Reform" he was overwhelmed with the shouts and applause of the more than six thousand in attendance.[1]

Greenville made every attempt to outdo Anderson. On his arrival Hampton was met in the evening by a throng of people and a regiment of torch-bearing horsemen. The Pendleton and Greenville Cornet bands filled the air with their music while the Robert E. Lee Fire Company strutted in bright new uniforms.

While the city of Greenville was filled with gaiety, Charleston erupted in a riot when two black Democrats on King Street were attacked and a mob of whites came to their rescue. Two black gangs, the Hunkidories and the Live Oaks, had instigated the melee under the direction of white Republicans. Men from several local rifle clubs arrived the next day to protect black Democrats.[2]

As the Rifle Clubs were arriving in Charleston, Hampton led a procession of fifteen hundred mounted men from the railroad station to the campus of Furman University where an estimated crowd of more than five thousand awaited. Former governor Perry presided over the event. Taking the speaker's stand, Perry announced he had recently spoken with a South Carolina Republican who was a confidant of President Grant. The man had told Perry that when he was with Grant he boasted that South Carolina was safe for the Republican ticket. Grant snapped, "It was safe until the

Democrats nominated Hampton. Now they'll carry it!" The crowd roared with excited and confident cheers. Following a torchlight parade that evening, Hampton, Simpson and others spoke to another large audience. All evening, cannons roared, rockets streaked across the sky, drums thundered and horns blared. It seemed that all Greenville was ablaze with excitement, and none would have denied redemption was nigh. If Greenville did not outdo Anderson, it wasn't because they had not tried.

Progressing deeper into the piedmont, Hampton arrived in Union County on 11 September. There another mass of mounted Red Shirts, some of whom were black, met and escorted Hampton's entourage. That night, the county Democratic committee entertained the crowd with a fireworks display that resulted in a fire. The small town had not yet formed a fire department, but the town's men and the visiting Chester Red Shirts quickly formed a bucket brigade and confined the fire to one store building. Responding to the effectiveness of the brigade, Hampton congratulated the men and pointed out the power of working together.[3] In every piedmont town along Hampton's campaign trail the people opened their streets and hearts to him, paying homage in a variety of ways, each town trying to outdo the other in rallies and celebrations.

The Republican state convention convened on 12 September. The floor remained relatively quiet and orderly until R.B. Elliott; chairman of the executive committee, rose to speak. Elliott was perturbed with Chamberlain's earlier flirtation with the Democrats and told the delegates he approved of Chamberlain's reform program, but did not believe the governor could be trusted in all matters. With that said, delegates "grew tumultuous and unmanageable." Elliott waved about a letter written by Chamberlain in 1870 when he was the South Carolina attorney general, replying to the question if he would be willing to accept a nomination for U.S. senator. Chamberlain replied he would accept the nomination if it would prevent the state "from being down-trodden by negroism." Elliott declared this sounded too much like Democrat thinking.[4] Continuing, Elliott accused Chamberlain of overstepping his jurisdiction when he opposed the appointments of Whipper and Moses, and revealed his racial prejudice by appointing only white men to the Board of Centennial Commissioners. Venting fully, Elliott charged the governor with making various attempts to usurp the powers of the legislature.

Though it was difficult to hear, Chamberlain knew Elliot was speaking aloud what many other Republicans were thinking. In that moment he faced the fact he was in for an uphill battle, even as he had at the April convention. Chamberlain came calmly to the podium and spoke with calm eloquence and in a straightforward manner. With dignity he responded to each accusation, moving the delegates to a standing ovation and loud cheers. After two days and a full session of fourteen and one-half hours the Republicans formed their state ticket with Chamberlain in the coveted spot[5]: governor — D.H. Chamberlain (white); lt. governor — R.H. Gleaves (mulatto); state treasurer — F.L. Cardozo (mulatto); attorney general — Robert B. Elliott (black); secretary of state — H.F. Hayne (mulatto); comptroller general — T.C. Dunn (white); supt. of education — John Tolbert (white); adjutant general — James Kennedy (white).

The day before Chamberlain received his nomination, the town of Chester held a spirited rally for Hampton though he was not present. Mounted companies of Red Shirts flooded into the courthouse town from all over the county. When the Rich Hill and the Blackstock companies, with a large contingent of black men, arrived they were given a rousing welcome. Other companies of mounted Red Shirts arrived from Lancaster, McAiley's Mill, Carmel Hill, Rossville, Lewis Turnout, Hazelwood and McConnellsville in York County. Colonel James Rion had opposed Hampton at the convention along with congressional nominee Colonel John H. Evins and Columbia attorney LeRoy F. Youmans; all put aside their reservations and gave their full support to the nominee. A parade of about two thousand filed through the streets to a grove where Evins exposed the "sins of the Republican Party," and Rion denounced Chamberlain's unwillingness to discuss political issues just to keep the black man ignorant. Rion assured the blacks in the audience that their rights were securely protected by the constitution and they should have no fear voting the Democrat ticket.

Noted for his speaking abilities, attorney Youmans delivered one of the most "eloquent and entertaining" speeches of his career. He caustically denounced the Radicals and made moving appeals to right the wrongs by voting the Democrat ticket and held President Grant and other Republicans up for the crowd's loudest scorn. In a dramatic appeal for black support, he assured them they would be protected from Republican vengeance "though the streets of our towns flow with the blood of white men in the endeavor to establish this right." Thundering applause filled the town grove.

Prior to an evening torchlight parade, a mounted company of men from Rock Hill arrived wearing sporty red sashes, and a cheering crowd from York arrived by train. At seven o'clock, the torchlight parade formed on Patterson's Green and began its march through the streets. Decorated wagons and companies of Red Shirts led the way, followed by hundreds of people carrying torches and lighted signs. Democratic sentiments were expressed on those lighted placards: "Rascality to the Rear — Honesty to the Front," "Wade Hampton: A Governor for Reform," "There is not five minutes more of good stealing in South Carolina," "D.H. Chamberlain — Hamburg Liar," and "We will protect the colored men from Radical Intimidation." The parade wound its way through town and returned to Patterson's Green, where the evening was filled with more speeches from local dignitaries.

Several days later, on 16 September, Hampton met privately with five Democratic leaders: W.D. Simpson, James S. Cothan, James A. Hoyt, Samuel McGowan and Robert Toombs at the Abbeville home of Mrs. Norwood. At this meeting Hoyt informed them that presidential nominee Tilden was highly dissatisfied with Hampton's being on the South Carolina ticket. This was no surprise to Hampton, knowing the bad blood between them. Judges Mackey and Cooke had counseled Hampton earlier that he would be better off excluding any mention of Tilden during the campaign. They reasoned with Hampton that he owed nothing to Tilden since he considered the South Carolina ticket to be nothing but "Southern Brigadiers" who were a liability to the party. Hampton and his team decided Hampton should get in touch with Manton Marble, chairman of the national Democratic Executive Committee, who was a friend to both Hampton and Tilden.[6]

From Walhalla, Hampton wrote a carefully worded letter to Marble making a political apology for creating a difficult situation for the presidential nominee and asked him if he might have suggestions on how to rectify the situation:

> How can we best relieve our friends at the North of their embarrassment? Of course we are most anxious to aid in the general election, but you can understand our solicitude to find out how we can best do this. Before our convention I wrote fully to Mr. Tilden, telling him what would probably be its action, and asking his advice so that we could promote the interests of the Democratic Party. He did not reply to my letter, and I was forced by irresistible public opinion to accept the nomination for governor. I have made the canvass thor-

oughly conservative, and it has been a perfect success so far. With aid from abroad, the State can be carried for Tilden. There is no doubt of its being carried for our State ticket, for our opponents would gladly agree to let us elect our men if we withdrew from the presidential contest. Of course we are most solicitude [sic] to find out how we can best do this. If our alliance is a load, we will unload. If our friends desire us to carry on the contest as begun, we shall do so.[7]

Two weeks passed before Marble responded in a one line telegram: "It is agreed here that your friend's persistence and his present efforts and plans are wise and advantageous." Though cool and cryptic, it was all Hampton could expect as an endorsement from the national party.

Judges Cooke and Mackey continued to counsel Hampton he could win without any help from the national party and were convinced the Republicans were willing to sacrifice South Carolina to maintain their control in Washington. Mackey told him he had heard the state Republican Party was planning to remain passive during the campaign under the pretense they were restrained by fear of the Democrats. Then, near the end of the race, they would incite a riot among the blacks, at which time Chamberlain would invoke federal intervention and martial law, giving black Republicans an opportunity to swamp the polls. Mackey assured Hampton that the national Republican executive committee had sanctioned the scheme.

Mackey went on to reveal that should the Democratic Party agree to withhold the presidential electors, the Republican national executive committee was willing to place $10,000 into his campaign coffers. Though no proof exists confirming that Hampton accepted the offer, it must have been tempting. Obviously the agreement would be good for the state, and it would give Hampton an opportunity to give Tilden a slap for being so arrogant as to think he had the state in his back pocket.

Political drums in western York County were rattling the day Hampton was conducting his strategy. A crowd of three hundred whites and fifty blacks gathered in the little unincorporated village of Hickory Grove to hear candidates at a joint stump meeting.[8] Dr. Robert T. Allison, a local physician, called the meeting to order at noon. Though not as eloquent as Youmans, who spoke at the Chester rally, Allison exhorted the same as he, saying the election would offer an opportunity to right the wrongs of the past eight years. The nominees, said Allison, are "exponents of honest principles and a faithful administration of the laws of the state." He quizzed, "Have you not been oppressed, your rights disregarded, your money stolen by exorbitant taxation, and squandered in a manner unexampled in the history of any State? The times demand a change; the people demand it, and we must have it."⁹

John Evins received a rousing cheer when he praised the unity of the state, saying he had never seen the people of South Carolina so determined "to rid our oppressed people of bad government." He charged the Republican Party of making the state poor through a corrupt legislature that had continually consumed the state's income. Turning to the blacks in the audience, he reminded them that Republicans had faltered on their promises:

> They promised a magnificent free public school system by which all colored people and their children could secure an education. But where are their schools? They tell you not to trust the white man, that they will return you to slavery, deprive you of your right to vote, etc. But I tell you that any man, white or black, who tells you these stories, lies when he tells them. Neither the white men as individuals, nor the Democratic Party, desire to deprive you of your freedom or your rights as citizens.... Your leaders tell you we want to keep you ignorant. This is false. We want you to acquire both education and property. But notwithstanding all the professions of your Republican leaders, have they shown that they want you educated, or that they desire you to acquire information and intelligence? No. They only want you for their dupes to keep them in place and power. They prefer that you remain in ignorance that they may steal from you, and through your votes, plunder all the people of the state.

Evins then turned his attention to Republican congressman Alexander S. Wallace, charging that Wallace's policies had created bad feelings and animosity between the races, and accused him of voting against every measure that would produce reconciliation. Hampton, however, he said, would be a governor for all, and would befriend the black man, and that proof was evident as Hampton was the first white man in the South to advocate Negro suffrage. "He has never done or said anything to deceive anybody," voiced Evins, "and would not deceive the humblest colored man in the state. He is pledged to honor, and he values his honor more than he values his life. You can trust him and implicitly rely upon what he says."

The next speaker, Nelson Davies, a black incumbent of the House of Representatives, denied Evin's charges of corruption, saying he had never voted for a corrupt measure, and had always favored reform. He denied the claims that the Democratic Party was a states'-rights party, and warned his black supporters that Democrats would surly ignore the black man's rights. Growing bolder, he declared that if Republicans were robbers and thieves like Evins said, then Democrats were murderers. Davies cautioned his people that if an all-white ticket were elected it would be by the "Mississippi Tiger Policy"—buying votes before the election and trampling down black men at the polls. In closing, Davies asked, "What has the Republican Party stolen from you? The Black Code, the whipping post, and the statute for a colored man to seek a chicken without the written permission of his employer."

Frank Edwards, a black Republican candidate for county commissioner came forward and, unlike Davies, spoke from his experiences rather than along party lines. He preferred not to recall the days of slavery, but believed it was best to let bygones be bygones. Yet he wanted to tell about an incident that took place shortly after emancipation. He said that while campaigning, he saw an old white man in the audience who had whipped him many times when he was a boy. Edwards suggested he may have deserved the whippings and probably was a better man for it; but to show he harbored no grudge, he approached the old man and asked him to vote for him for old times' sake. Edwards went on to say he believed there were good men on both tickets and hoped everyone would be allowed to vote and be satisfied with the outcome. Without admitting the Republican Party was guilty of corruption, Edwards agreed morals and ethics were improving.

Democrat Thomas J. Bell, a Yorkville attorney, was the last to speak. The *Yorkville Enquirer* reported he had spoken "in his most scathing style, arraigning the Republican Party for misrule and corruption." Like other Democrats he tried to assure the black voter that Democrats were their "best and truest friends" and should they be elected to power would "enact only wholesome laws, under which both races could live peaceably and prosperously." Bell's hope for peace was short lived.

Just two months after the Hamburg Riot the little town of Ellenton erupted into a bloody riot. The situation came about when two black men broke into a house of a white farmer and clubbed his wife and nine-year-old son in a robbery attempt. The woman drove them off with a shotgun and within a short time a dozen neighbors formed a posse. It was not long before one of the accused was apprehended and placed in jail, but he soon made a bold escape and was wounded in flight. During the night the escapee hid at a friend's home where he was joined by other black men offering protection. When a large group of armed white men arrived with an arrest warrant, a gun battle ensued in which six white men were killed. The fleeing black men turned to rioting, tearing up railroad tracks, wrecking a train, cutting telegraph wires, and setting fire to a cotton gin. The violence spread into an adjoining county and before federal troops could intervene, thirty black men had been killed, one of whom was black state representative Simon Coker, who had been killed in execution style while on his knees in prayer.[10]

Ellenton continued to be a powder keg. In mid–September, trial justice Frank Arraim notified Chamberlain that more than five hundred armed white men had crossed the Savannah River from Georgia and were camped near Hamburg, ready for a fight. Arraim requested the governor appoint a man "to collect and take charge of all the arms and ammunition, now scattered and belonging to the State, [and] to use them to protect the citizenry."[11] Chamberlain conferred with his political bosses and sent U.S. district attorney David Corbin to Ellenton to investigate the state of affairs in Aiken County.[12] In his report Corbin used terms reminiscent of the Ku Klux Klan days: "These clubs have created and are causing a perfect reign of terror. The colored men are, many of them, lying out of doors and away from their homes at night. Many of them have been killed, and many have been taken from their beds at night and mercilessly whipped, and others have been hunted with threats of murder and whipping, who thus far, by constant watchfulness and activity, have escaped. The white men of these clubs are riding day and night, and the colored men are informed that their only safety from death or whipping lies in their signing an agreement pledging themselves to vote the democratic ticket in the coming election.... I fix the number of colored men killed in this county alone, by white men of these clubs, during the past three weeks, at thirteen certainly, and at probably twenty-five or thirty.... Aiken County rivals the worst demonstrations of the Ku Klux Klan in 1870 and 1871."

In conclusion, the district attorney general told Chamberlain he owed it to himself "to exercise, and at once, all the powers vested in you as governor of the state." Immediately Chamberlain proclaimed a state of insurrection and telegraphed President Grant for additional troops. Grant, however, was in California and several weeks would pass before Chamberlain would get a reply. In the meantime, parts of the state were simmering with racial anger. Contributing to that anger were strikes among rice field laborers in the Low Country. Numerous outrages flared across the state.

It was at this time that James Conner, the Democratic candidate for attorney general and commander of ten rifle clubs, received word that a secret shipment of Remington rifles and ammunition was bound for Charleston from Washington by way of Columbia. After arriving in Charleston the arms were to be sent by boat across the Ashley River, where they were to be distributed at Yemassee to black laborers.

When the shipment arrived at a depot in Charleston, Conner was ready with a plan to seize the rifles. Under cover of darkness twelve men boarded two pleasure yachts moored at Vanderhost's Wharf on the Cooper River. About midnight the *Eleanor* and the *Flirt* left their moorings, slipped down the river, around the Battery and up the Ashley, arriving at the depot at 1:30 P.M. The two guards on duty were overtaken, bound and gagged, and for about an hour Conner's men worked swiftly and quietly loading the arms onto the yachts. From there they sailed to a wharf owned by J.E. Adger & Company and were met by two employees, Thomas Darcey and James Moore, who were waiting with wagons. As soon as the arms were secured in a warehouse, Conner was notified, and distribution was made among the rifle clubs before dawn.[13]

Though never proven, it was widely believed that someone in the Washington War Department was responsible for the shipment of arms. This person, or persons, dared not make a complaint of the raid for fear of being discovered, so no search for the raiders was made.[14] The Remington was a superior weapon in 1876, capable of delivering a bullet twice as large and heavy as those developed for World War I. Had these rifles been distributed as planned, a bloody civil war might have occurred.

The press had plenty to say about the political situation. The *New York Tribune* on 14 October offered a description of South Carolina's political scene and suspected methods Democratic candidates were using to secure votes:

> The air is filled with reports of outrages and murders that never appear in print. No prominent Republican of either color can safely leave a town. Let a hint that he intends to ride out into the country get wind and he is sure to be ambuscaded. But more than this, whites regard a Republican of their color with tenfold the vindictiveness with which they look upon the Negro. Scores of white Republicans are hurrying in alarm to the newspaper offices to insert

cards in which they renounce their party and profess conversion to democracy. If these men hang back and refuse or neglect to join the precinct club or the nearest military company, their conduct is reported to the township meeting. A committee is appointed to request an explanation. They call on the suspected man at their earliest convenience. If he is sensible, he will submit profuse apologies and regrets and hurriedly take up his rifle and follow them to the drill-room. Three or four white circuit judges have been dragooned into conformity, and the crowd of lesser lights threatens to absorb every white Republican in the State, except Governor Chamberlain and the United States Senators.... If a white man refuses to join a precinct club, if a white man's loyalty to the party is suspected, if a white Republican persists in his opinions, he is spotted, marked, doomed. He is scowled at if he walks abroad. If he passes a crowd of loitering whites at a street corner, an ominous silence falls on them till he is out of hearing. No warning is given him. No midnight visits are now paid, or Ku-Klux missives dispatched. The whites have found by bitter experience that such things are boomerangs, which return with tenfold force to injure the thrower. They manage the matter better now. They wait till an obnoxious man whom they had deemed as a victim chances to stand, or pass near them, say on the public square, at the post-office, in a bar-room, on the street. A crowd of white desperadoes will cluster near him or follow him. They appear to be drunk, and begin to quarrel over some silly matter having nothing to do with politics. Several bystanders come up and take sides. Finally blows are exchanged, pistols drawn, and a regular free fight occurs. All parties fired shots. Yet, strange to say, when order is restored, it is found that not one of the combatants is injured, while the poor Republican has been struck by several random shots and killed. An account of the affray appears in the press (the press is almost wholly Democratic) under the heading, "Street Row — One Man Killed." Not only are single men picked off this way, but some fights are arranged by white ruffians on some nonpolitical pretense, which swell to the proportion of riots, and in which several Republican bystanders are killed by chance shots, while none of the combatants are hurt. Of course the authors of these deeds go unpunished. In the first place it is impossible to tell who fired the shot. Then it is unsafe for any one to indict anybody about it, or for officials to be too zealous in investigating or prosecuting. But if an assassin does get into trouble by imprudence, his comrades, who of course compose most of the bystanders, are called as witnesses, and swear him out safely by giving in doctored testimony.[15]

In the midst of civil strife Hampton's campaign was going well. Many black Republicans were convinced to switch over to the Democratic Party as well as a number of white Republicans who followed the lead of Judges Cooke and Mackey. This practice became known as "Crossing Jordan." In spite of Hampton's supporters prematurely referring to him as "governor,"[16] he knew he had to strengthen ties with the national party.

Three days after the Ellenton riot, a stump meeting took place in the

Four. All the Redeemer's Men 97

agricultural community of Blairsville that would be called "the last grand stand of the Republicans in York County." Before noon a crowd of about four hundred assembled at Wilson's Chapel Church, representing both political parties and equally divided racially. A sizable delegation of Democrats led by Major Hart came from Yorkville and several Democratic Clubs of the area came bearing the banners of Hampton and George D. Tilman, nominee for the 5th Congressional District.[17]

The Democrats appointed J.C. Chambers to confer with J. Hannibal White, the chairman of the county Republican party, on how he wanted to proceed. Chambers and White met privately for about half an hour and agreed to several conditions. All banners except for the United States flag were to be furled and put out of view, the utmost courtesy was to be shown to all speakers, and both parties would feature three speakers with a thirty-minute time limit. Congressman A.S. Wallace was to make the closing address.[18]

Senator I.D. Witherspoon began his speech by flattering the black voters, saying how much he appreciated the two races coming together for

The Witherspoon House. Located at 121 North Congress Street, this villa-style home was built in 1860 by Colonel William Wright for his niece, Margaret, and her husband, Judge Isaac D. Witherspoon. The judge and his wife lived out their lives in this home and their daughter, "Miss Leslie," occupied the home until her death in 1959 (courtesy of Culture & Heritage Museums).

the day. Continuing to flatter, he remarked how "the colored man" was owed a great debt of gratitude for his conduct during the war while the white man was away from home. Witherspoon tried to assure them that white Democrats were not their enemy, that he could guarantee the party was committed to the state constitution, which protected them so securely that it was an "utter impossibility" to deprive them of their freedom and their rights to vote and sit as jurors. In an apologetic tone, he confessed that the Black Code had been a mistake and had been formed "under the peculiar circumstances of the situation, thought to be for the best, but had proved to be for the worst."[19] He attempted to make the Black Code a moot point by saying it was never put into effect.

Witherspoon disputed the power of Lincoln's Emancipation Proclamation over the Confederate states, claiming that it really did not free the slaves since the Confederacy was a separate and sovereign nation. Hoping to entangle the Republicans, he recalled that Senator Wallace had voted for parts of the Black Code, along with others who would later defect to the Republican Party. Facetiously he excused them, saying he was sure they "did it honestly." He praised the Democratic candidates, who were pure and honest men, unlike Republican candidates, who, if they had not stolen from the state themselves, had stood silently by while others did.[20] In closing, he denounced the Republican controlled state legislature and the administration for have burdening the state with exorbitant taxation, and he promised that if the reins of government were given to the Democrats, they would "abolish unnecessary offices, reduce salaries, and thus lighten the expenses of the State government."

In glowing terms Witherspoon introduced the next speaker, Republican J. Hannibal White. After the necessary pleasantries White assured his black listeners that their fear of Democrats was justified. He predicted that should the Democrats gain the majority of both Houses of the Congress they would "declare the amendments to the Constitution and the Reconstruction Acts null and void" and a bloody war would ensue. White did not believe Witherspoon was a "bitter Democrat," yet he did believe if Witherspoon was elected he would become a servant to his party and do all its bidding. Unable to sit quietly, Witherspoon leaped to his feet and denied belonging to any man and said that only his conscience would dictate his decisions.[21] White ignored the Yorkville lawyer, emphasizing his own concerns for civil rights, and warned if Democrats gained control

Four. All the Redeemer's Men 99

of the government, the Dred Scott case would "be pronounced in full force" and the black man would have no rights a white man would respect. White characterized the South Carolina legislature immediately following the war as being one "onerous to the colored race" that never enacted legislation that favored the black man.[22]

Isaac Donnom Witherspoon
February 8th, 1833
March 24th, 1901

Isaac Donnom Witherspoon (courtesy of the Museum of Western York County, Sharon).

Democrat James Hart followed Witherspoon's lead, saying he appreciated the peaceful gathering of the two races and crediting the wisdom of Providence for offering an opportunity to "work out our destinies together." Remarking that Republicans feared blacks would lose their rights if Democrats were in power, he pointed out that since Democrats had not been in control of the government since the war, they could not be blamed for bad legislation.[23] Giving more credit than it was due, Hart said it was white men in the South Carolina general assembly who created the first law emancipating slaves in August 1865 and approved the Fourteenth Amendment, but he failed to mention how the general assembly hemmed and hawed until Congress offered statehood to South Carolina only if its general assembly ratified the amendment and abolished all laws dealing with slavery.[24]

As previously agreed, Representative Wallace closed the meeting. Seeing that the crowd was growing tired, he made only a few optimistic remarks about the upcoming election, saying he would "bottle and cork" his opponent, Colonel Evins. Wallace warned the Republicans that they had much to do to secure "the liberties of the colored people," and for that reason alone voters should support him to ensure the work would be done.²⁵

As hypocritical and patronizing as some of the speeches made by Democrats were, they were electric and effective, as the election would show. No doubt the candidates were sincere, knowing they needed the black vote to oust the Republican government. The local newspaper reported the meeting was conducted in a "most friendly spirit," though old prejudices remained intact on both sides.

Hampton's campaign was going well, and his strategists wanted an opportunity to have Hampton and Chamberlain face off in a series of public debates. On 28 September Alexander Haskell penned a ten-page letter to Governor Chamberlain inviting him to attend their mass meetings scheduled in each county and join in the "discussions." "You are aware," Haskell wrote, "that your part and your own official course are charged with having inflicted great wrongs upon the people whose interests it was your duty to promote." The invitation extended an opportunity to refute "the slanderous charges which constantly are published against our party in some newspapers which claim to be your political organ, and also in the Northern papers, backed by the name of Senator Patterson or some other person who claim to be your political friend."²⁶

Chamberlain agreed to debate Hampton on ten occasions, five of which were to take place in the piedmont beginning in Yorkville on 12 October and five in the predominately black areas of the Low Country. Haskell specifically wanted to confront the governor about the secret shipment of firearms sent to arm Charleston blacks. Other party leaders wanted to hear his explanation of why he claimed Haskell, Hampton, Gary and ex-governor Perry were promoting rebellion, why he thought Hampton was head of the Hamburg Riot and that twenty thousand armed Democrats were patrolling the state.²⁷

Tempers and threats continued into October, convincing many Republicans that the only way to preserve peace and insure a free election was through military force. Chamberlain warned the Democrats, saying, "The Executive of the United States will do his duty, and I shall do mine." At the same time, he was trying to assure Republican freedmen that neither he nor the president would allow the Constitution and laws of the state and nation to "be trampled under foot by any combination or party of men in this state."²⁸

Four. All the Redeemer's Men

Chamberlain's words may have seemed empty to Democrats, but a few days later he issued a proclamation demanding the disbanding of all rifle and saber clubs, and that all weapons be delivered over to the government within three days. He threatened that if his proclamation was ignored he would "put into active use all the powers with which, as governor, I am invested by the constitution and law of the state."[29] The following day Chamberlain wrote President Grant on the state's condition, particularly Aiken, Barnwell and Edgefield counties. Without specifically asking for military intervention, he asked the president to aid him in suppressing "insurrection and domestic violence."[30] Grant, however, was still in California and Chamberlain would not hear from him for about two weeks.

Chamberlain's proclamation and threats did little more than infuriate the Democrats. An editorial in the *Yorkville Enquirer* called Democrats to "obey the command ... in so far as it relates to the existence of the clubs as quasi-military organizations," but to ignore the part that demanded the surrender of arms since it violated the constitutional right to keep and bear arms.[31] To get around the governor's order, the rifle and saber clubs underwent a cosmetic makeover, dropping their military titles and using nonthreatening though sometimes ridiculous names. At Allendale, one hundred and fifty mounted men renamed themselves the "Allendale Mounted Baseball Team." Another became "Mother's Little Helpers," and still another called itself the "First Baptist Church Sewing Circle."[32]

Meanwhile the South Carolina supreme court was studying whether Chamberlain's proclamation and threat of armed force was constitutional. It was also looking into the charges that Democrats had instituted the violent Mississippi Plan. Chief Justice Moses was on friendly terms with the leaders of the Democratic Party and believed, or at least claimed to believe, the party was innocent of promoting violence. He assured Hampton his report would be supportive of Democrats, saying, "I saw in no instance any exhibition of arms or any behavior inconsistent with the strict propriety. I shall require very strong evidence to satisfy me that South Carolina is an armed camp."[33] In a letter to Haskell, Associate Justice A.J. Willard reported the same: "I can only say that I have witnessed nothing beyond the circumstances generally characteristic of an excited political canvass. I have seen no violence; on the contrary, so far as I have had intercourse with gentlemen of your part, I have observed less disposition to excited statements and personal bitterness than during any of the previous political campaigns of this state."³⁴

Chamberlain would not accept the court's conclusion. Reports of threats and violence as well as petitions for protection were constantly arriving at his desk. Only recently he had received a petition from Union County asking for troops to protect Republicans who were being threatened and party meetings disrupted. The signers of the petition claimed that Trial Justice John Ray was inciting Democrats against black Republicans, telling them "to shoot their damned hearts out." The petitioners claimed local Democrats were planning to carry guns to the polls the night before the election and if the black voters refused to vote with the Democrats, to make a slaughter.³⁵ The situation in Greenville County was no better, and toward the end of the month county Republicans were requesting a peacekeeping force.³⁶

While Chamberlain was occupied with complaints from around the state, Hampton continued to keep his campaign machinery rolling with "Hampton Day" rallies in towns across the piedmont. The rally in Rock Hill was a typical "Hampton Day" filled with parades, bands and pageantry.³⁷ Shortly after Hampton's afternoon arrival a special train from Charlotte brought four hundred to greet Hampton — among them the Charlotte Cornet Band.³⁸ As the train pulled into the depot, a loud cheer rose from the waiting crowd and was quickly answered by cheers from the train passengers. While the North Carolinians shouted the name of Wade Hampton, South Carolinians enthusiastically cried out the name of their governor, Vance. Amid shouts the two names were united, creating a unique slogan: "Wade-in and ad-vance!" A second train arrived from Chester, carrying many from that town as well as a detachment of the Stonewall Fire Company. An hour later, the Chester Saber Club commanded by General W.A. Walker rode in from Chester to take part in the welcome.³⁹

A parade of mounted Red Shirts with the Lancaster Club heading up the column was formed and led Hampton and other dignitaries into town. It was nearly four o'clock before the parade halted near the Gordon Hotel on Main Street where a crowd pressed in to shake the general's hand and delayed his arrival at the home of R.M. Sims for some time. That evening, Chief Marshall W.S. May formed a mile long torchlight parade of eight hundred mounted Red Shirts and another two thousand people on foot.⁴⁰

From a dais in a large field near the residence of J.R. London, Hampton stood and spoke to the crowd for nearly an hour. By this time Chamberlain's order to disband the rifle and saber clubs and surrender their arms had become a joke among the Democrats. Hampton had a bit of fun that evening when he jokingly commended the Rock Hill Rifle Club for having "promptly boxed up all the arms they possessed — an old flintlock musket, a broken saber and a worn-out holster pistol ... [reporting] that were all the arms they possessed, and he was welcome to them." On a more serious note Hampton said, "But I need not tell you that private arms are your own individual property. They belong to you, and you have the right to retain them."

While preparing for his ten-mile trip to Yorkville, Hampton received a telegram from Indiana's governor Hendricks notifying him his state had elected a Democrat. That same evening he learned West Virginia had elected two Democratic senators, and Ohio's Republican nominee had carried the state with only a small majority. The next day he would tell his supporters in Yorkville that "These are tidings which should stir us all. They tell us that the system of oppression and misrule — of Grantism — with which the whole country has been afflicted for the past eight years, is going down, and shall go down." Another message, not quite so thrilling, was received from Chamberlain advising Hampton he was unable to leave Columbia and would not be joining him in Yorkville for the first debate. Hampton quickly rewrote his speech.[41]

By 10 o'clock the streets of Yorkville were filled with people from all over the county. A mile and a half east of town, the chief marshal, Colonel Asbury Coward, was forming a company of Red Shirts into a column. During the war, Coward had commanded the Fifth Regiment of South Carolina volunteers known as the Palmetto Sharpshooters and had been called "the best colonel in the Confederate Armies" by General R.E. Lee. For many years he had been principal of the King's Mountain Academy in Yorkville and afterward superintendent of the Citadel in Charleston.[42]

At eleven o'clock Hampton stepped off the train from Rock Hill and was met by the now familiar cheering crowd. After greeting the throng of people and shaking a few hands, South Carolina's messiah mounted a magnificent charger next to Colonel Coward. They led the column of Red Shirts up Liberty Street, turned onto Congress and passed through the business district and the grand homes of the elite. All along the tree lined streets Hampton was greeted by cheering men, women and children. Nearing the park where a speaker's stand had been erected, he was met by the uniformed Arlington Hook and Ladder Company and two groups of young boys. "Hampton Boys" were dressed in white pants and red shirts, and "Evins Boys" were sporting black pants and blue shirts trimmed in red.[43]

Hampton dismounted and ascended the stand with former sheriff James Brian, the county's fourth and oldest living sheriff, and H.F. Adickes, the county's oldest merchant. Hampton waved and smiled at the shouting crowd as a shower of bouquets from adoring ladies filled the air and fell at his feet. Two little girls from the Female Academy Institute — Hattie Lowry and Cora Lee Kuykendal — rushed forward and handed him a magnificent bouquet. As the cheering ebbed, Yorkville's noted photographer, John R. Schorb, began playing an organ as the "Hampton Boys" burst into singing a song specially written for the occasion and sung to the tune of the old revival hymn, "Hold the Fort."

> Ho! My comrades, see the signal
>   Waving far and wide;
> Hampton and the boys are riding,
>   For honest rule they ride.
>
> Hold the fort, for they are coming,
>   Hampton leads us still;
> Send the answer o'er the country,
>   By God's help we will.
>
> See the mighty host advancing,
>   Simpson leading on;
> Rogues and thieves the State are leaving;
>   Soon they'll all be gone.
>
> Hold the fort, for they are going,
>   Hear the bugle blow,
> In our leader's name we'll triumph
>   Over every foe.
>
> See our glorious banner waving,
>   Proudly in the air;
> Victory will crown the efforts
>   Of those who do and dare.
>
> Hold the fort, for we are coming,
>   Hampton signals still;
> Send the message o'er the nation,
>   Yes, indeed, we will.

Four. All the Redeemer's Men

Long our "Prostrate State" has suffered,
   But our help is near;
Onward comes our great commander,
   Cheer, my comrades, cheer.

Hold the fort, for we are coming,
   Hampton leads us still,
Send glad tiding o'er the nation,
   By God's help we will.

Similar to speeches he had made at other rallies, Hampton attacked Chamberlain's record of supporting a corrupt government and accused him of personal corruption, saying he had a paper in his pocket that would prove the governor was a felon. For the benefit of the blacks, Hampton said he had served with Representative A.S. Wallace in the 1858 South Carolina legislature, and the only bill Wallace introduced during his term made provisions to sell freedmen back into slavery: "Yet you have voted for that man who wanted to pass a law to sell free men into slavery; and if you could trust him, why can you not trust one who opposed so iniquitous a measure? For further information on this subject, I refer you to the Journal of the House for that year. That is all about A.S. Wallace, and he is not worth the time I have given him."

John R. Schorb. Locally Schorb became notable in the fields of photography, education and music. Many of York County's elite and middle class flocked to his Yorkville studio to be captured by his camera for history. Collections of his pictures (whether the subject is known or not) are prized (courtesy of the Museum of Western York County, Sharon).

Captain E.W. Mosie of Sumter, candidate for adjutant and inspector-general, followed Hampton and spoke for nearly an hour, mostly to African Americans. Mosie reviewed the origin and rise of slavery, pressing the point that the present generation had nothing to do with what had been established before their time. As other Democrats had done, Mosie assured freedmen that the Democrats would protect their constitutional rights.

That evening the park was brightly illuminated with blazing torches and filled to overflowing with both blacks and whites. Promptly at seven o'clock, the band struck up the moving strains of "Dixie" and after the music ended, a large Tilden-Hendricks balloon rose above the park. Following the music and lift-off, Colonel Evins spoke, denouncing Chamberlain for resorting to the "iron hand of military despotism to propel himself into power." He likened the governor to Lewis Merrill, who had arrested many York County men on suspicion of Ku Kluxing, "brought from his hiding place to once more do the dirty work of incarcerating citizens of this state."

Captain Mosie was next at the lectern; finished with vilifying Chamberlain he turned his attention to Senator Wallace. He delivered numerous scathing remarks and charged that Wallace was in league with Chamberlain to intimidate black Democrats and had traveled over the state telling black voters that there would be a revival of the Ku Klux Klan if they did not vote the Republican ticket. Moise reviewed the record of various Republicans, accusing them of robbing the state of millions of dollars through the corrupt land commission.

Hampton addressed the people and later in the evening the crowd called for him again. When he pleaded fatigue, the crowd called for Senator Witherspoon, who humbly submitted to their demands. After reviewing the last eight years of corrupt Republican rule, Witherspoon assured his audience that "under the Hampton banner we will get home rule once more, and under the honest administration of a home government, administered by our own men, peace and prosperity will again smile upon our proud old state." The senator closed with an appeal to work for the good of the state by voting the Democratic ticket that the country might be redeemed from "despoilers' rule." "This can be done," he said, "if we are true to ourselves and true to our honored dead."

The festivities came to a close near eleven o'clock with Colonel Coward thanking everyone for coming and making the rally an enthusiastic event. The *Yorkville Enquirer* later reported it was the largest and most enthusiastic political gathering ever held in the town. York then joined in with Abbeville, Edgefield, Greenville, Spartanburg and Sumter counties in arguing who had entertained Hampton more royally.[44]

As it had done in other piedmont counties, Hampton's Yorkville campaign distilled new hope in the hearts of York County Democrats. A Democratic Club meeting in the tiny agricultural community of Bullock's Creek on the county's southwest boundary sharply illustrates the new hope. At that meeting one hundred and forty-five whites and twenty-three blacks were in attendance; these figures sharply contrast with a similar meeting held two years earlier when only five men attended. A number of the whites attending admitted they had not voted since the war.

Remarkable in its nature, Hampton's campaign drew the state Democratic Party into a solid unit not seen since the beginning of the war. An eyewitness aptly describes the workings of Hampton's campaign and platform: "So far as study of history tells, there never has been in the world a political campaign so nearly flawless in execution as that of the Democrats in 1876 in South Carolina nor a people steered and led so successfully through so many intricate difficulties and dangers, over so many obstacles that looked to be insurmountable. Design and plan ... were wonderfully fitted to the needs."[45]

Upon Grant's return from vacationing in California, he studied the reports from South Carolina and ordered General Sherman to telegraph Brigadier General Thomas H. Ruger in Columbia on October 14: "We are all back from California. If you want anything say so. I want all measures to originate with you. Get along with the minimum force necessary, but you shall have all we can give if you need them." Two days later Ruger telegraphed Sherman: "Think I have troops sufficient unless circumstances change. Have nineteen companies in the state now in stations of one to four companies. Have some companies still in reserve. No special disorder has occurred since Ellenton Riot last month. If I need more troops I will ask for them." Grant ignored Ruger's reply and, in support of Chamberlain, ordered all available troops in the Atlantic military district to be sent to South Carolina. He also strengthened Chamberlain's proclamation by issuing a presidential order for all Democratic Rifle Clubs to disband.

Hampton and Haskell were dining in a private home in Sumter when they received a telegram notifying them of Grant's message to Chamberlain.[46] They knew without a doubt that Chamberlain was not bluffing and would not hesitate to bring the state back under martial law. Many Republicans were willing to use force to keep the state in their control, but some, like Zion Collins of Greenville, believed it was the wrong approach. He warned the governor that the use of military force, though lawful, would be "injurious" to his campaign since the people might "use it as a weapon to keep back many Democrat votes that you are likely and most sure to get."[47]

Throughout the month complaints of violence continued to arrive at Chamberlain's desk. From York County, L. Hotchkiss of the town of Fort Mill wrote Chamberlain reporting he had been threatened "in plain open view of the officials of the town," who did nothing to help. He explained that while doing business at the local post office two men came up cursing him, saying, "Old Lethey, you are a damned old black hearted Radical!" Hotchkiss accused a member of the town council of hearing the commotion and seeing the assailant pull a pistol with cursing and threats but that he did nothing and walked away.[48]

There were other troubles in Fort Mill Township. Under some complaint, a number of men from the area petitioned the governor to remove Republican Trial Justice Murray and replace him with Democrat W.S. Stewart. Justice C.J. Pride of nearby Rock Hill opposed the suggested replacement and wrote Chamberlain explaining: "W.S. Stewart is a Radical Democrat of the worst stripes, spells Negro with two gg's and wants Jeff Davis for President, and his appointment will injure our cause very much."[49]

Charleston had been on the verge of violence all summer, and finally, on 16 October it erupted at Cainhoy, a waterfront suburb. At a mass meeting where men of both parties gathered, arguments and tempers soon developed into a shouting match spiked with threats. According to a preconceived plan, a number of black Republicans ran for a nearby thicket where rifles had been hidden and opened fire. Six whites and one black man fell dead; sixteen other whites were wounded. Martin Delany, who had come with hopes of converting other blacks to the Democratic Party, escaped into a building while others ran to excursion boats. As expected, a local rifle club arrived in the evening and patrolled the streets until federal troops arrived the next day. Republican officials saw an opportunity to gain votes. Republican senator "Honest John" Patterson would later boast that the "Cainhoy massacre was a godsend to us, we could not have carried Charleston County without it."[50]

Four. All the Redeemer's Men

Ten days after the Cainhoy riot Hampton came to Beaufort. Heavily populated with black Republicans, it was one of the more difficult stops and required careful planning. Hampton opted to enter Beaufort without the usual pageantry. A crowd of five hundred, two-thirds of them black, gave Hampton the usual respect and allowed him to speak without any interruption. When LeRoy Youmans came to speak, the crowd jeered and called him names. Unable to silence the crowd, he yielded to Thompson Cooke; but Cooke, too, was shouted down. When it seemed the crowd was about to riot, a "marvel," as one newspaperman termed it, occurred: "Hampton advanced again, and once again there was silence as he spoke quietly and without show of resentment, like a man rebuking a crowd of disorderly children. He said those before him might be interested to know that a large party of naval officers from the fleet at Port Royal was in the club house and had seen all that had happened and would be able to tell their friends at the North what the conduct of the Negroes and Republicans and the officials had been."[51]

The rest of Hampton's Low Country campaign was aflame with cheering crowds, especially at Charleston, where he was met at the railroad station by hundreds who followed him to the Charleston Hotel. The city was decorated in flags, banners and "Hampton Red." Nearly half of the city filled the streets along with numerous rifle clubs and hundreds of Red Shirts, making the event the state's most magnificent rally.

Leaving Charleston, Hampton made short visits to Georgetown, Summerville, Orangeburg and Lexington before arriving in Columbia for its "Hampton Day." At the Elmwood Avenue fairgrounds, before thousands, Hampton said, "My work is done. I have gone throughout the whole state in obedience to your command.... God save the State and bless the people of Richland."[52]

CHAPTER FIVE

Casting Out Satan

In preparation for the November 7 election Democratic leaders across the state were instructing Red Shirt companies to make a show of solidarity through parades, newspaper ads, rallies, and especially at the polls on election day. Following party instructions, chairman James F. Hart of the York County executive committee placed an ad in the *Yorkville Enquirer* inviting "white men, colored men, Democrats, Republicans, American citizens, all come, join with us in our great struggle for reform and redemption."[1] The federal government was making preparations as well, sending extra soldiers to several upstate military garrisons. Thirteen arrived in Yorkville.

Just three days before the election, York County Democrats staged a grand rally and parade in Yorkville. Six to nine hundred Democrats were in attendance and about six hundred mounted men paraded through the heart of town. J.M. Leach of North Carolina arrived by train and "enchanted" his audience for three hours with "the most eloquent and stirring speech delivered in this place." Typical of Democratic speeches, his recalled and denounced the oppressive rule of the Radicals and urged the people of York County to "rise in their might and secure the election of the peerless Hampton."[2]

On the morning of the election the Yorkville Red Shirt Regiment, under the command of Colonel Asbury Coward, began to form at the depot. Virtually every corner of the county was represented: Bethany, Bethel, Blairsville, Bullock's Creek, Mount Holly, Tirzah, Cherokee, Clay Hill, Coates' Tavern, Ebenezer, Fort Mill, Hickory Grove, McConnellsville, Pride's Old Mill, Rock Hill and Yorkville.[3] Of course a circus was on hand, a proven tactic for exchanging ballots for tickets.

The all-white Straight-Out Democratic ticket made a clean sweep of York County. The *Yorkville Enquirer* reported the election had "passed off quietly at every precinct in the county" and that there had been "no cases of intimidations or violence reported." There may not have been any *reported* events, but there certainly were incidents that would not be tolerated today. Years later some recalled seeing ballots sold, as well as subtle demonstrations of force. In 1926, a York County man denied wholesale irregularities but suggested meddling was common: "[Y]ou often hear people bragging how they voted a half a dozen times during the day, and also how seventeen year old boys voted. There was some of that; but most of it ... [was] just stuff, blowing off hot air. Most people voted only once, and very few boys voted at all." He claimed to have witnessed one incident in Yorkville that might have incited "real trouble" had it not been for the intervention of a lieutenant from the garrison. According to this man's account, Joe M. Nichols had come of age to vote shortly before the election and when he proceeded to cast his ballot, Jim Wagoner, a black trial justice, challenged his age. John Nichols, the young man's father, became very indignant along with other whites that were nearby and sides were quickly taken. Wagoner appealed to Lieutenant Benner of the garrison, but seeing his duty was only to keep the peace, he refused to interfere without the consent of the sheriff. Tempers gradually cooled and Nichols was allowed to cast his ballot. In circumspect, the man believed Lieutenant Benner made the right decision, that had he allowed the troops to interfere there would have "been real trouble around the polls that day."[4]

W.O. Guy, of the Blairsville community, recalled in 1922 that the people of York County in 1876 were "determined at all hazards to rid themselves of the political situation" and, at least at the Blairsville precinct, bordered on wholesale tampering.[5] According to Guy, Republican ballots were printed in red ink with a spread eagle and the words "Union Republican Ticket" across the top. In order to confuse illiterate black voters, the Democrats had thousands of tickets printed in red ink with a spread eagle and the same words across the top, but with the name of the Democrat candidates. Various methods, Guy stated, were used to put them into the hands of illiterate black voters.[6]

Throughout the state each polling place had three managers: two Republicans and one Democrat. At the Blairsville precinct William Kell (white) and Dave Crosby (black) were Republican managers with Samuel Blair (white), the Democratic manager. During the count, Crosby took the ballots from the box while Blair called out the names and Kell did the tallying. Kell soon noticed that Blair was calling out the names of Democrats from red tickets and said, "Now Sam, we were boys together, been friends all our lives, and I did not think you would attempt to cheat me." "Well, Bill, what do you mean?" asked Blair. "Sam," Kell replied, "you are calling Democrat names from a Republican ticket." "I beg your pardon, Bill, see for yourself." Kell took a look at the red ballot, the spread eagle and the names of Democrats and retorted, "Well, that beats all!" and took no further notice of the count.[7]

Guy was at the Blairsville precinct during the voting when Democrats became fearful they might not carry the box because of the tremendous turnout of black voters. As the day wore on, about four o'clock someone decided to send for help from a nearby community. Guy and Samuel Brown were dispatched to Hickory Grove, about four miles away, to explain the developing situation at Blairsville. Defying voting regulations that voters must vote in the precinct where they were registered, ten to fifteen Red-Shirt Democrats rode posthaste to Blairsville to cast their ballots. When the Blairsville ballots were tallied, Democrats had carried the box by only seven votes.[8]

In Charleston, the heaviest populated area in the state, Republicans had made plans to insure victory for their party. City streets were patrolled by Republican-appointed deputy sheriffs and marshals armed with clubs and guns. Black voters who had aligned themselves with Hampton and the Democratic ticket were the main targets.[9]

In Edgefield County, where General Ruger had sent six companies of troops to keep peace, it was the Democrats who were doing the threatening. Gary and Butler had assembled eight hundred Red Shirts along with arms, baggage wagons and rations to the county seat.[10] In previous years it had been a practice of Republican blacks to assemble en masse at the voting precincts and crowd out white voters; then near the end of the day, they would rush to their appointed polls and cast at least one ballot. Determined to break this practice, fifteen or more Democrats were sent to each polling place in the county.[11] Most of the day passed peacefully as whites voted at the Edgefield Courthouse and blacks a half mile away at a schoolhouse.

The day's tension heightened when Republican poll manager Richard H. " Daddy" Cain announced there would not be enough time for all voters to cast their ballots. Many black voters became infuriated, believing they had been duped out of their rights. Cain led a huge mob in excess of two thousand men armed with clubs and pistols toward the courthouse to demand access to the white polling place. Nearing the courthouse the marchers could hear singing drifting though the chilling rain. When they arrived at the courthouse grounds they came upon a sight that chilled their blood more than the weather. The grounds looked like an army camp. On one side were squadrons of mounted horsemen looking very much like a cavalry ready to charge. The building itself resembled a fortress with armed Red Shirts lining the steps and filling the doorway. Cain halted his advance and sent someone for General Ruger, who was nearby. Ruger, dressed in his blue uniform, walked across the space separating the two forces; his uniform buttons, braid and insignias of rank gleamed in the dim light. Out of the mass of Red Shirts stepped Martin Gary dressed in military riding boots and a gray frock coat of a brigadier general. For a moment time froze.[12]

Ruger informed Gary of the situation and said, "You must make your men give way and let these Negroes get to the ballot box. My orders are to see that there is no obstruction to voting." Gary, suspecting a scheme to throw the election, exploded: "By God, sir, I'll not do it! I will keep the compact I made with you this morning, that whites and Negroes should vote at separate boxes, and if you think your bluecoats can make way for these Negroes to vote again, try it!" Behind Gary a roar of Rebel yells filled the air and withered the courage of Cain and his men. Seeing the mob begin a retreat, Ruger realized the decision had been made for him; he too, retreated.[13]

After managers tabulated ballots, results were sent to the county board of managers, who would prepare the necessary papers before sending them and the returns to the State Board of Canvassers. According to the South Carolina law, which had been created by Radical Republicans, the State Board of Canvassers was to be composed of the state treasurer, comptroller-general, secretary of state, and attorney general. This board was required to meet on the third day after the election and complete their examination of the returns within ten days. Once the examination was complete and certified, the results of the Senate and House races were then given over to the secretary of state. After the senate and house was organized, they were to request the votes of the gubernatorial race and in joint session examine the results and declare the winner. The problem in 1876 was that Republicans dominated the entire process.

Under the terms of the Twelfth Amendment of the U.S. Constitution, state presidential electors were to meet on 6 December, vote and send their certified ballots to the president of the U.S. Senate. These would then be opened in a joint session and the winner announced.

As night closed in on South Carolina and returns were posted, it was evident from the beginning that Hampton and the Straight-Out ticket were carrying the state. On the national scene, there was a high turnout of voters and the results were one of the closest votes in American history. Tilden won the popular vote 51 to 47 percent — a margin of about two hundred and fifty thousand votes. He needed 185 electoral votes but had garnered 184.

Later in the evening, John C. Reid, managing editor of the *New York Times,* a pro–Republican paper, began to study the electoral votes. Reid knew that four states with twenty electoral votes were still in dispute: eight in Louisiana, seven in South Carolina, four in Florida and one in Oregon. It dawned on Reid that if verification was delayed in these states, electoral votes might be swung to Hayes' favor. He rushed to Republican headquarters at the Fifth Avenue Hotel and awoke several key party members to explain the situation. Party chairman Zechariah Chandler, not wanting to be bothered, told Reid to do whatever he thought best. Reid rushed to the Western Union office and fired off identical telegrams to Republican leaders in three of the four states: "Hayes is elected if we have carried South Carolina, Florida, and Louisiana. Can you hold your state? Answer immediately." Chamberlain received Reid's message early in the morning and began putting into motion his plan to manipulate the Board of Canvassers. Under his direction the board challenged the legality of enough Democratic votes to delay tabulation.

The day after the election, a number of newspapers announced a Democratic victory for the South Carolina state race. As might be expected, pro–Republican papers declared the election was fraught with illegalities and that the victory was the result of rifle clubs and intimidation. Frances Dawson of the *Charleston News and Courier* was so sure the Board of Canvassers would throw the election in favor of the Radicals he boldly published his opinion that South Carolina remained in the Republican fold.

Hampton, however, was so confident of the outcome that he made a formal acceptance statement on the evening of 10 November. Projection of the results also predicted the House of Representatives would consist of sixty-four Democrats and sixty Republicans and Democrats would take twelve new seats in the Senate, making a total of fifteen. This tabulation gave Republicans a majority of only three in the Senate; but in joint session with the House, Democrats had a majority of one.[14]

While Democrats in Columbia rejoiced over Hampton's acceptance statement, the city of Charleston was riotous. Hampton appealed to the Republican mayor for a joint intervention of federal troops with local rifle clubs acting as backup. Although Hampton's plan quelled the riot, when Grant learned federal troops had acted in conjunction with rifle clubs, the commander was promptly relieved of his post and transferred.[15]

A week after the election Democrats across the state were still waiting outside telegraph and newspaper offices to hear a final tabulation of votes. Alexander Haskell, fearing the Board of Canvassers would report whatever results it desired, appealed to the state supreme court to issue an order demanding completion of the tabulation and issue certificates of election to those elected to the house and senate. Republicans dominated the court, but two of the justices favored Hampton and the third was known to be fair-minded. Chief Justice Franklin J. Moses, Sr., the father of the "Robber Governor," and his family had been close friends and admirers of the Hampton family for years. Justice A.J. Willard, a New York carpetbagger who originally came to South Carolina to work for civil rights, admired Hampton's support of black suffrage and had been one of Hampton's neighbors at Cashiers Valley. Once, when Willard's children were sick, the Hamptons extended a kind hand to the family and the Willards never forgot that kindness. The third justice, J.J. Wright, was a black man who had come from Pennsylvania; and though he owed his appointment to the Radicals, he had proved he had a mind of his own and the moral courage to use it. As Haskell had requested, the court issued a writ of mandamus compelling the Board of Canvassers to certify the votes, document any irregularities and report to the court all candidates who had received the majority.

Hearing that the supreme court was about to issue the writ, the board quickly reassembled on the morning of the twenty-second. The board discovered the "face of the returns" gave Hampton 92,261 votes to Chamberlain's 91,127, with the majority of the House going to the Democrats. To reverse the returns in favor of the Republicans the board disqualified all votes from Edgefield and Laurens counties under the guise of voting irregularities.[16] Their nefarious task done, the board quickly adjourned before receiving the supreme court writ.

The supreme court was outraged over the board's action and charged the members with contempt and issued warrants for their arrest. In total disregard to the board's report the court issued certificates of election to every elected Democrat, including those from Edgefield and Laurens counties.[17]

As it happened, Judge Hugh L. Bond[18] of the U.S. Supreme Court was in Columbia when the board members were arrested. After a discussion with Republican leaders he ordered their release. Prior to the board's release, Representative Benjamin H. Massey of Fort Mill wrote his son what he expected would happen:

> The Board of State canvassers are now in Jail, for contempt of court. I heard the sentence pronounced on them by the Chief Justice, that they each pay a fine of $1500 and remain in Jail until released by this court, how long they will remain in Jail we cannot tell. The Supreme Court has ordered certificates of Election to be issued to the Dem. Members elect from Edgefield and Laurens, which we think, secures their seats to them. If such should prove to be the case we will have a majority of four in the House, hence we will elect our Officer in the House and also declare Gen. Hampton the governor and inaugurate him as such as soon as possible. We are hopeful not Sanguine. They are fighting hard and will put everything possible in our way. Everything depends on Tuesday next, the very moment the clock strikes 12, the house will be called to order and a motion made for such a man to take the chair, each side will endeavor to have his man in the chair, if we get ours in all will be right with us, but if they get theirs in the chair and he refuses to recognize and swear in the Edgefield and Laurens Delegations, then we expect to retire from the House to another Room and claim that we are the Lawful House of Representatives of the State of South Carolina. Then we will most probably have two Legislatures and two governors. But at this time it is impossible to say what will occur. Our leaders urge the people to be quiet by all means and bide our time, it is hard to tell what a day or an hour may bring forth. We may be in Revolution and shedding Blood like Rivers of water before another Sabbath day. But God forbid that such may occur. We heard many rumors but things are to all appearances quiet now. I have just been in consultation with Gen. Butler and he asks me to say to the people to be quiet and stay away from Columbia at least for a few days....
>
> We intend to do everything in our power to have Gen. Hampton inaugurated governor of South Carolina and by the help of God we will do it or die. But don't infer from this assertion that we intend to fight the United States troops for we believe that a majority of them are with us. It is believed by some that the State House will be surrounded by Bayonets on Next Tuesday and no person be permitted to go in that has not a Certificate of Election from the Board of Canvassers, which would deprive us of Edgefield and Laurens. If

such should be the case none of the Democratic members will go in to be qualified. Consequently there would be no quorum and nothing could be done.[19]

On the same day Massey wrote his son, General Ruger in Charleston received a telegram from U.S. Secretary of War James D. Cameron, sent under orders of President Grant:

> D.H. Chamberlain is now governor of the State of South Carolina beyond any controversy, and remains so until a new governor shall be duly and legally inaugurated under the Constitution. The Government has been called upon to aid with military and naval forces of the United States to maintain republican Government in the State against resistance too formidable to be overcome by the State authorities. You are directed, therefore to sustain Governor Chamberlain in his authority against domestic violence until otherwise directed.[20]

Attached to Grant's message were additional instructions from Secretary Cameron: "In obeying these instructions you will advise with the governor, and dispose of your troops in such a manner as may be deemed best in order to carry out the spirit of the above order of the President.[21]

Ruger immediately placed himself and his troops at the disposal of the governor and during the night of November 27 quietly moved a company of infantry into the State House. A small detail was placed at the doors of the house under command of A.O. Jones, former clerk of the house, and J.B. Dennis, the former superintendent of the penitentiary. Jones and Dennis were given strict orders to allow no one to enter without a certificate from the Board of Canvassers. This order was meant to exclude Democrats from Edgefield and Laurens who held certificates from the supreme court. With armed troops strategically placed in the State House and convening of the state legislature scheduled for the next morning, the scene was set for a showdown.

The State House was a sorry sight for a seat of government. Construction had begun prior to the declaration of war but was abandoned in 1861. When Republicans took possession of the government, the unfinished building was no more than a shell, and as soon as a floor and roof were added it was occupied. There were no granite steps, porticos or dome, and the building looked more like a stone barn than a seat of government. Around the bleak building the grounds were a maze of muddy paths crisscrossing patches of weeds, large blocks of granite and unfinished stones.[22]

Shortly after nine o'clock on Tuesday morning, 28 November, two

Democrats approached the State House doors and asked for admission. Dennis approached and asked to see their passes. When they produced certificates from the supreme court, Dennis denied them entrance. Not long after this Hampton and Haskell arrived at the State House, but not having certificates from the secretary of state they too were turned away.

Democrats from all over the state had assembled in Columbia with happy expectations for the convening of the legislature. When they found Hampton and Haskell had been denied entrance by armed guards a huge mob of angry men gathered on the capitol grounds. Someone sent telegrams to the leaders of the Edgefield Red Shirts ordering them to come to Columbia and await further orders. Though the telegram could not be traced to Martin Gary, he approached Hampton saying he had ample support and was ready to storm the State House. Hampton declined.

Having been provided with certificates from the Board of Canvassers signed by the secretary of state, Republican house members gained easy

South Carolina State House. When the Civil War commenced, the state was in the process of building a new State House to replace an older one that had been destroyed by fire. General Sherman's artillery unit used the building as target practice; five bronze stars today mark the damage.

Five. Casting Out Satan

access into the State House. At noon, clerk A.O. Jones called the house to order and declared, "I hold in my hand an official list of the determination of the State Board of Canvassers of those legally elected members to the House of Representatives to South Carolina. Members will answer to their names."[23] Fifty-nine of the sixty elected Republicans answered, but not one Democrat was present to answer. Jones announced, "Fifty-nine members have answered to their names. One hundred and sixteen members have been chosen, of which fifty-nine is a quorum, and the House is now prepared to proceed to business."[24]

With the roll call complete, the house proceeded with organization. Edward W.M. Mackey was elected speaker of the house, A.O. Jones clerk, Henry Daniels sergeant-at-arms, and W.R. Marshall reading clerk.[25] As required by the state constitution, a message was promptly sent to the senate notifying them that the house had been organized and was ready to conduct the business of the state. The senate responded with recognition and notified Governor Chamberlain the general assembly awaited his orders.

Believing they had out-foxed the Democrats, the senate quickly adjourned until noon on Wednesday, while the house remained in session. Thomas Hamilton,[26] a well-to-do black Representative from Beaufort, made a lengthy speech questioning the house's organization without the Democratic representatives, urging that all duly elected representatives should have been admitted. He reasoned that if the people of these counties paid taxes and were subject to the laws of South Carolina, then the state constitution guaranteed representation, and without representation from all counties the election of the speaker and other officers was illegal. Hamilton was ignored and the Republican house continued with its business.

Within an hour of being turned away from the State House, the Democrats went into caucus at Carolina Hall.[27] Here they discussed the situation and decided to attempt entry into the State House en masse. John Sheppard and Martin Gary led all sixty-four members down the street and to the doors of the State House. When Sheppard asked for entrance Dennis requested to see his certificate of election signed by the secretary of state. Sheppard replied, "I have the certificate of the Supreme Court of the state." When Dennis refused Sheppard entry a heated discussion ensued. Watching from his post the captain of the guard came over and took Dennis aside. When Dennis returned he agreed to allow the Democrats to pass following a surrendering of firearms.

Having gained entrance into the state house lobby, the men proceeded to the doors of the house chamber and found a detail of twelve soldiers and two officers standing guard. Each member was again asked to show his credentials. Only two who had certificates from the Board of Canvassers were allowed to enter. When they walked into the house chambers they found the Republicans had already organized the house.

Meanwhile a crowd of five thousand had assembled on the muddy grounds of the state house and when they learned the elected Democrats had been barred from entering they grew menacing toward the soldiers standing guard. From the governor's office Ruger and Chamberlain could see a riot developing. When an assistant heard the governor say he believed the only man able to squelch the mob was Wade Hampton, the assistant rushed out of the office to find Hampton and luckily ran into him in the hallway.[28] The governor-elect stepped out onto the grounds to make an appeal for peace. Hampton fixed his blue eyes on a farmer who appeared to be one of the agitators and said:

> My friends, I am truly doing what I have done earnestly during this whole exciting contest — pouring oil upon the troubled waters. It is the greatest importance to us all, as citizens of South Carolina, that peace should be preserved. I appeal to you all, white men and colored, to use every effort to keep down violence or disturbance. One act of violence may precipitate bloodshed and desolation. I implore you then to preserve the peace. I beg all of my friends to disperse, to leave the grounds of the Capitol, and I advise all colored men to do the same, keep perfectly quiet, leave the streets and do nothing to provoke a riot. We trust to the law and the constitution, and we have perfect faith in the justice of our cause.[29]

Having suffered the stench of Radical rule for years, and now, with the fresh smell of victory in their nostrils, the crowd was ready for a fight; but Hampton's plea for peace caused them to moan with disappointment and fall silent as if in deep concentration. Momentarily the mob gave a rousing cheer for Hampton and turned away onto Gervais Street. Within minutes the grounds were evacuated, though uneasiness lingered over the city. General Butler and Judge Mackey continued to urge peace; but Gary, who nearly had the blood bath he wanted, busied himself urging violence.

When the Democratic representatives filed out of the State House, W.H. Reedish of Orangeburg, a black Republican who refused to have anything to do with "the Bayonet House" was with them. When the

Democrats took their seats at Carolina Hall they were in for a long session that would not end until eleven o'clock that night. Having decided to ignore the organization of the Republicans they began their own organizing. Acting as speaker, General William H. Wallace of Union County called the house to order and proceeded with a roll call. Sixty-four Democrats, including the elected members from Edgefield and Laurens, replied. Not one Republican responded until Representative Reedish's name was called, and he rose amid applause and cheers. He announced he was ready to change parties and asked to be received into their body. His request was quickly granted. Having completed the roll call, Wallace declared the Democrats to have the majority and with a quorum present was ready to conduct its business. The house elected Wallace as speaker, John T. Sloan, Jr., clerk, W.B. Williams reading clerk and John D. Brown sergeant at arms. From that time and for many days afterward, South Carolina would have two houses of representatives. Aptly named, they would be known as the Wallace House and the Mackey House. Uncertainty hung over the state.

J.W. Westbury, a black Republican from Sumter, had grown disgusted with the actions of the Republican house and was considering throwing in with the Wallace House. In the afternoon he came to Carolina Hall and presented himself and he, like Reedish, was received into the fold, bringing the total of the Democratic house number to sixty-six.

Just before the Wallace House adjourned that night, a communiqué was sent to the senate giving notice they had completed their organization and were ready to process the votes for governor and lieutenant governor. It would be mid-morning of the next day before they learned the senate, by a vote of seventeen to thirteen, had recognized the Mackey House and directed the secretary of state to deliver the votes to them.

General Ruger sent a message to Hampton saying Dennis had been mistaken in barring Democrat members from the house chambers and should have allowed them to pass on supreme court certificates. Ruger apologized and promised he and his men would remain neutral in the future. The message gave Hampton hope that the stalemate might be settled peacefully; but again, Martin Gary came to Hampton urging him to use the Red Shirts to storm the state house. Again, Hampton flatly rejected Gary's proddings.

At ten o'clock in the morning of 29 November the Wallace House assembled at Carolina Hall. When Westbury did not answer the roll the house was disturbed by the absence of their newest member. It was not until later they found that Westbury was being held captive at the State House. When he returned to the State House to retrieve his election certificate he had been taken captive by Republicans.[30]

The senate convened the same day at noon with intentions of meeting with the Republican Mackey House at 2:00 P.M. to count the votes for governor and lieutenant governor. The only Democrats in the Senate were T.B. Jeter of Union County and Stephen S. Crittenden of Greenville County. They valiantly argued the Mackey House was illegal since it had not been formed with the whole membership. As the argument was ongoing, Speaker Wallace sent word to the senate's president saying he would like to meet with him and discuss the situation. Not only did the president refuse to speak with Wallace, he would not accept any message from him. Just prior to the two o'clock appointment with the Mackey House, a motion was passed to postpone the matter until the following Friday and the senate adjourned.

The Republican house continued with its business and proceeded to hear a report from the Committee on Privileges and Elections. The chairman reported on the contested election of Republican representatives from Barnwell County and called for all five candidates — Fred Nix, Jr., Scipio Bennett, Silas Cave, A.S. Jackson and William Brabham — to be seated.

N.B. Meyers and Thomas Hamilton, both from Beaufort, were concerned that only four of the seven committeemen had signed the report and both men made lengthy protests against its adoption. Hamilton called the report "cut and dry" and argued the committee had no evidence whatever that these men had been legally elected. He reminded his fellow Republicans that the Democrat representatives of Barnwell County had been adjudged elected by the Board of Canvassers and had received certificates from the secretary of state.[31] Representative Ferriter of Sumter joined with Hamilton and Meyers, calling the report "unconstitutional and void." In spite of their objections the report was accepted and prepared to be sent to the senate. When Mackey called for the Barnwell men to come forward and be sworn into office, Ferriter rose and warned, "I am a Republican of longer standing than any present, even since the days of John C. Frémont, and I speak to you now as a Republican. We are nothing more than a Rump Parliament at best, and now when the legality of your organization is being contested, I beseech you not to do this, which will be the last straw that will break the camel's back. The eyes of the whole country are upon us. Pass this iniquitous measure, and the moral support of the Northern people, upon which alone we rely for countenance, will be withdrawn, and those bayonets from yonder door. I say unto you, Beware."32

When the sun rose over Columbia on Thursday, November 30, little did the people of South Carolina realize how close they were to a civil war. Both the Wallace and the Mackey houses convened. Shortly after their convening, the Wallace House began leaving Carolina Hall in groups, walking steadily toward the state house. Not sure of what was taking place, but sensing their representatives were about to take action, a crowd of armed men followed. The crowd was still confused on the facts of why the Wallace House had deserted the State House and they and many Democrats across the state were seething with anger. Upon their arrival at the main doors to the State House the federal troops allowed them entrance without question. Led by Alexander Haskell and James Orr, they ascended the stairs but were stopped at the chamber doors by two doorkeepers. When asked for identification several men at the front presented their certificates signed by the secretary of state and when they were allowed to enter, Haskell grabbed one of the doorkeepers and shouted, "Come on men; let's get at it!" In an instant, the entire body rushed into the chambers. For about five minutes the Republicans were in a state of shock. Hampton and a small group came to the chamber door and requested permission to enter but the Republican sergeant at arms refused him. When a scuffle ensued, Hampton realized his presence was making bad matters worse and he withdrew his request and left the scene. Momentarily Mackey, Jones, Detective Hubbard and others came through the doors. As they neared the speaker's stand, Wallace rapped the gavel and called the house to order. Mackey demanded Wallace remove himself. Wallace ignored the demand and informed Mackey he had been duly and constitutionally elected. The chamber became a din of angry shouts from infuriated Republicans and replying Democrats. When Wallace again refused Mackey's demand, Mackey called for his Sergeant at Arms and ordered him to remove Wallace. Wallace then called for John Brown, his Sergeant at Arms, and made a similar demand. Both sergeants at arms walked up the aisle together and when they began struggling with Mackey and Wallace, several Democrats and Republicans rushed forward to assist their respective speakers. Arthur Glover of Edgefield, who was not a member of the house of representatives and had twice been defended by Martin Gary for murder, took a position behind Mackey and said, "If anything happens, I will kill you."[33]

Neither side budged an inch and both speakers began their duties. From the Democrat side came a motion for a committee of six to be appointed to work out the situation. When Wallace began making appointments, Mackey called out to his side that no one was to take any notice of Wallace and ordered a roll call. A second motion came from Representative Gray of Greenville moving that Wallace appoint a committee to inform authorities that the house was being disturbed and usurped by a band of insurgents. Wallace quickly appointed William D. Simpson, W. Scott Allen, H.A. Shaw, Thomas Hamilton, N.B. Meyers and John Gibson. Gibson, an avid Radical, declined to serve.

At this point several Republicans and Democrats rose to be recognized by their respective speaker. While these speeches were in progress, Mackey had a conversation with Dennis ordering him to go to Chamberlain and tell him that nonmembers were disturbing the house and to send troops to evict them from the chambers.

When the first two speakers finished, Democrat Gray and Republican Gibson stood to make speeches before their party cohorts. Mackey called Gray to order and Wallace called Gibson to order; neither responded. When these finished, Democrat Sheppard and Republican Minor rose to speak. Mackey commanded his sergeant at arms to silence Sheppard and Wallace called on his to silence Minor. Both sergeants at arms attempted to follow their orders but failed and the double speeches continued.

Crossover representative Meyers rose and spoke to the divided body, saying he had come to the house of representatives as a Republican, but because he loved South Carolina more than the party and the men who had brought the state to ruin, he threw his lot in with the Democrats. "I am satisfied," he said, "that General Hampton has received the highest number of votes, and I am in favor of South Carolina being ruled by South Carolinians."

Just as Meyers finished speaking, a forlorn Dennis returned to the chamber and went directly to Mackey and spoke to him in low tones. By the look on the Mackey's face, it was obvious Chamberlain was not sending military support. Not to be out done, Mackey shouted, "I am determined to have order. The Sergeant at Arms will demand all persons not sworn in here to leave their seats and go behind the railing." As the sergeant carried out the demand, Wallace counterordered: "Every member of this house who has been sworn in will remain seated."

The two houses remained in deadlock. The Democrats suggested the situation be reported to U.S. senators Thomas J. Robertson and John B. Gordon for them to end the deadlock. Since both senators were Democrats, the Republican house refused. Mackey commanded, "Any person in this House disturbing its peace will be put out for contempt." Wallace rose and echoed, "Any person in this House disturbing its peace will be put out for contempt." A Republican moved to suspend the three o'clock adjournment. Representative Gray of Greenville rose and made the same motion on the Democratic side. This would begin one of the longest sessions in history.

After six hours Mackey and Wallace came down from the speaker's stand. Wallace turned his duties over to James Orr, and Mackey relinquished his to Thomas of Newberry.[34] Speeches by members from both sides followed the transition, one of which was by Republican C.S. Green of Georgetown. Green entertained both houses with a humorous speech and in closing compared the Republicans' work that day as having had more effect on the Democrats than Moses' miracles on the pharaoh.[35]

S.J. Keith of Darlington addressed the weary assembly: "If times don't get better, I will have to leave Columbia for want of money. We can't afford to stay here all day and all night. I propose that speaker Number One and speaker Number Two adjourn their two houses, and all come back tomorrow at the same hour.... [I]f we don't adjourn I shall stay here until I rot, and hold the fort for Hayes and Wheeler and Chamberlain, and wave the answer back to Tilden he shall never win!"[36]

Democrats holding certificates from the secretary of state were allowed to come and go from the house chambers, but those who held certificates from the supreme court knew if they left they would be barred from reentering. Word began to circulate that General Ruger was considering using force to remove those who held court certificates. Hampton telegrammed President Grant informing him of what Ruger was considering and warning him of the probability of violent consequences. Hoping to convince the president it was in the best interest of his party not to use military force, Hampton assured Grant that Democrats had no plan to overturn the electoral vote for Hayes, but only wanted to have a peaceful and legal house of representatives. Later that night Ruger received orders not to interfere.[37]

When the sun sat on that bleak Thanksgiving Day, winter settled in with a blast of frigid air that broke a forty-five year record. Conditions inside the State House were little better. Due to Republican mismanagement of state funds, the gas supplier had denied credit and for some time service had been suspended. By ten-thirty house members had settled down and more or less quit trying to outdo the other. Candles had been stuck to desks for a bit of light and the iron stove was stoked until it was red hot. Perhaps as proof of their legality and power, the Democratic executive committee was able to convince the gas supplier to open the valves to the State House. For the first time in many sessions lights brightened the halls and chambers and the warm glow of gaslight seemed to renew the flagging spirits. Feeling more comfortable, nearly half of the members were asleep or sat in stillness; others, however, continued their haranguing to about three o'clock in the morning.

When word flashed across the state that Democrats had stormed the State House and taken their seats in the house chambers, some county leaders ordered Red Shirt companies to gather in Columbia in anticipation of trouble. Throughout the night, armed Democrats arrived in the capital ready to support their party. Others, unable to make the trip, gathered around local telegraph offices to hear the latest word.

When dawn came to Columbia, coffee and rolls were sent in to the Democrats, who graciously shared with the Republicans across the aisle. Outside a crowd had gathered and just before noon James Orr moved that the Wallace House session of November 30 be adjourned; the motion carried. Minutes later, as the chamber's clock began chiming twelve, the house was called to order and another day of so-called business began. The Republicans followed suit — adjourning and reconvening. Both clerks called their rolls and when that was accomplished both speakers announced they were in session.

Shortly after the call to order, cracks began to appear in the Republican armor when Thomas Hamilton, who was siding with the Democrats, declared, "This thing is going too far, and I am afraid it will break up in a row." Republican George Reed agreed with Hamilton, saying that no one wanted to avoid a row any more than he and he was ready to do anything right and just to secure peace. Taking the floor again, Hamilton condemned the Republicans' "outrageous conduct" of seating the Barnwell members. Furthermore, he knew the Committee on Privileges and Elections was waiting to seat other uncertified members, though it would take six weeks to get proof of their election. That said, Reed leaped to his feet declaring, "If you mean that the committee intends to seat more illegal members, I will put my foot down on that!" Hamilton warned his colleagues to take care they did not bring the enmity of the American people upon themselves and the party. Reed was moved to tears when he spoke of the shame his own race had brought upon South Carolina.

Across the aisle Robert Aldrich believed he sensed the timing was right for a bipartisan effort and he proposed that a committee be formed consisting of six members from the house and six from the senate, selected equally from each party, and both houses adjourn until the committee reached a decision. Republicans, however, refused to have anything to do with Aldrich's proposal.

By Saturday evening, 2 December, Republican Thomas Hamilton had endured enough of his party's shenanigans. He took the floor and ridiculed the idea of disqualifying the returns of Laurens and Edgefield just because of the number, since his own county had cast three thousand more votes than it had done two years before. He ended his lengthy speech by condemning the "bob-tailed legislature" for trying to force their "unlawful body as a genuine, *bona fide* legislature" upon the people of South Carolina. Finished, he promptly went to Speaker Wallace and requested to be sworn into the Democratic house. N.B. Myers followed Hamilton's lead. While Hamilton and Myers were being sworn in, many Republicans were shouting death threats. Things continued to look bad for the Republicans when Democrats learned that Republican Silas Cave of Barnwell County had never been in the chamber and that someone had been answering the roll call for him. They also discovered that several Republicans from Abbeville County had false certificates.

Early on Sunday, at 9:00 A.M., Democrat Benjamin H. Massey began addressing a letter to Drakeford, Massey & Company, in Fort Mill, a business in which he was a partner. Massey's letter gives us a rare play-by-play account of the day's happening:

We were in session all night and likely to remain so for several days. The Republican side was very stiff yesterday evening, but tempered down considerably last night and seems to be very quiet this morning. Discussions have ceased on both sides at present. We think we have exhausted that point. We are now trying other and I hope more effective means. The military failed to appear to put us out yesterday, and now the impression is they will not eject us from the hall. If they do not we are masters of the situation. The Republicans did not canvass the votes yesterday for governor, according to their appointment; postponed until 2 o'clock today and I don't think they will reach that point today. The difficulty with us is we have no recognition from the senate. They have recognized the other side of the house. If we are under the necessity of retiring from this hall we will have to create a senate before we can operate. We have twelve Democratic senators seated and three who have not yet been seated. That number does not constitute a quorum, consequently we would not have a lawful assembly; but if the worst has to come to the worst we will have to take that course and organize a bogus senate. That we are trying to avoid if possible and that will be our last resort, for we are now in the bounds of law, and our object is to remain so. One thing I can say that if we should fail it will not be our fault for this house is determined to stand up for our rights as long as there is a glimmer of hope. It is a sad sight to see sixty-four intelligent gentlemen on one side and fifty-five Negroes and five mean, low white men on the other side assembled in the house of representatives of this state — a sovereign state of the United States — arrayed against each other and sometimes to all appearances ready to kill each other. Then again, we are laughing and talking together, on friendly terms, as we are at this writing, as Gen. Wallace, our speaker, Mackey their speaker, are now sitting together near me laughing and talking together.

1 o'clock P.M.— The Republican side has just passed a resolution postponing the counting of votes for governor until Monday, 2 o'clock P.M.

2 o'clock P.M.— Hamilton, a Negro from Beaufort, now speaking in favor of Hampton, claims that Chamberlain has not received a majority of votes and that he is not elected. Hamilton is a Radical. Myers is also with us on the same principle. Democrats brightening up. Republicans depressed.

3 o'clock P.M.— Great excitement. Another man sworn in by our speaker. We are getting the advantage of them. We find they have been claiming a member from Barnwell who has not been here yet. We received a telegram stating that this member has not left home yet. The discovery of that fact produced great confusion amongst the Republicans.

7 o'clock P.M.— Rather quiet at this hour. Myers of Beaufort is now speaking on our side. There seems to be a general depression on the Republican side whilst the Democratic side brightens. W expect to remain in the house tomorrow, and until we gain our point, if not driven out by the military, which we now think will not be done.[38]

Like Ben Massey, the other house members stirred from their fitful sleep. Men on both sides of the aisle lolled about at their desks reading newspapers and chatting with one another as they waited for several invited black ministers to arrive and preach to a stalemated congregation. The morning passed without a sermon or prayer and it was supposed the ministers were too afraid to walk into such a volatile situation. At noon both houses adjourned and reconvened and settled in for another long day.

No one thought very much about the ministers not showing up until it was learned Hampton had received an anonymous letter warning him that Chamberlain was planning to bring more than a hundred Hunkidories from Charleston on Monday. The author outlined the governor's plan to appoint these hooligans as constables and strategically locate them throughout the State House as random spectators or sneak them in as Republican house members. At a given signal the Republicans would leave the chambers and the armed Hunkidories would rush in and evict the Democratic members or gun them down on the spot. Some theorized Chamberlain was hoping a scuffle would ensue, giving him an excuse to bring in federal troops. When members of the press in the State House heard about the letter they mentally began rehearsing a quick escape should shooting begin.[39] Others in the chambers were eager for a fight. Twenty-five-year-old Claude E. Sawyer, the youngest Democratic house member, and other hotheads were ready to back against the walls with pistols in hand and fire at anyone who dared to enter.[40]

Among the Democrats there was a growing consensus that Chamberlain's devil-may-care attitude toward violence indicated he was not getting the support from Washington he so desperately wanted. Hampton and top party leaders clung to the belief that Washington's hesitancy to send additional troops indicated the National Republican Party was willing to sacrifice South Carolina to retain power in Washington. Yet they understood they were in a precarious position; if a bloodbath occurred in the house of representatives, it would enflame the nation and once again the state would fall under martial law.[41]

The state was inching ever closer to the edge of civil war. Coded messages were being sent to Red Shirt companies across the state similar to one sent to Greenville: "Ship first train 200 game chickens state fair, with sufficient gaffs."[42] While waiting for support to arrive, the Red Shirt companies already in Columbia sprang into action. One company trained a loaded cannon on the doors of the State House while a fire department stood ready with ladders to rescue the Democrats through the upstairs windows. All night and into the next day the city waited, not knowing what the next hour might bring.[43] A reporter described the scene: "By noon there were twenty-five hundred to three thousand and before night between four and five thousand, enough to annihilate all the Hunkidories Mackey could bring, and the troops also, if necessary.... In the hall the Democrats were smiling and jubilant, Republicans bewildered, depressed, demoralized. The sudden show of strength too overwhelming to be resisted made it evident that an attempt to expel the Democratic members by force would result in the death of every prominent Republican in the city, if not in the state."[44]

Inside the State House both houses adjourned and reconvened at noon on Monday. Wallace rose and read from a carefully prepared statement scripted by himself and Hampton: "I have just been officially informed that there are now in readiness upwards of one hundred armed men who are about to enter the hall for the purpose of ejecting certain members upon this floor." A number of Democrats chuckled at the idea, a hundred Hunkidories against thousands of Red Shirts! Wallace continued: "With a view of preventing a collision upon this floor in which lives may be lost and blood shed, with a view of preserving the public peace, and a view of submitting to proper and legal arbitration all the rights we claim on the floor, the Chair is of the opinion that this House should withdraw from this hall."[45] Loud protests from the Democrats resounded in the chamber. Trying to calm the uproar, Wallace explained that leaving the State House did not mean they were abandoning their offices. "I recommend," said Wallace, "that we do adjourn to another hall in this city." A number of Democrats pleaded with their fellow delegates to hold their ground and fight against all odds, but logic prevailed and the Wallace House slowly filed out of the State House.[46]

As the house members stepped out on the State House grounds, they were greeted with roaring waves of cheers from a sea of Red Shirts. The mood, however, changed when the crowd learned their representatives were again abandoning the State House: elation turned to ire. Hampton then made another of his sudden appearances. Leaping upon one of the massive building blocks discarded in the construction of the State House, he gestured toward the fairgrounds and shouted, "I am glad to see you all here to see the State Fair. There is a very good stock out there and I hope you will all go to see it, and be very particular to behave in an orderly and quiet manner. I want you all to remember I have been elected Governor of South Carolina; and by the God above I intend to be governor. Go home and rely on that. I'll send for you whenever I want you."[47] Magically the crowd fell silent and turned away in quiet obedience. Not only was Hampton South Carolina's redeemer, he was also their prince of peace. When the Democrats abandoned the State House, the gas was shut off, leaving shivering Republicans to root hog or die.[48]

The following day, Tuesday, 5 December, with the Republican house rid of the Democrats, they sat in the still, cold air in joint session with the senate canvassing the votes for governor and lieutenant governor. As expected, they threw out the votes from Edgefield and Laurens, to insure a positive Republican outcome.[49] Their tally gave 86,216 to Chamberlain and 83,071 to Hampton. For lieutenant governor, Gleaves received 86,620 and W.D. Simpson 82,521. Republicans Chamberlain and Gleaves were declared winners.

Earlier the Wallace House had convened at eleven o'clock. During this session, black Republicans Daniel Bird and John Gibson of Fairfield County announced their defection from the Mackey House and were sworn into the Wallace House. Bird and Gibson's defection gave the Wallace House sixty-two members exclusive of representatives from Edgefield and Laurens counties.[50]

Telegraph offices were busy sending word that Democrats had vacated the State House and Chamberlain and Gleaves had been declared winners by the Republican controlled general assembly. When outlying towns received the news, more Red Shirts headed to Columbia. The York County companies, however, were ordered to remain at home. Years later Clark R. Starnes explained: "After the tickets were counted, each side claimed the election. Our 'Red Shirt' crowd wanted to go down to Columbia and put Hampton in office, but we were advised to act differently. They told us to keep quiet and everything would work out right."

Amid angry shouts and demands for action, Martin Gary was in his element. In front of Hampton's office at Carolina Hall, Gary cheered on the masses' denunciation of the Republican government and urged immediate purging of the state. Hampton stepped out of his office and confronted the angry mob. He was met with an odd combination of cheers and frantic shouts of action against Radical rule. One angry man called out, "We'll leave everything we've got with you and tear down the State House with our hands if you'll just give us the word, General!" Hampton again pleaded for peace and assured the mob that nothing could be gained by violence. He made them a promise: "When the time comes to take the State House, I'll lead you there."[51]

CHAPTER SIX

Redeemed!

On 1 December, Rutherford Hayes met with Colonel Roberts of the *New Orleans Times*. Roberts shared the political views of Senators Walthall and John Lamar of Mississippi, John Gordon of Georgia and Governor-Elect Hampton of South Carolina. That evening, in his personal diary, Hayes quoted Roberts: "'You will be President. We will not make trouble. We want peace. We want the color line abolished. We will not oppose an Administration, which will favor an honest administration and honest officers in the South. We will favor measures to secure the colored people all of their rights. We may not, and probably will not, leave the party of opposition, but such an administration as you can have, we will support as men of the opposite party can. We want nothing of you in the way of promise or pledge.'"[1]

In South Carolina, Republicans were making hurried preparations to swear Chamberlain and Gleaves into office. To expedite the swearing in, the senate introduced a bill empowering anyone with the authority to administer an oath equally qualified to install a governor and lieutenant governor. This bill diametrically opposed the state constitution, which required the chief justice or, in his absence, one of the associate justices to perform the service. When the bill was put before the Mackey House for its first and second reading, it passed with few objections.

On 6 December, the supreme court formally recognized the Wallace House as the legal house of representatives with one hundred and sixty-four legal members. Finding that the necessary quorum of sixty-three had been present when William H. Wallace of Union County was elected speaker, the court declared "William H. Wallace as the legal speaker of the lawfully constituted House of Representatives."[2] This recognition entitled the Wallace House to receive the returns of the election for governor and lieutenant governor for inspection. Henry E. Hayne, secretary of state, was ordered to deliver the returns to Wallace. President Grant did not like the situation in South Carolina. Unwilling to accept a Democratic government in South Carolina, he ordered an additional six hundred troops to Columbia on the same day of the supreme court decision.[3]

Representative Benjamin Massey of York County wrote one of his constituents in Fort Mill, Captain T.J. Cureton, informing him about Grant's sending additional troops to the city:

> The action of Grant has stiffened up that party very much and they are more defiant now than ever. Our leaders express themselves as still hopeful, but I must admit that matters look gloomy to me. We are holding on hoping to accomplish something. We balloted for U.S. Senate today but did not elect, merely went through the form to kill time. I have not heard from the Rump House but suppose they are balloting for Senator also. Our Robertson trick seems to be played out. The Rump speaks of adjourning on Friday week. I understand they are debating that question today. If they adjourn, we will do so too. I can't say when Hampton will be inaugurated governor. No one seems to know. I will stop writing until night when I may be able to give you more news. 7 o'clock P.M. The Radical House and Senate elected Corbin to the U.S. Senate.[4]

The Mackey House convened at noon on 7 December with fifty-one members. Their first order of business was the passage of a bill that would empower anyone who was authorized to administer an oath the authority to swear in both governor and lieutenant governor. As expected, the bill passed the house and with its passage the Mackey House agreed to go into joint session with the senate. Republicans began preparations to swear Chamberlain and Gleaves into office — the bill had not yet come before the senate.

The Wallace House was called to order at the same time the Mackey House went into session. Several resolutions went into committee; one of the committees was appointed to meet with General Ruger to notify him that the Wallace House consisted of a constitutional quorum and that he should remove troops from the State House and allow the Democratic representatives to enter. A second resolution requested a joint meeting between the Wallace House and the senate to take place on 12 December, to vote on a U.S. senator to replace T.J. Robertson, whose term would expire on 4 March. During the afternoon session, the Democrats passed a third resolution, this one to seat the Edgefield and Laurens counties delegates. That resolution passed sixty to three.

Six. Redeemed!

No sooner had the Republicans taken their seats, in joint session, than Chamberlain entered the chambers and went directly to the speaker's stand where Probate Judge Boone was waiting. Without hesitation the judge swore Chamberlain into office. The governor stepped forward to make his inaugural address, which read in part as follows:

> I regard the present hour in South Carolina as a crisis at which no patriotic citizen should shrink from any post to which public duty may call him. In my sober judgment our present struggle is in defense of the foundations of our government and institutions. If we fail now, our government — the government of South Carolina — will no longer rest on the consent of the governed, expressed by a free vote of a majority of our people. If our opponents triumph — I care not under what guise of legal forms — we shall witness the overthrow of free government in our state....
>
> I stand appalled at the crimes against freedom, against public order, against good government; nay, against government itself, which our recent political experience here has presented. And I am the more appalled when I see the North, that portion of our country which is secure in the freedom and civil order, and the great political party which has controlled the republic for sixteen years, divided in its sympathies and judgment upon such questions. It is written in blood on the pages or our recent national history, that no government can rest with safety upon the enforced slavery or degradation of a race. In the full blaze of that great example of retributive justice which swept away a half million of the best lives of our country, we see the American people divided by party lines upon the question of the disfranchisement and degradation of the same race whose physical freedom was purchased at such a cost. And, what is more astonishing still, there are Republicans who permit the errors which have attended the first efforts of this race in self government to chill their sympathies to such an extent that they stand coldly by and practically say that the peace of political servitude is better than the abuses and disquiet which newly acquired freedom has brought.
>
> I denounce the conduct of the recent election, on the part of our political opponents in this State as a vast brutal outrage. Fraud, proscription, intimidation in all forms, violence, ranging through all its degrees, up to wanton murder were its effective methods....
>
> The gentleman who was my opponent for this office in the last election, has recently declared, as I am credibly informed, that he holds not only the peace of this city and State, but my life in his hand.... My life can easily be taken. I have held it, in the judgment of all my friends here, by a frail tenure for the last three months. But there is one thing no man in South Carolina can do, however powerful or desperate, he may be, and that is to cause me to abate my hatred or cease my most vigorous resistance to this attempted overthrow and enslavement of a majority of the people of South Carolina. Here I stand; I can do no otherwise; God be my helper. Wife and children, nearer to me than are the ruddy drops that visit my sad heart — all other consideration must

give way before the solemn duty to resist the final success of that monstrous outrage under whose black shadow we are assembled today.

That night an angry crowd demanded Hampton explain why Chamberlain remained governor. As usual, he counseled them to have self-control and patience, and to strive for peace; he closed with a stirring declaration: "The people of South Carolina have elected me governor, and, by the Eternal God, I intend to be their governor."[5]

The following day the Wallace House and the Mackey House, as well as the senate, were at work. When the Wallace House convened at Carolina Hall, Representative Sheppard introduced a resolution requiring the Committee on the Judiciary to inquire into the proper procedure for "bringing to justice D.H. Chamberlain, late governor of this State." The resolution charged Chamberlain had made "treasonable proceedings in bringing war against the State by filling the State Capitol with armed men and thereby obstructing the meeting of the General Assembly."[6]

Another committee questioned General Ruger about who ordered the State House to be occupied with federal troops in November. Ruger did not want to speak off the cuff and asked to submit his statement in writing. He was granted his request and delivered his statement to the committee: "I am ... the commander of the troops in Columbia, and they act under my orders. My orders to them come from the President of the United States and I act as I understand those orders. Governor Chamberlain applied to the President for troops to preserve the peace against violence and insurrection. President Grant recognized Chamberlain as the Governor of South Carolina and ordered the troops placed at his disposal." Secretary Cameron had engineered Ruger's statement; it was obvious the Republican Party was fulfilling its part of the Hayes-Hampton agreement.

S.J. Keith of the Mackey House presented a resolution citing those who had been "duly elected as members of this House, but have neglected and refused to appear and qualify as members." The resolution also stipulated that those who had joined "another body of men calling themselves the House of Representatives of South Carolina, which said body is wholly without legal or constitutional validity," must appear before the house by 11 December. If these did not appear within three days, their seats would be declared vacant and the speaker would be asked to issue writs of election to fill the seats. Their demand was ignored.

The day after Chamberlain was sworn into office, the senate took up the oath bill. Republican W. Beverly Nash opposed its passage on the premise that it would be an admission that the inauguration the day before was unconstitutional. Either he had the right or he did not. Nash's argument must have been convincing since a motion to indefinitely postpone the bill passed eighteen to twelve. Sometime during the senate's session the Congressional Investigating Committee from Washington made their appearance. The committee's visit was expected to last some time, but they departed after fifteen minutes without explanation.

The decision seems to have been spontaneous. It may have had something to do with the communiqué Saylor sent to Speaker Wallace. Saylor excused the committee from appearing at the Wallace House: "owing to the delicacy of the relations the committee abstains to the contending parties in this State." Saylor continued, citing it was their "desire that no act of theirs as such committee should imply a recognition of the validity of either of the acting legislative bodies of this state." It may have been that as long as the committee sat in the Republican controlled senate it could be interpreted that they were lending an (unintentional) assent.

Within a few days the congressional committee had completed its investigation of voting irregularities and concluded the state had indeed elected Hayes and Wheeler by about seven hundred votes and that Hampton and the entire Democratic state ticket were elected by a majority of a thousand.[7]

Since the election, rumors had been circulating that Hampton had been indifferent toward Tilden and his election. Some Democratic Party leaders were troubled by "face of the returns," which showed a Democratic majority for the Straight-Out ticket but a Republican majority in the presidential race. It was explained that many white and black Republicans had cast their ballots for Hampton but remained loyal to their party on the national level.[8] Pennsylvania senator Simon Cameron, the father of Grant's secretary of war, believed it was "due to the personal appeal of Hampton to the colored people, who, being many of them possessed of property, believed his promises of retrenchment and lower taxes."[9]

A committee headed by Chief Justice David K. Cartter, was sent to South Carolina to investigate the matter. From their study they concluded that South Carolina Democrats were satisfied with the election of Hampton and Republican Hayes. They also determined that the blame for the narrow election of Hayes over Tilden rested squarely on Hampton's shoulders.

The committee cited that Hampton neglected Tilden during his campaign. They further said they could verify only one occasion that Hampton approached the subject of national issues, and at that time he said he would vote for Hayes and Wheeler.[10] The committee reported that South Carolina Democratic leaders were more concerned about their party in South Carolina than they were the party in Washington. At a campaign speech in Abbeville Hampton frankly stated, "I am not in that big fight, however, I am in this little fight to save South Carolina."[11] Judge Mackey testified that he heard Hampton say in Winnsboro that he saw no reason why Republicans and Democrats could not support both Hampton and Hayes. Mackey himself had been more outspoken, saying he supported Hampton in the state but Hayes on the national level.[12]

As if South Carolina politics could not become more muddled, another emotional situation developed during mid–December that disturbed many of the state's Democrats. A rumor began to circulate that Hampton was eyeing the congressional seat that was to be vacated by Robertson. A reporter from the *News and Courier* asked Hampton if he would accept the position if it was offered. He replied as follows:

> When the Democratic nomination for governor was made, my position was that I should be governed solely by the wishes of the people. They were to judge where and how I could best serve them. If everything had gone smoothly, and the people had deemed that I could serve them in the Senate of the United States better than I could as governor, I should have abided by their wishes; but, since the recent complications, and in view of the troubled condition in which affairs are at present, I am strongly inclined to think that our people, all over the state, prefer me to remain as governor.[13]

The reporter pressed, asking if he was given his preference as to which position he preferred — governor or senator. Hampton replied, "I am not the one to determine this; but I feel that I could do little or nothing in the Senate, while I may be able to do some good here as governor."[14]

No sooner was Hampton confirmed as governor than the rumor surfaced again. Much of the general population was disturbed about the possibility of his leaving the state, fearing they were being abandoned without clear leadership. Whether this rumor had any basis or not, Hampton remained in the governor's office and was reelected for a second term in 1878. What does seem to give some validity to the rumor was the fact that soon after his reelection he agreed to serve in the U.S. Senate when the general assembly asked. By this time the people in South Carolina were feeling more politically secure at home and were happy to have Hampton standing guard in Washington.

On 13 December John S. Richardson of Sumter requested from the secretary of state certified copies of the 1874 and 1876 elections. Secretary Hayne assumed Richardson was preparing to contest his unsuccessful bid for U.S. Representative. When the secretary gathered together the requested papers, he inadvertently included the election results of both Edgefield and Laurens counties. The next day, the Wallace House sat in joint session with the Democratic senate and studied the returns. By counting the returns from Edgefield and Laurens counties along with the rest of the returns, they found that Hampton had received more than a thousand votes more than Chamberlain.[15] They declared Hampton to be the elected governor and plans to inaugurate him sped forward.

At three o'clock in the afternoon, about the same time Hampton and Simpson were being escorted by James L. Orr, John C. Sheppard and Thomas Hamilton to the inaugural platform in front of Carolina Hall, six hundred troops ordered by President Grant arrived.[16] Their arrival was hardly noticed for the cheering of Hampton's black and white supporters that filled the streets and sidewalks and the thundering of cannons from Arsenal Hill. South Carolina's day of redemption seemed near. Governor-elect Hampton came forward to give his inaugural address, denouncing the last eight years of corruption the state had endured at the hands of the Reconstruction regime:

> When the corrupt party which for eight years has held sway in this State, bringing its civilization into disgrace and make its government a public scandal, saw that the demand for reform found a responsive echo in the popular heart ... they appealed to Federal intervention.... We have witnessed a spectacle abhorrent to every patriotic heart and fatal to republican institutions — Federal troops used to promote the success of a political party. [He then promised to work for reform, establish good government, maintain a system of public education and protect the rights of both races.]
>
> To the faithful observance of these pledges we stand committed, and I, as a representative of the Conservative party, hold myself bound by every dictate of honor and good faith to use every effort to have these pledges redeemed fully and honestly. It is due not only to ourselves but to the colored people of this state that wise, just and liberal measures should prevail in our legislation. We owe much of our late success to these colored voters, who were brave enough to rise above the prejudice of race and honest enough to throw off the shackles of party in their determination to save the State. To those who, misled by their fears, their ignorance, or by evil counselors, turned a deaf ear to our

appeals, we should not be vindictive, but magnanimous. Let us show to all of them that the true interest of both races can best be secured by cultivating peace and promoting prosperity among all classes of our fellow citizens.[17]

Having completed his address, Hampton turned to Judge Mackey and said, "Now sir, I am ready to take the oath of the office to which I have been elected."[18] Following the oaths of Hampton and Simpson, the crowd again erupted into celebration. The guns on Arsenal Hill, called the "Hampton and Tilden Glee Club," thundered over the city time and time again. Hampton, seated in a chair provided by Edgefield County, was hoisted and carried through the streets to the Wheeler House amid a cheering crowd.[19]

For the next four months, South Carolina would have two governments, each claiming the right to govern. On the national scene the election hung in the balance. Twenty-two electoral votes were in dispute, including seven from South Carolina.[20] However, when the South Carolina electors had met in Columbia on 6 December and voted, it was clear Hayes had won by a slight margin. Party leaders urged Hampton to make a statement announcing Hayes as the winner in South Carolina, thinking Hayes would immediately remove the troops; but Hampton believed to do so would be premature. Not only did South Carolina have a competing set of electors, Florida and Louisiana did also. Too, Oregon's one electoral vote was being challenged. If any one of the four states were to be counted for Tilden, it would take the pressure off Congress and he would be automatically elected.[21]

In preparation to govern, Hampton set up an office over a downtown store and chose his nephew, Wade Hampton Manning, as his secretary.[22] Long before the results of the canvassing had been announced, and as early as the previous November, Hampton and the members of the legislature were being inundated with requests for official appointments.[23] Hampton asked party leaders from each county to submit a list of incumbent officeholders by party affiliation — an obvious plan to purge every Republican officeholder from the government and be replaced by a Democrat. He began working on his agenda by commissioning two black men, Ed Henderson and Martin Delaney, the former to the position of Jury Commissioner of Abbeville County and the latter as trial justice.[24] Hampton began purging the government by relieving several Republican trial justices in several counties and appointing Democrats in their place. Hannibal

White of York County argued that these officeholders were only suspended, and claimed Hampton had no legal power and any charges brought against them had to be investigated by the senate before they could be removed. Hampton found no reason to argue with White.

On December 18 Hampton sent a letter to Chamberlain demanding him to vacate the executive offices, surrender the state seal, the State House, all public records and things pertaining to the office of the governor. Chamberlain flatly refused. That same day the Republican senate passed a bill to "prevent, punish, etc. any person or person setting up a state government in opposition to the legitimate and legal state government." When Lieutenant Governor Simpson advised the senate he was ready to begin his duties as presiding officer, the Republican controlled senate ignored him. But Simpson was not outdone. He called the Wallace House and senate into general assembly and set about to elect a senator to replace Robertson. They would also nullify the Mackey House election of David Corbin. When the general assembly began their voting for senate replacement, Martin Gary was the favorite, followed by Samuel McGowan, William H. Wallace, Benjamin F. Perry and Matthew C. Butler. Before the second roll call Gary and the other nominees were swept aside in favor of Butler, who had received only eleven votes on the first ballot but sixty-four of the seventy-nine on the second.[25] Gary's rejection might be explained by the party's need for him to remain in the South Carolina senate. Too, it may have been that Gary's hatred of Republicans would have hindered him from forging the much-needed deal with Hayes.

The election of Butler must have caused some northern congressmen to suspect South Carolina's old regime was back in power. Certainly Butler's record had to be disturbing. Six years earlier, during the 1870 election when a riot erupted in Laurens, the general had sent a company of armed men from Edgefield who systematically hunted down blacks and Republicans, killing about a dozen men.[26] When questioned by a congressional investigating committee he said he had a "passive indifference" toward the activities of the Ku Klux Klan, "[and] I, for one, do not intend to raise my hand against [the violence]."[27]

Within hours of his election Butler boarded a train bound for Washington, arriving three days later. While Butler's term would not begin until March 4, Hampton wanted him to stand guard in Washington while he himself worked on the home front.[28] The first hurdle Hampton had to clear was a lack of state funds. The treasury was empty and the government was having difficulty getting credit extensions. To compound the situation, many across the state were not paying their property taxes, due to the confusion of two governments.[29] A few days before Christmas the Wallace House requested all property owners to withhold property taxes from the Chamberlain government and submit 10 percent of what their property had been assessed the year before to the Hampton government.[30] In response, mass meetings were held in every county, with taxpayers pledging to support the Hampton government. Charleston led off on 21 December, followed by a number of piedmont counties. In spite of one of the worst winters in history, every section of York County was represented at a mass rally in Yorkville and declared to support Hampton and "no other person claiming authority in this state." They further resolved "to adopt such peaceable measures as may be regarded as proper and effective, to secure the full recognition and necessary maintenance of the government of South Carolina, to be administered by Wade Hampton, the legally elected and duly qualified governor."[31] After a few preliminaries and a speech by I.D. Witherspoon, Major Hart introduced a resolution similar to those being submitted across the state:

> Whereas, the general election held in South Carolina, on the 7th day of November, last, resulted by a majority of the votes cast, in the election of Wade Hampton for governor, and of W.D. Simpson for Lieutenant Governor, and in the selection of a democratic majority in the House of Representatives. And, whereas, efforts are being made to deprive the people of the results of this election, by setting up a rival government under the administration of one D.H. Chamberlain, without authority of law; and whereas, it behooves all classes of the people to declare their position in reference to said usurpation. Therefore,
>
> *Resolved*, That we recognize in Wade Hampton and W.D. Simpson the duly elected and rightfully installed Governor and Lieutenant Governor respectively, of this State, and will recognize and regard no other person as filling those offices.
>
> *Resolved*, That we recognize the House of Representatives, presided over by the Hon. W.H. Wallace, as the regularly organized House of Representatives, and will regard no other.
>
> *Resolved*, that we will cordially uphold and support, by all lawful and peaceful agencies, by our means and influence, and by our united determination, the persons and official bodies herein endorsed, and will refuse to countenance any other usurping persons or bodies.
>
> *Resolved*, That it is the sense of this meeting that all the citizens of York County should promptly respond to the recent request of Governor Hampton for funds to relieve the pressing demands on the State government; and we

would urge this upon our fellow citizens as the simplest solution of our present political complications.

This and similar resolutions became known as the "starve 'em out policy."[32] Ten miles east of Yorkville a group of Rock Hill Democrats met and resolved "that the Chamberlain government is a usurpation, achieved by fraud and the sword. We loathe and despise him and his abettors. It is no government of ours and we will pay to it no cent of tribute."

By February Hampton's treasurer had received something between $40,000 and $50,000 from only twelve counties. Economists projected that the month's total could rise to $100,000 but that estimate was exceeded by nearly $10,000.[33] Not only were Southern Democrats willing to make advance payment, some Northerners living out of state were instructing their agents to pay the 10 percent on property they held in the state.[34] Before the end of March, more than $120,000 had been placed within the state coffers; $38,000 was paid out to settle immediate needs and the remainder was placed in several banks.[35]

With money flowing into the coffers of the Democratic government and none into Chamberlain's, Hampton had a definite advantage. The Republican government was denied credit from every corner of the state; and to make bad matters worse, heads of some departments came to Hampton for funding and payment of salaries.[36] Without a cash flow, the Chamberlain government existed in name only, supported by a military presence.

Following the example of Democrats, Republicans across the state attempted to counteract the lack of money by holding rallies in support of Chamberlain. At one such rally in Yorkville, about one hundred and twenty-five blacks led by J. Hannibal White assembled and heard White call for support of the Chamberlain government as the only legal government in the state. White addressed a rumor that certain Republicans were proposing to buy land and colonize blacks. White told his audience that Grant had recommended such a plan, but he was not in total agreement.[37] A second rumor contained hearsay that the year's poll tax was being used to purchase land in Ohio where blacks might emigrate. Historically White had opposed the colonization of blacks in foreign countries. In 1871, at a Southern States Convention in Columbia, he had denounced the emigration of blacks to Liberia and had gone so far as to prevent several York County families from moving to Africa.[38] In Yorkville, he said the only way he would favor emigration was when an appropriation was made that would enable "all the colored people to go, and when the government says there is no further use for the Negro in the United States."

Hampton, Chamberlain, and all of South Carolina continued to wait for election results from Washington. Hampton and his team continued their persuasion campaign with President Grant, Tilden, Hays and a large battery of other politicians.[39] Congressional Senator John Gordon of Georgia, who was acting as an intermediary between the Hampton administration and congressional Republicans, presented a memorial to Congress that reviewed the situation in South Carolina since the November election and the introduction of federal troops. Gordon requested Congress to order the removal of the military, uphold the decision of the state's supreme court and declare the Chamberlain government illegal. After the reading, Gordon submitted a resolution declaring the lawful government of South Carolina and every assistance should be given "to the end that the laws may be faithfully and promptly executed, life and property protected and defended, and all violators of law, State or national, brought to a speedy punishment for their crimes." The resolution was laid over until 2 January.

As the Christmas holidays approached it became evident that the standoff between Republicans and Democrats on both the national and state levels would drag on into the new year. With so much work ahead of them Congress decided not to take their usual Christmas recess. In South Carolina the Democratic leadership was frustrated over the troops not being recalled and began to believe there was little hope of their being withdrawn before the end of the year. Four days before Christmas the Wallace House went into secret session to consider sending a dispatch to President Grant and Congress making one last plea to withdraw the troops. On the same day, Senator Butler sent a message to Hampton, disclosing that the president's cabinet would meet the following day; he said he had all confidence they would agree not to support Chamberlain's government. Butler was wrong.[40]

The weather remained bitter, keeping the piedmont of North Carolina and South Carolina in the grip of frigid temperatures. In York County, on 19 December, the thermometer rose to only fifteen degrees above zero. Rivers were frozen eighteen inches thick, while an equal amount of snow covered the ground. On New Year's Day Chester County was still covered by several inches of snow, and two days later Anderson County reported a temperature of minus two, the coldest day in twenty-one years. Toward the middle of the month, two men froze to death in Lexington County, and in Greenville County a farmer reported he lost sixteen hogs and goats to freezing temperatures. The Broad and Saluda rivers were frozen solid to within a few feet of the middle and immense cakes of ice tumbled along the open areas. Further south, the Congaree was icy in spots.

During the last week of December, Judge Mackey traveled to Ohio and met with Hayes. On 30 December Hayes wrote in his journal: "The political event of the week is the visit made me by Judge T.J. Mackey of Chester, South Carolina, with a letter from General Wade Hampton. Mackey is a fluent and florid talker. His representations are such as leads one to hope for good results by a wise policy in the South."[41] Hayes' remarks on the contents of Hampton's letter reveal little: "The letter is not of much importance except as it indicates General Hampton's views of duty in case of armed resistance by the Democrats."[42]

William A. Sheppard, in his *Red Shirts Remembered*, seems to think there were two meetings between Hayes and Mackey, one on the first of December when the judge delivered one letter to Hayes and a second (shortly after 19 December) when Mackey was supposed to have carried three letters. Hayes' diary, however, mentions only one meeting that occurred during the week of 30 December. It is possible that Mackey took three letters — the first one for Hayes that indicated Hampton's view of his duty in case of an armed resistance; the second a news release containing a copy of Hampton's inaugural address and statements about the internal condition of South Carolina reporting that "profound peace prevails throughout the State" and "the laws for the protection of the inhabitants, in all the right of person, property and citizenship, are being enforced in our courts"[43]; and a third to Tilden.

According to Sheppard, a Washington correspondent from the *New York Herald* was in town and heard about the meeting between Mackey and Hayes. The next day an article appearing under the heading "Turning the Enemy's Flank" reported that "T.J. Mackey of South Carolina, a relative of Mackey, the Speaker of the Chamberlain House of Representatives, arrived here last night and spent the evening with Governor Hayes. During the recent canvass [Judge] Mackey was a warm supporter of Hayes and

Hampton."[44] Though the media had few facts, the New York and Washington papers had a heyday reporting Hampton was supporting the Republican nominee. Two in New York attacked Hampton for what was termed "deplorable actions [that] added to the demoralization of the Democrats."[45] The *Louisville* (KY) *Courier Journal* condemned Hampton for his support of Hayes: "[The letter] fell like a wet blanket on the Democrats in Washington City. General Hampton's Southern friends and admirers are deeply mortified at the step he has taken. The opinion of the best observers is that the situation is rendered deeply critical by these utterances, and so far from the prospect of a collision being lessened by letters like these, it is greatly increased. The Republicans are justly encouraged by these demonstrations."[46]

Hampton demonstrated his severance from the National Democratic Party when William Preston telegraphed the governor that he should deny any charges of supporting Hayes. Hampton replied, "No one is authorized to make declarations for me or our party here, we abide by the decisions of legitimate authority and hope for a peaceful solution."[47] Hampton's own political machinery rushed to control the damage and advised him to deny the reports, while Judges Mackey and Cooke worked in secret. Soon after, Hampton met with members of the press and denied having sent Mackey to Ohio or authorized him to speak for him. The judge, he explained, had gone to Ohio on private business and any view he expressed was his own.[48]

Many Democrats found it hard to believe their hero could be so devious and preferred to believe it was a scheme contrived by Republicans to sully Hampton's character. One Chester Democrat, however, liked the possibility of a compromise and told a correspondent from the *Yorkville Enquirer* that the "irrepressible Judge [Mackey] has, doubtless, presented the claims of Hampton in the strongest possible light, and done all in his power to secure a promise from Hayes to recognize the Hampton government in the event he shall be declared and inaugurated President."[49] Others, like General Jubal Early, believed Hampton wrote the letter; but Early also protested that anyone who knew Hampton would have to "admit that he is incapable of anything savoring of dishonor."[50]

While Hampton denied knowing anything of the Hayes-Mackey meeting, the "irrepressible" Mackey openly told a group in Yorkville that he had met with Hayes for the better part of three days and had given the

Ohio governor a full review of the political events in South Carolina. Mackey said he was sure Hayes would be declared president, and that his first official act would be to recognize Hampton as the legally elected governor of South Carolina.

The northern press rushed to interview Senator Robertson, whose term had not yet expired; but they received little from him. He explained that he thought it odd that the media had created such a furor, that Hampton had openly said throughout the campaign that any South Carolinian could vote for Hayes and Wheeler if they desired. In defense of Hampton, Robertson said he doubted Hampton would ever put his state's affairs behind the selection of a president.[51]

The *Augusta Chronicle and Sentinel* produced a lengthy article styled as an expose on the secrets of the 1876 campaign. The ill feelings between Hampton and Tilden were recounted; but overall the writer stressed the shenanigans of Tilden, pointing out that he had sent an agent to the state convention to prevent Hampton's nomination. The reporter accused Tilden of having refused to give Hampton the support deserving of a same-party candidate, nor did the chairman of the National Democratic Party offer financial support to the Democrats in South Carolina. According to the reporter, Tilden had cut his own throat when he did not reply to Hampton's letter, which was the reason Hampton had not tried to garner votes for Tilden. Even as late as the canvassing of votes, wrote the reporter, Hampton had agreed to Judge Cooke's suggestion to drop Tilden's name and let the canvass be only Hampton and Hayes — for the promise of funds to be furnished by the Republicans.

Hampton continued to deny any knowledge of the letters or the meeting. When asked about the *Chronicle and Sentinel*'s report, he replied:

> The writer has fallen into many grave errors. I have no agency whatever in Judge Mackey's visit to Ohio and he bore no proposition. No message came from me. He says so himself. A proposition was made to withdraw our electors, and the Democratic Executive Committee knows that I took strong ground against it. A subsequent proposition was made on the same subject, and this I also declined. Judge Cooke spoke for Tilden and voted for him. Judge Mackey spoke with me at but two places, and he will doubtless say how he voted in the Presidential election. Whether the canvass was a mistake or not is not for me to say; but I do say that I supported Tilden thoroughly and heartily throughout. The Democratic electors can speak on this point, and especially can General [Samuel] McGowan, who is referred to, and who will, I hope, answer for himself. The leaf of history has been so secret that no one in the

States knows anything about it, and it is as utterly unreliable as history as it is as a secret.⁵²

When questioned later by another reporter, Hampton again denied ever having any consideration of withholding the Tilden electors or using his influence to motivate the state Democratic Party to do so. He admitted that unnamed Republicans came to him with a proposition that if he publicly acknowledged Hayes federal troops would be withdrawn and he would be recognized as governor. Hampton further admitted that the offer was tempting, but his character would not allow him to give any consideration to this proposition.

While Governor Hampton was denying any association with Hayes, Judge Mackey was trying to convince Democrats how they needed Hayes. After Mackey adjourned court in Yorkville on 16 January, some of the men who were at the courthouse urged him to speak to them about the developing political situation. He openly confirmed meeting with Hayes and said he was convinced it would be beneficial to South Carolina to "lay before him facts" about the political situation in the state and "have an impartial judge" if he was declared president.

Mackey said that no matter who went into the Oval Office, not everyone would be pleased. Northerners would say Tilden had won through violence and intimidation, and if Hayes were inaugurated, Southerners would scream "fraud!"⁵³ and might explode in a bloody revolt. Mackey went on to say that he believed it would be significantly better for South Carolina if Hayes were elected since he would need to have a policy of reconciliation toward the South, whereas Tilden would direct his policy to pacify the North. Too, Tilden would have to contend with a Republican majority that was bent on punishing South Carolina. Hayes, a Republican himself, would be friends with the Senate majority and could afford to adopt the easiest way to work out the state's problems.

Hampton's damage control chiefs were caught off guard when a letter appeared in the 10 January issue of the *Augusta Chronicle and Sentinel*, written by "A Tilden Democrat." The writer accused Hampton of being indifferent to Tilden throughout the campaign and claimed that he had flirted with and had been willing to make a deal with the National Republican Party. Hampton was accused of "repudiation of the plan of campaign adopted" by Gary and the Straight-Outers and had instead supported a "milk and cider, peace and prosperity, conciliation of Radicals and flattery of Negroes policy."

Although he could not prove it, Hampton was sure the letter's author was none other than Martin Gary, who had become disenchanted.[54] Whoever the "Tilden Democrat" was, he obviously had access to the inner workings of Hampton's campaign. The writer disclosed reports of intrigues in which Tilden would be denied the presidency and how Hampton had become disillusioned with the Democratic nominee. He even mentioned how W.Y. Pelton, Tilden's nephew, urged leaders of the state Democratic convention to nominate a man less prominent than Hampton, because Hampton would "injure the party at the North." The supporters of Pelton were John Bratton, John D. Kennedy, James H. Rion and James A. Hoyt. Private discussions, known only by the top level of leadership, were exposed as well as how Hampton had tried to appease Tilden but was ignored. The letter disclosed how Cooke and Mackey devised the plan to aid the Democratic cause in South Carolina by abandoning Tilden and withdrawing the presidential electors, and that "General Hampton was willing and anxious that such an agreement should be made."[55] South Carolina's pro–Democrat newspapers were furious and Alexander C. Haskell went into a rage, saying the letter would never have been printed in South Carolina. In a bitter letter Haskell denied Hampton was "willing and anxious" but did not deny the charge that Hampton withdrew from Tilden.

Both South Carolina and Louisiana had submitted two sets of certified ballots to the Senate—one Democrat and one Republican; the question before the Senate was which ballot was to be counted. The U.S. Constitution made no provision for deciding between two sets of returns. William McFeely, in his biography of Ulysses S. Grant, wrote pointing out that "The Constitution calls for the electoral votes to be opened in the presence of both houses of Congress, but it does not say who should do the counting. If the Republican Senate majority decided the county went one way; the Democratic majority of the House of Representation might decide it went the other. Another possibility was a Senate filibuster, begun before the count could be made, might extend past Grant's last day in office, leaving the United States without a president."

In January Congress passed the Electoral Commission Law establishing a body to decide which votes from the several disputed states should be counted. That commission was to be composed of five members from the House of Representatives, five from the Senate and five from the Supreme Court. Of these, seven were to be Democrats and seven Republicans, with the deciding fifteenth vote to be cast by Illinois supreme court justice David Davis. Both parties had confidence Davis could make an impartial decision, but before the commission could be seated Davis was disqualified when Illinois elected him to the U.S. Senate. Republican justice Joseph P. Bradley was appointed to replace Davis. Democrats suspected they had been hoodwinked.

Both houses of Congress met on the first day of February to count electoral votes. When the roll call got to Florida the fifteen-member electoral commission paused and debated for nine days on who should get the votes. Justice Bradley voted with his fellow Republicans and awarded the four electoral votes to Hayes and made the same decision when Louisiana's votes went into discussion. Louisiana's Republican Governor Packard was clinging to office, eating and sleeping in the State House; but when Bradley made his decision to give the state's electoral votes to Hayes, it gave Packard renewed hope. Believing Justice Bradley was going to decide everything in favor of the Republicans, Tilden and the Democrats fell into despair.

Meanwhile, President Grant continued being concerned about armed rifle clubs and the possibility of their being used against Chamberlain's shaky government. The dismissal of Republican judges and other law enforcement officers was particularly worrisome to Grant, and even more so, word that local residents were requesting Hampton to commission the rifle clubs. With Washington's birthday approaching, Hampton commissioned several clubs to march in a Charleston parade alongside federal troops. Grant's fear of armed Democrats led him to issue an order forbidding white militia units to march, explaining the clubs were no more than armed political bands that had never respected his order to disband. The president concluded:

> I must say that while I believe the Democratic leaders would have done all that was possible to prevent an outbreak, yet, on an occasion of that kind, men sometimes indulge too much in strong drink, and while under its influence might so express themselves against their political opponents as possibly to provoke retaliation, and thus incite a riot with serious, if not fatal consequences, and which disturbance might extend to other localities. Therefore, entirely apart from the propriety of observing the day, it was thought better that the military demonstration should be prevented for the reasons stated, rather than run the risk of a riot.[56]

Grant's order incensed many white Democrats, but once again Hampton stepped in with his persuasive way and brought calmness to the situation.

Chairman Saylor of the Congressional Investigating Committee made his committee's report on South Carolina to the U.S. House of Representatives, giving good news for Hampton and the Democrats. In agreement with the Republican Party's plan to scrap the Chamberlain government, Saylor reported Chamberlain's government, "like its predecessor, has no power to protect the people, and is so utterly weak that nothing but the moral powers of the support of the general government keeps it in existence a single day." The report hammered a nail into Chamberlain's political coffin by asserting it would be "wrongful support" to use the military to prop up the Republican government, as it would "quickly vanish like the dew before and sun, and will no longer disturb the peace of an oppressed and long suffering people."[57]

Toward the end of the month, the *Philadelphia Times*, an Independent Republican newspaper, predicted Hayes would be declared president though two-thirds of the people of the United States would maintain that he was not elected honestly. The *Times* columnist speculated on the probable policies Hayes would adopt toward the South, saying that he would (1) cast aside the men and agencies that would declare him president and form an entirely new cabinet, (2) recognize Nicholls of Louisiana and Hampton of South Carolina as governors, (3) recall the troops from the South "and invite carpet baggers and plunderers to play by themselves," (4) "cast from him the dregs of the Grant administration," and (5) attempt to bring both houses of Congress into harmony with the White House.[58]

The *Times* ended its predictions with a lengthy prophecy: "The organs of the Republican Party which have been proclaiming Hampton and Nicholls from day to day as conspirators, assassins and usurpers, and which had been flaming with hate and vengeance against the South, will, within thirty days, declare Hampton and Nicholls to be estimable gentlemen and lawful governors, and they will pay tribute to peace and universal brotherhood as the shrines at which every patriot should bow."

When the U.S. House of Representatives met on March 1 it began one of the more turbulent sessions in history. House Speaker Samuel Randall, a former Tilden supporter, enraged other members when he stalled the vote of the Electoral Commission. During this session Randall began developing the powers of the Speaker of the House and is responsible for the authority the officer enjoys today. For eighteen hours the House was in turmoil; some members mounted their desks, brandishing pistols and shouting their disapproval amid vulgar oaths and insults. Tilden feared this turmoil might erupt into a civil war, and for the good of the nation he telegrammed his supporters to submit to the decision of the Electoral Commission. Shortly after four o'clock on the morning of 2 March, the Senate president counted the disputed electoral votes of Florida, Louisiana, Oregon and South Carolina as being all in favor of Hayes, who was elected to the White House by one hundred and eighty-five votes to Tilden's one hundred and eighty-four.[59] Only a few days after the *Philadelphia Times* had made its prophecy, Rutherford B. Hayes, who had suffered indignities such as "His Fraudulency" and "Rutherfraud," became the 19th president of the United States.

Previously, when the House had been called to order on 1 March, Hayes, his wife, and a small entourage left Columbus, Ohio, for Washington on two private railroad cars. Earlier in the day Hayes and his wife were honored with a large reception at Ohio's State House and upon leaving for the train station they were led by college cadets and followed by a large crowd. En route to Washington they were greeted by crowds in Newark, Dennison, Steubenville and other points along the line. Hayes and his wife were awakened near Harrisburg and given the news he had been elected.[60]

Reaching Washington about 9:30 in the morning they were met at the depot by General/Senator Sherman and were driven directly to Sherman's home for breakfast. Hayes and Sherman later called on President Grant at the White House. On the advice of Secretary Fish, a state dinner was arranged at the White House where Hayes would be sworn in by the chief justice "to prevent an interregnum between Sunday noon and the inauguration, Monday."[61] On Saturday, March 3, Hayes took the oath in the Red Room of the White House, and for the rest of the day and Sunday the new president met senators and representatives, many of whom had suggestions for cabinet members. On Monday, he took a public oath on the East Portico of the Capitol and gave his inaugural address.

Lucy Webb Hayes, the wife of President Hayes, would become a popular first lady and was the first president's wife to have a college degree. She and Hayes were married in December 1852 and had eight children, three of whom died in infancy. While in the White House they set the highest standard for the nation. Smoking was not allowed; alcoholic beverages were banned even at state dinners. This prohibition on alcohol earned Mrs. Hayes the teasing nickname "Lemonade Lucy." Though she was not a prohibitionist, she supported the standards of her husband. There were no lawn parties, dances or card playing. Daily prayers and hymn singing were the rule of the household.

Twenty-four hours after the inauguration, Alexander Haskell stepped off the train in Columbia and proceeded to the State House. Haskell was delighted to deliver a letter to Chamberlain from Senator Matthews with a postscript by secretary of state William M. Evarts. The letter relayed disappointing news to Chamberlain: "[A]n arrangement could not be arrived at which would obviate the necessity for the use of Federal arms to support either Government, and leave that to stand which is able to stand of itself."[62]

Feelings of betrayal rested heavily on Chamberlain. He knew too well that his government would collapse without the support of federal troops. Knowing nothing else to do, he began calling for help from those who had been his supporters. He telegraphed Senator David Corbin to intercede but there was no response.[63] The silence was sickening. He then telegraphed Matthews that there had to be a better way to appease South Carolinians than by removing the troops from the State House: "To permit Hampton to reap the fruits of a campaign of murder and fraud so long as there remained power to prevent it is to sanction such methods."[64]

The *New York Journal of Commerce* published a dispatch from Washington on 9 March regarding the Republican governors of South Carolina and Louisiana:

> Before taking final action in the matter of the withdrawal of the Federal forces from Columbia and New Orleans ... the President has decided to give Messrs. Chamberlain and Packard an opportunity to voluntarily retire from the positions which they cannot possibly maintain. Unmistakable intimacies have been conveyed to both these gentlemen.... If after a reasonable lapse of time it is found that these gentlemen are determined to attempt to maintain their positions, orders will be issued to Generals Ruger and Auger, directing them to withdraw the Federal troops ... thus leaving it to the people of South Carolina and Louisiana to decide for themselves which of the dual governments they will sustain. If either Packard or Chamberlain entertain the belief that any senator or combination of senators, can prevent the President from inaugurating and carrying out the policy enunciated in his letter of acceptance and in his inaugural address, they are doomed to serious disappointment, and this they will realize within a few days.[65]

Indeed, they would realize the truth though no official announcement was made; Hayes' inaugural address gave every indication of being conciliatory toward the South, to bring peace and unity to the nation. The following day Judge Mackey met with President Hayes and his nominee for secretary of state, William M. Evarts. During this meeting Evarts wanted to know, if Chamberlain came to Washington to meet with the president, whether Hampton and the Democrats would take advantage of his absence and take the government by force. Speaking for Hampton, Mackey gave his word that the status quo situation in the state would continue without intervention. Judge Mackey warned the president that should Chamberlain be recognized armed elements of the Democratic party would resist and peace would be lost. As Mackey left, Evarts privately told Mackey he had no doubt a decision would be made by 15 March.[66]

The day after Hayes and Evarts met with Mackey the *Journal of Commerce* reported Chamberlain had "about made up his mind to resign all pretensions to gubernatorial honors in South Carolina." While it is uncertain who spoke with the *Journal*, ex-governor Fenton of New York was in Columbia and had lengthy conversations with both Hampton and Chamberlain. The president had the advice of a number of men from his party who were not willing to leave South Carolina. Senator John Patterson advised the president that a new election was needed in South Carolina. Others believed the Democrats would yield the state if the president recognized the Chamberlain government. Hayes and his cabinet continued to seek peaceful ways to end the deadlock.

While Washington remained silent, Hampton continued to busy himself replacing Republicans with Democrats amid protests and denials of his authority. To fill a trial justice seat in York County's Bullock's Creek Township vacated by the death of J.M. Smarr, Hampton appointed Samuel Davidson. Republican R.J. Willie Peacock complained to Chamberlain that Davidson was "a man who the Republican Party is bitterly opposed to" and he should not be recognized because Hampton had no authority.[67]

Hampton's request for the names of officeholders and their political affiliation alerted Magistrate James L. Strain of Union County. His letters to Hampton and Chamberlain serve as a case study of those Republicans who wanted to keep their employment. Unknown to Strain, several petitions signed by those living in Gowdysville, Skull Shoals and other communities in Strain's jurisdiction requested he be replaced by Democrat J. Rufus Pool.[68] In January Strain wrote Hampton telling him that he had received his appointment from Chamberlain in February 1875, and that the law stipulated the term of office for trial justices were for two years, though he recognized the governor could terminate the term prematurely. Strain went on to tell Hampton he had served in the Confederate army and had lost a leg that rendered him unfit for manual labor and in dire need of the "petty remunerations of my office."[69]

When Strain heard about these "secret" petitions he wrote the governor on 6 February. Again, he mentioned his handicap and how much he depended on the income of a trial justice. He believed the petitions were a product of prejudice and pleaded for an opportunity to vindicate himself. On the outside of Strain's letter a secretary summed up the contents: "Asks to be heard before his head is cut off."[70] Just one month before Chamberlain left office, Strain was playing up to the Republican in hopes of saving his salary. Strain confided in Chamberlain, saying he refused to recognize Hampton's claim. Hoping for an appointment to a clerical job he cited his knowledge of *Munson's System of Phenography* and the fact that he had five years' experience in shorthand.[71] To ingratiate himself to Chamberlain he sent a copy of resolutions adopted by local Democrats, saying it "may be used as evidence that our people were compelled to vote contrary to their wishes to save themselves from harm."[72] Strain's head was cut off and his office given to another. Some years later, after Hampton had left office and Strain had proved to be a loyal Democrat, he was reappointed and served in that capacity for many years.

Strain was not the only Republican trying to save his appointment. Benjamin Briggs, a York County Republican who would later be appointed county auditor, wrote the governor a straightforward letter about being a Republican but assured Hampton that he was not a Radical and, like him, opposed Black Rule and Carpet Bag Rule.[73]

Across the state Republicans were feeling the impact of a developing Democratic government. Rubin Gains, a barber in Yorkville, complained to Chamberlain about his particular situation and asked for "ever so little [money] to keep me from suffering." Pleading for his wife and four children—two were sick. He said of the Democrats, "They have shut me out so that I have no means of making a living."[74] Some fifteen miles away, in Fort Mill, Republican Sandy White had greater concerns than making a living — he feared for his life. White had received a note that evoked memories of the reign of terror by the Ku Klux Klan:

> He[a]d Quarters
> KKK
> Sandy White, you have ten days to get out of the State or well [sic] will have your head.
> *Fear Notice*
> KKK[75]

Four hundred miles to the north, in Washington, President Hayes announced the formation of his cabinet. The news did not sit well with Radical Republicans, especially the appointments of D.M. Keys of Tennessee to postmaster general, William M. Evarts of New York to secretary of state, and Carl Schurz of Missouri to the Department of Interior. On 14 March Hayes made an entry in his journal: "The chief disappointment among the influential men of the party was with Conkling, Blane, Cameron, Logan and their followers. They were very bitter.... [S]peeches were made, and an attempt to combine with the Democrats to defeat the confirmation of the nominations only failed to be formidable by the resolute support of the Southern Senators.... After a few days the public opinion of the country was shown by the press to be strongly with me. All of the nominations were confirmed by almost a unanimous vote."[76]

South Carolina Democrats saw the appointment of Keys as an encouraging sign, but when Hayes' decision declaring Hampton governor was not forthcoming, they began to suspect the administration was wavering. A reporter from the *News and Courier* described their feelings: "depressed with the deferred hope which maketh the heart sick, can only patiently wait the interminable delays of those hands our political destiny seems to be placed."[77] When Butler wired Hampton on 21 March, he expressed the same heartsickness, believing the state was at the mercy of the Electoral Commission: "Everything looks blue; there seems to be no hope for South Carolina. It looks like another game of eight and seven."[78]

Two days later Colonel W.K. Rogers, private secretary to the president, sent letters to Hampton and Chamberlain inviting them to come to Washington to discuss their situations and "put an end as speedily as possible to all appearance of intervention of the military authority of the United States in the political derangements which affect the government and afflict the people of South Carolina."⁷⁹ Both men promptly replied to the president that they would immediately proceed to the White House.

Chamberlain left on Sunday, 25 March, two days before Hampton. On the same day Hampton was preparing to board a train for Washington, Chamberlain had arrived and met with the president. The *New York Herald* reported that Chamberlain had said Hayes wanted to know if there was any way he and Hampton could come to an amicable decision. Chamberlain firmly protested he had been legally elected as governor and would keep the office. The *Herald* however, was of the opinion that Hayes was giving Chamberlain a last chance to back out gracefully. Chamberlain insisted it was obvious he was the true governor since there had been no recognition of Hampton except by the South Carolina courts that were now controlled by the Democratic party. Although Chamberlain publicly insisted he was the true governor, the newspaper gave the idea that Chamberlain really had no confidence he could hold the position.⁸⁰

There had been a wide range of opinions among the Democrats as to whether Hampton should accept Hayes' invitation. Some emphatically believed he should decline; but others figured that even if the meeting produced nothing good, it probably would do no harm. Mackey briefed Hampton about his conversation with Hayes' secretary of war, George McCrary, and said that McCrary had told him that the real reason for Hayes' invitation was to learn the policy Hampton would pursue as governor. Mackey told Hampton that McCrary had referred to him as "governor and expressed hope that your administration would prove the wisdom of the President's policy."⁸¹

Hampton boarded a train in Columbia accompanied by Butler and others. At Florence they were joined by a delegation from Charleston and the entire trip was spiked with grand welcomes and rousing ovations. At Wilmington, North Carolina, a crowd of three thousand gathered at the depot to catch a glimpse of the hero from South Carolina. Speaking to the crowd, he said, "I go there to say to him that we [the people of South Carolina] ask no recognition from any President. We claim the recognition from the votes of the people of the state. I go there to assure him that we are not fighting for party, but that we are fighting for the good of the whole country. I am going there to demand our rights, nothing less, so help me God, to take nothing less! I go to tell him the condition that South Carolina has been in for years past, that our people have been under disadvantages never encountered by any other people on this continent; that they carried the election, were successful, and that they propose to enjoy the fruits of their victory."

All along the route through North Carolina — at Magnolia, Mount Olive, Goldsboro, Wilson, Rocky Mount, Enfield, Halifax, and Weldon — hundreds cheered and clung to every word of the Carolina hero.[82] The sky was ablaze with rockets as the people of Petersburg welcomed Hampton to Virginia. He told the Virginians that "the time was near when South Carolina would take her place with her sister states, equal to any of them"

When the train arrived in Richmond at 8:30 P.M. a crowd of five thousand was waiting. Hampton addressed them:

> The people of South Carolina are in earnest. We have tried compromise in vain, and so last fall we planted our feet firmly on the Constitution and began to battle for our rights. We remembered that ours was one of the original thirteen states, and strong men and noble women joined hands in the struggle, declaring that by the Almighty God they would sacrifice everything to win.... You cannot imagine what those people had to bear to win their constitutional victory; but they won, and fully twenty thousand colored men cooperated with them, and now thousands and tens of thousands of colored men are paying taxes to my government. All we ask, and all I am going to Washington to ask, is that the Federal troops be with drawn from the State House of South Carolina, the only place in the State where my authority is not respected. Send the soldiers to the barracks, where they belong. Leave the government of the State to the men who are strong enough to sustain it. My people tell me to hold on, and so long as they have a right to give me such advice, so help me God, I will hold on![83]

Hampton arrived in Washington on Thursday morning, 29 March, and after settling in at Willard's Hotel, he notified Hayes of his arrival:

> Sir: In compliance with your invitation, I am here for the purpose of uniting my efforts with yours to the end of composing the political differences, which now unhappily distract the people of South Carolina. I beg you to believe that my anxiety to bring about the permanent pacification of that State, a pacification in which the rights of all shall be safe and the interests of all shall be protected, is as sincere as I feel assured is your own for the accomplishment of the same ends. My position for years past in reference to the political rights of colored citizens, and my solemn pledges given during the late canvass in South Carolina, that under my administration all their rights should be absolutely secure, should furnish a sufficient guarantee of my sincerity on these points which appear to be the subject of special anxiety; I have the honor to ask at what hour it will be your pleasure to receive me. Wade Hampton.

The president sent an immediate reply by Colonel Rogers saying he would see him at one o'clock. South Carolina Attorney General Conner and Georgia Senator John B. Gordon accompanied Hampton to the White House, where they were met by the president's son and were escorted by him into the library. They were soon joined by the president. After a short informal meeting the president took his visitors into the cabinet room, where they were introduced to the presidential cabinet. The president led the three men back to the library, where they discussed the situation at length. Mrs. Hayes came into the library and was introduced by her husband, who invited his guests to dinner. Withdrawing into the dining room, the First Lady was escorted by Governor Hampton. After dining they parted company and Hampton went back to his hotel to wait on word from President Hayes.

That afternoon the president met with a delegation from Charleston to be briefed on the financial and political conditions in the state. The businessmen explained that an immediate decision on the South Carolina government was necessary since the planting season had arrived and farmers and planters were not able to obtain credit from merchants due to the instability of the government. They explained that due to the lack of credit the labor system was rapidly disintegrating and due to idleness of laborers the Chamberlain government was constantly making breeches in the peace by inciting riots and other disturbances.[84]

The following day the Charleston businessmen separated into subcommittees and met with various department heads while the cabinet met in a three-hour session and discussed the situation in South Carolina. They did not come to a conclusion on the government to take control of the state, but all were in agreement on recalling federal troops from the state. That evening Hampton sent a message to President Hayes: "Several telegraphic communications have come to me today from Columbia demanding immediate answer, but I can give none until I have a conference with yourself."[85] Hampton penned a lengthy letter the next day hoping to reassure the president that no violence would follow the removal of the troops and that his administration would protect the rights of every citizen in South Carolina.

Hampton was again invited to the White House on Sunday. Hayes gave Hampton the news he was looking for — Washington would no longer support the Chamberlain government and troops would be moved from the state. A jubilant Hampton wired his lieutenant governor: "Everything satisfactorily and honorably settled. I expect our people to preserve absolute peace and quiet. My word is pledged for this. I rely on them." Before leaving Washington Senator Patterson and some contrite South Carolina Republicans called on Hampton to formally concede and offer their support to his administration.[86]

Sometime earlier, the secretary of war reported to the House of Representatives that the entire U.S. Army roster totaled twenty-seven thousand. Of these, more than three thousand were soldiers and officers stationed in the South, with nearly half that number in South Carolina alone. Just over a thousand were in Columbia and an equal number in New Orleans.[87] Before the question of removing troops from the South was satisfactorily answered, congressional Democrats had refused to vote on a military appropriation bill so long as Republicans were guarding Packard and Chamberlain with federal troops.

In a closed meeting McCrary and General Sherman prepared a dispatch to be sent to General Ruger on the following Wednesday with orders to remove the troops from the South Carolina State House. The reason for sending the orders several days later was to allow Hampton time to notify his party leaders and ensure peace would be maintained. As a formality, the War Department issued the following order on 3 April: "To Gen. W.T. Sherman, Commanding the United States Army: GENERAL: I enclose herewith a copy of a communication from the President of the United States, in which he directs that the detachment of troops now stationed in the State House at Columbia, S.C., be withdrawn and returned to their previous barracks or camping ground. You are hereby charged with the execution of this order, and will cause the withdrawal of the troops on Tuesday next, the 10th of April, at 12 o'clock, M. Very respectfully, your obedient servant, Geo. W. McCrary, Secretary of War."

President Hayes would later write of the situation in his journal: "We have got through with the South Carolina and Louisiana [problems]. At any rate, the troops are ordered away, and I now hope for peace, and what is equally important, security and prosperity for the colored people. The result of my plans is to get from those states by their governors, legislatures, press, and people, pledges that the Thirteenth, Fourteenth, and Fifteenth Amendments shall be faithfully observed; that the colored people shall have equal rights to labor, education, and the privileges of citizenship. I am confident this is a good work. Time will tell."[88]

The Democratic leaders of South Carolina were busy making plans

Six. Redeemed!

for Hampton's triumphant return. An invitation was extended to every state citizen to come to Columbia on 6 April to give the governor the welcome he so richly deserved. A train was chartered to meet Hampton in Charlotte and escort him into the state and the capital city.

After a stopover in Charlottesville, Virginia, to see his sister, the governor arrived in Charlotte, North Carolina, at 8:30 P.M. on 5 April and was met by a group of sixty friends from Columbia. Hampton disembarked amid the cheers of thousands and was hustled into an awaiting carriage. The Hornet's Nest Rifles and cadets from the Carolina Military Institute, as well as the city's uniformed fire brigade, escorted the governor to the Central Hotel. A band followed Hampton and his escorts, who were followed by a multitude shouting, "Hampton!" "Hampton!" The next morning the cadets and the rifle club reassembled to lead the governor back to the depot. The entire chartered train had been heavily decorated with banners, streamers and flags with brilliant colors. The smokestack, wheels, driving rods and cowcatcher were nearly hidden by wreathes and ropes of evergreens.

Passing into South Carolina a crowd waited to greet their governor at the Rock Hill depot. Hampton spoke to the people for about twenty minutes amid a bower of greenery and flowers erected for his welcome. At Chester, a triumphal arch was erected over the tracks and the rifle clubs were poised for his arrival. There, Judge Mackey stepped forward to welcome him as the governor alighted onto the platform. The judge was at his best that day and delivered a rousing speech. A small brass cannon blasted away amid the blare of a band and a cheering crowd that did not fall silent until the train pulled away. A detachment of Chester Rifles boarded the train and continued on with the governor. A similar welcome was made at Winnsboro.

At 4:30 P.M. the train pulled into the Columbia depot where hearty cheers and thundering salutes from assembled artillery batteries shattered the air. When the passengers stepped from the train they were immediately enveloped by a mass of humanity that filled the streets and squares surrounding the depot. Amid the pressing crowd Hampton was guided to a flower-covered carriage drawn by four magnificent bays. The Hampton entourage with various civic and military organizations was led by the band of the 18th U.S. Army down Blanding and Main streets to Carolina Hall.

Every house along the way was decorated with wreathes and pictures of Hampton, and a multitude of flags waved from ropes strung across the streets. At Carolina Hall the governor's carriage slowly drew up to the foot of a carpeted platform canopied with a huge United States flag. Hampton, clad in a gray suit, stepped onto the stand, and as soon as he could quiet the crowd he began to speak:

> Mr. Chairman and my countrywomen and countrymen of South Carolina: Travel worn and weary, I have come back amongst you to make my report to my constituents. These constituents are the true people of South Carolina; and coming here, to my surprise, I find a welcome which has stirred my heart to its inmost depths. It is not the welcome that a conquered people would give to a conqueror. I bring no blood stained ensign. I bring no trophies from the battlefields; but I come to say that the cause in which we fought, the cause in which you made me your standard-bearer, the cause of truth, has been victorious, and once more the banner of South Carolina, not carried through bloody fields, but through those more glorious ones of peace, floats over a State, free, disenthralled, regenerated and redeemed. And how has it been redeemed? My friends, not by blood, not by violence, but by the potential agency of the ballot. It has been redeemed because the honest men of South Carolina of all races and of all parties determined to wipe away the scandal which had hung so long over her history....
>
> You fought a battle that has never been equaled on the American Continent. I scarcely realized in those days of peril and gloom, the grave issues which were hanging on this contest. I did not realize them until I went to Washington. I tell you that a musket shot in this town would have meant civil war on this continent; and what stopped it? ... [I]t was because the people of South Carolina were the most law-abiding people in this country, and because they had risen above consideration of party, and had determined to save their State....
>
> I wish to say to you, forget for the next four years, everything about politics. Forget that you are Democrats or Republican; and remember only that you are South Carolinians. Go to building up the material interests of the State, invite immigration, show the people of the North that we have no proscription in our hearts; that we will welcome him here who comes as a citizen, no matter what his politics may be; that we are striving for the redemption of our State, not for petty office of government; and then you will see the era of peace, and a new prosperity will dawn upon South Carolina. Labor will be employed, you will see whites and honest colored men improving, happy, prosperous and united, if you will only forget politics for awhile and devote yourselves to the great interests of the state....
>
> Now, my friends, how can we bring about this consummation so devoutly to be wished? How can we bring happiness, peace and prosperity to our people? We can do it but in one way, and that is that you must observe the law. I enjoin it upon you. I do not issue a proclamation. I do not give an order. But I ask my friends of South Carolina, the people whom I have trusted and who have trusted me and won me more honor than any other man, the people whom I love better than anything in this life, I ask them to carry out my wishes. I want

every man to constitute himself a conservator of the peace, to see that there shall be no violence; to go around and tell your neighbors that, if there is bloodshed or violence, we shall lose what we have gained; to appeal to them in the name of South Carolina to carry out this policy of peace.

The only difficulty that seemed to stand in the way at Washington was the fear that, when the troops were taken out of the way at the State House, there would be violence. They asked me about it; and I pledged my honor; mark me, my friends! I pledged my honor that not one single man would go into the State House unless he had some business there; that I would place two unarmed men there simply to inform the citizens that I requested them not to go there, and I felt assured there would be no violence or excitement and that the laws would be obeyed. Have I asked too much? You have never deceived me; I know you will carry out this promise. I beg, I beseech you! You have trusted me, trust me a little longer. It is important for you. It is doubly important for Louisiana, and for the whole country, that you do what I have asked you.

I requested of the President that the troops should not be removed until I got here. When that order comes, let nobody go to that State House. Just let it stand until I want it, and I will tell you when I want it....

You can, by imprudence or violence, undo the labor of months, and bring back to us all the scenes of anarchy, corruption and misrule which have prevailed; or if you are prudent and discreet, as you have been, you can soon place yourselves upon a higher and better plane, and will see peace, honor and prosperity opening on your State. You will see both races and both parties willing for a while to forget the bitterness of the past strife, and ready to clasp hands, and move on, and lift up our old state. You will see capital brought here. Immigration will flow in, and you will find your old state once more exercising that controlling influence for good, in the nation politics, which she has long enjoyed and honorably employed. I beg you to be true to that record in the past, to try every means in your power to cultivate good will between both races and parties. I beg you, white men, to show to the colored men that what I have said for twelve years is true: that you are the best friends they have in this world. I appeal to the colored men to recognize the government which is now firmly established, to trust us for a while, and as they are still in the majority, if the government I have established does not carry out the pledges I have made, then throw out all the men in office at the next election, and put in anybody you please.[89]

Amid the celebration, Chamberlain was forgotten. Even as the state was raising its voice in celebration, Chamberlain was choking on the news, and in spite of what was happening around him he maintained he was still the true legal governor. Twenty minutes before noon on 10 April two members of the press were admitted into the State House under the glares of special constables who watched their every move. Inside were about one hundred and fifty men, mostly black, who were milling about, and a detachment of twenty soldiers of the Second Regiment, under the command of a Lieutenant Haynes. The men were dressed in full accouterments and stood at rest in two ranks. Prepared for evacuation, rifles were stacked behind the door of the comptroller general's office, which had been used as the officer's quarters since the siege. One solitary soldier paced back and forth in front of the executive office while Colonel Black and Adjutant Potter stood by patiently. General Ruger's aide had already arrived with the evacuation order, but Black was determined to comply with the precise instructions.[90]

At five minutes before noon, Hampton's representative, Wade W. Manning,[91] approached the door of the executive office and was met by C.J. Babbitt. Manning requested the surrender of the office in the name of Governor Hampton, but Babbitt replied that he had been instructed by Governor Chamberlain to surrender the office precisely at twelve o'clock and he would do so not one minute before.[92]

Whether Manning knew it or not, Chamberlain had left the State House an hour earlier. When the Republican returned from Washington he was determined not to surrender the office, and only in the last 24 hours had he decided to go peacefully. Earlier that morning he spoke to his supporters:

> By the recent decision and action of the President of the United States, I find myself unable longer to maintain my official rights with the prospect of final success, and I hereby announce to you that I am unwilling to prolong a struggle which can only bring further suffering upon those who engage in it....
>
> While the long struggle for the Presidency was in progress, you were exhorted by every representative and organ of the National Republican Party to keep our allegiance true to that party in order that your deliverance from the hands of your oppressors might be certain and complete. Not the faintest whisper of the possibility of disappointment in these hopes and promises ever reached you while the struggle was pending. Today, April 10, 1877, by order of the President whom your votes alone rescued from overwhelming defeat, the government of the United States abandons you; deliberately withdraws from you its support, with the full knowledge that the lawful government of the state will be speedily overthrown.
>
> By a new interpretation of the Constitution of the United States, at variance alike with the previous practice of the government and the decision of the Supreme Court, the Executive of the United States evades the duty of ascertaining which of two rival state governments is the lawful one, and by the withdrawal of troops now protecting the state from domestic violence, abandons the lawful state government to a struggle with insurrectionary forces too powerful to be resisted. The grounds of policy upon which such action is defended are startling....

It is said that if a majority of the people of a state are unable by physical force to maintain their rights, they must be left to political servitude. Is this a doctrine ever before heard in our history? If it shall prevail, its consequences will not long be confined to South Carolina or Louisiana.

It is said that a Democratic House of Representatives will refuse an appropriation for the army of the United States if the lawful government of South Carolina is maintained by the military forces. Submission to such coercion marks the degeneracy of the political party or people which endures it. A government worthy of the name, a political party fit to weld powers, never before blanched at such a threat....

My strict legal rights are of course wholly unaffected by the action of the President. No court of the state has jurisdiction to pass upon the title to my office. No lawful legislature can be convened except upon my call. If the use of these powers promised ultimate success to our cause, I should not shrink from any sacrifices which might confront me. It is a cause in which, by the light of reason and conscience, a man might well lay down his life. But, to my mind, my present responsibility involves the consideration of the effect of my action upon those whose representative I am. I have hitherto been willing to ask you, Republicans of South Carolina, to risk all dangers and endure all hardships until relief should come from the government of the United States. That relief will never come. I cannot ask you to follow me further. In my best judgment, I can no longer serve you by further resistance to the impending calamity.[93]

After finishing his speech, he bade his chief officers farewell and entered a waiting carriage with J.G. Thompson and was driven to his home. At that hour the streets were filled with people who had turned out to see the circus parade and only a few noticed the carriage as it made its way down Main Street. Other Republican officers decided to remain in their offices, until a decision by the Supreme Court would come. Democrats who had been elected to these offices moved into the State House and occupied vacant rooms until the Republicans cleared out.

Hampton assumed the office of the governor at noon on 11 April 1877 and by the first of May the Hampton administration was in full possession of the South Carolina government.[94] On that day, South Carolina was redeemed from Radical Republican Rule and Reconstruction. The state and its people owed their deliverance to Wade Hampton and his Red Shirts. Redemption was full. True Reconstruction could get under way and the New South was about to emerge. The *New York Sun* carried a poignant line in an editorial: "Chamberlain's piratical ship goes down defiantly with the bloody shirt nailed to its mast."[95]

Epilogue

The National Republican Party abandoned the South to the Democrats with little regret and satisfied themselves with having regained control of the Old Northwest (Ohio, Indiana, Illinois, Michigan, Wisconsin, Minnesota, and Iowa). The Republican Party now had little need or care for the Southern black man. The Northern antebellum idealism that had seemed so important for two decades had gone out of fashion and Federal Reconstruction came to an end.

As soon as the Democrats gained hold of the government reins in 1877, they set about cleaning house, the Democrats wanting to publicly expose the corruption that had gone on under the Republicans for the past eight years. The general assembly authorized a joint committee to search records for proof of what the Democrats had been accusing the Republicans of for years. The committee's report began with a fraud in 1869. That year the general assembly authorized Governor Scott to use treasury funds to arm the militias he raised all over the state.[1] The report revealed a second major fraud enacted on 28 July 1871 when Governor Scott used a proclamation offering $200 for each person arrested and convicted under the Enforcement Act. Over $30,000 was paid out through this proclamation.[2] Historian John A. Leland wrote that Colonel Lewis Merrill was instrumental in getting an appropriation of $35,000 from the 1871–1872 legislature. Of this sum, Merrill received the lion's share—$21,800 for one hundred and nine convictions.[3]

The report of eight years of corruption incensed many South Carolinians, who expected and demanded that those Republicans who had participated in criminal activities be brought to trial and convicted.[4] Hampton knew, however, that if these men were arrested and brought to trial, it would do little more than revive old animosities and the Republican press would demand retaliation. In a speech at Anderson, Hampton proposed, "If we give general amnesty, we shall have amnesty for our own people."[5]

When Hampton took office, the state was in a precarious position in regard to justice. Three men from South Carolina still remained in prison for Ku Klux Klan charges and many others were separated from their families in a self-imposed exile, fearing arrest if they returned.[6] Another eight hundred men were under federal indictment placed by U.S. Attorney General Corbin during the 1876 campaign.

Negotiations to work through this morass began with a telegram to President Hayes from Hampton in May 1877. Hampton strived for amnesty for those charged with Ku Kluxing and for those who were in the Hamburg and Ellenton riots. Hayes expressed his hesitation in a letter to Hampton, saying he was concerned that amnesty might be extended to more serious crimes. Governor Hampton replied with a lengthy letter detailing how he had worked to minimize prosecution of Radical Republicans in the state and had sponsored a resolution in the general assembly giving him the power of nol-pros in any political case. "My position has been a very difficult one," wrote Hampton, "for besides the opposition to me from political opponents, I have had to meet and control that of the extreme men of my own party."[7]

By mid summer Hampton and Hayes came to an agreement, with Hampton getting the presidential amnesty he wanted. Not bringing the Radicals to prosecution was a bitter pill to swallow for South Carolinians; yet, it was the best course for the state and the nation. With amnesty secured for both Democrats and Republicans, Reconstruction came to a peaceful end. During the fall of 1877, Hayes made a tour of the South, becoming the first president to make a gesture of reconciliation since the war. Hampton accompanied the president on his tour and introduced him to Kentuckians as a "noble and patriotic man" and said of him, "He serves his party best who serves his country best."[8]

When Hampton was elected for a second term in 1878, it was with the majority of both black and white voters. Out of 169,763 votes cast, the incumbent received 169,550. He was so popular that the Republicans came close to endorsing him for reelection, and while they failed to do so, they did not nominate anyone to oppose him.[9] Yet all was not well during his administration. He had continuous quarrels with white supremacists, most particularly the leader of that faction — General Martin Gary. With men like Gary forever in the background stirring the racial pot and diligently watching for a time to express their most hateful element, the advances Hampton had made in racial harmony and civil rights came under attack as soon as he left Columbia to take a Senate seat in Washington.

Hampton's departure from Columbia for the United States Senate left the state open to the advocates of white supremacy. His suffrage plan for African Americans was disassembled to comply with extremist views advanced by Martin Gary. It took years to completely dismantle Hampton's midstream policies, but the African American voter began to feel the crippling results almost immediately. Just four years after Hampton's departure for Washington the general assembly in 1882 enacted a rigid registration law and instituted the "Eight Box" voting system to defraud black voters. The system effectually served as a literacy test. Voting required separate ballots for each candidate, with each being placed in the appropriate box. To confuse the illiterate the law provided for the shuffling of the ballot boxes at the discretion of the poll manager.[10] Eventually black voters became frustrated and discouraged, and after a few elections, deserted the polls.[11] Since ten to fifteen thousand continued to vote in South Carolina through the turn of the twentieth century, the "eight box" law had not defrauded all black men.[12] Generally speaking, the North's rabid abolitionists and fire-eating Republicans eventually forgot the black man. In due time the Civil Rights Act of 1875 was repealed and through a series of other repeals the black population lost federal guarantees. Though the Fourteenth and Fifteenth amendments remained on the books, African Americans were without equal rights. This was happening not only in South Carolina but throughout the South. For nearly one hundred years, the black population in both the North and the South remained only half emancipated.

Sitting in the White House on the evening of 12 November 1878, President Hayes wrote in his journal about the Southern states' successful attempts to disenfranchise the black voter: "In South Carolina and Louisiana, and perhaps in some of the other cotton states, grave charges are made that the constitutional provisions which guarantee equal citizenship have been practically nullified; that by fraud, or force or intimidation, colored citizens have been disfranchised."[13] Black congressman Joseph H.

Rainey of Georgetown had earlier warned the president that whites in Sumter and other counties were resorting to intimidation and violence to prevent blacks from organizing for the election. Hayes noted: "The division there is still on the Color line. Substantially all the whites are Democrats and all the colored people are Republicans. There is no political principle in dispute between them. The whites have the intelligence, the property, and the courage, which make power. The Negroes are for the most part ignorant, poor, and timid. My view is that the whites must be divided there before a better state of things will prevail."[14] Of course, this did not happen.

Aristocrats in South Carolina had enjoyed social and political prominence for three or more generations. Most of them were graduates of the South Carolina College or the Citadel and had distinguished themselves as Confederate soldiers. Many of the Bourbons, like Hampton, were successful in blending the old with the new and laying the foundation for the New South. Although the years following Reconstruction allowed Hampton and other Bourbons to restore their old style of government, it was not to last, eventually giving way to a more equal society.

Indeed, the aristocrats may be accused of laboring to regain what they had before the war, but most of the state's residents believed the state would run best with whites at the wheel. At the same time, they were able to forge a viable state out of the rubble of war and supplied a long-lived romantic imagery of the times. That imagery remained unquestioned through the 1950s. Until then South Carolina and its Confederate sisters were termed the "Solid South"—white Southerners had built the Democratic Party into such a holy institute that only the bravest would question it or suggest another ideology.

The Red Shirts who paraded across South Carolina brought a definitive end to the state's Reconstruction regime and effected an agrarian revolution. Each in its own time—the Conservative Clubs, the Klansmen and the Red Shirts—succeeded in their fight for supremacy. For all its efforts, Reconstruction did not destroy the South's socioeconomic structure. The slavery plan was merely replaced by the sharecropper system, which was as effective as slavery but less costly to the landowner. Most of the upper, ruling classes survived the era intact, while poor whites and blacks remained in landless dependence upon large landowners.

A clash of Civil War titans occurred in 1880 as South Carolina was unraveling civil rights for African Americans. Senator Sherman before the national Republican conference in New York, cajoled the committee: "And now you are asked to surrender all you have done into the hands of Wade Hampton and the Ku Klux, and the little segment in the North that is called the Democratic party." In a letter to Sherman dated 17 September, Hampton requested an "early reply" as to whether Sherman meant to connect him "directly or indirectly to what is known as the Ku Klux Klan." Sherman did not flinch from Hampton's demand and sent to Hampton's Washington address a barn-burner:

> I no doubt spoke of you as a leading representative of the Democratic Party in the South, and referred to the Ku Klux Klan as representatives of the barbarous agencies by which the Democrats have subverted the civil and political right of the Republicans of the South.
>
> I did not connect you personally with the Ku Klux Klan. Indeed I know that you had, in one or two instances, resisted and defeated its worst impulses. I appreciated the sense of honor, which makes you shrink from being named in connection with it. Still you and your associates, leading men of the South, now enjoy the benefits of political power derived from the atrocities of the Ku Klux Klan, in which phrase is included all the numerous aliases by which it has from time to time been known in the South.
>
> Your power in the Southern states rests upon the actual crimes of every grade in the code of crimes, from murder to the meanest form of ballot-box stuffing, committed by the Ku Klux Klan, and its kindred associates, and, as you know, some of the worst of them committed since 1877, when you and they gave the most solemn assurances of protection to the freedmen of the South. These crimes are all aimed at the civil and political rights of the Republicans in the South, and as I believe, but for these agencies the very State that you represent, as well as many other States in the south, would be represented both in the senate and House by Republicans. But for these crimes, the boast attributed to you that the 144 solid Southern votes would be cast for the democratic ticket, would be but idle vaporing; but now we feel that is sober truth.
>
> While I have no reason to believe that you or your Northern associates personally participated in the offenses I have named, yet while you and they enjoy the fruits of these crimes, you are joint co-partners with the Ku Klux Klan in a policy which so far has been successful in the South, and which it is hoped, by the aid of a small segment of the Democratic party in the North, may be extended to all departments of the government. It is in this sense that I spoke of you, the Ku Klux Klan and the Northern Democratic party.

Hampton's October response to Sherman was little more than an acknowledgment mailed from Charlottesville, Virginia, on his return to Columbia. Upon his return Hampton made a speech that was published by the *News and Courier*; in this speech Hampton evidently disclosed the contents of Sherman's letter and denied its claims. In a response, Sherman wrote Hampton on the 18th:

> [T]his morning [I] read what purported to be an extract of a speech made by you and published in the *News and Courier*, and upon your general reputation had denied that you made such a speech or written such a letter as is attributed to you in that paper. What I stated to you in my letter of the 21st of September, I believe to be true, notwithstanding your denial, and it can be shown to be true by public records and as a matter of history. As you had, long before your letter was delivered to me, seen proper to make public a statement of your views of the correspondence, I will give it to the press without note or comment, and let the public decide between us.

Hampton had more to say in his defense to the Reverend Dr. Howe of South Carolina, who had written to Hampton regarding the published letters,

> Mr. Sherman forgot the propriety of his official position as well as of mine, when he made a scandalous charge against me in a public speech.
> I called his attention to the language he was reported to have used, in a courteous letter, thus giving him the opportunity to disclaim or explain his utterance. In reply, he not only reiterated his charge, but he took that opportunity to vilify not only the people whom I represented, but also those of the whole South. I could not condescend to notice his slanderous attack upon the South, and I simply denounced his charge connecting me with the Ku Klux Klan as false. I could do not less than this, for there never was a falser charge made, nor have I ever known a grosser violation of personal courtesy or of official propriety than that of which he was guilty.
> It has been my good fortune never to have been involved in an "affair of honor" in any way, save as a peace-maker, and it is a source of deep gratification to me to know that I have been instrumental in settling many difficulties amicably.

In the spring of 1899, when Hampton was eighty-two years old, his home on Camden Road was destroyed by fire. Friends of the Carolina Redeemer raised the funds to build him a handsome home at 1800 Senate Street in Columbia. Though he made protest over their generosity, he eventually accepted the house and resided there until his death. Exactly twenty-five years from the day he redeemed South Carolina from Radical rule, Wade Hampton III died, at 8:50 A.M. on Friday, 11 April 1902. Following his last words, "Tell my people, black and white — God bless them all," he was laid to rest in the Trinity Episcopal cemetery in Columbia. He had requested a simple funeral, with as little pomp and circumstance as possible. His body did not lie in state at the capitol as one would expect, but thousands viewed his body at his home and 20,000 followed the casket to the cemetery. Among the mourners that attended his funeral were a large number of blacks who paid homage to their former master and crusader of civil rights. South Carolina mourned like it had not done in fifty years, when John C. Calhoun died. Hampton's passage was quiet and simple for such a highly praised man who was owed so much by his beloved state. To ensure Hampton's work as liberator was remembered, before his body was cold plans began to jell for a state monument, and fund-raising began immediately.

The Wade Hampton bronze monument was erected in 1906 on the State House grounds. The statue says a lot. Astride a muscular horse sat a relaxed, powerful man, chest thrust out and head erect, with full control over his powerful mount, symbolizing how he had restrained his Red Shirt followers after the election of 1876.

In the end we might ask what South Carolinians had learned from Reconstruction and the eventual overthrow of Republican rule. A simple answer cannot be made, unless we reply, "Probably nothing at all!" Mostly it depended on who you were. For years afterward, white conservatives called themselves "Redeemers"; and in their minds that meant they did not want to lose their redemption by the return of Republican rule — it was still an "us or them" situation. Political speeches well into the twentieth century used fear of the return of liberals to strengthen the resolve of whites to prevent any real change in politics. Most whites viewed Reconstruction as proof that African Americans were not ready for civil liberties, much less a seat in government.

Southern blacks came though Reconstruction with hardly a flicker of hope. During the summer and fall of Hampton's campaign they might have seen some hope for reconciliation, but they soon felt the hangman's noose slipping over their civil rights. In 1940, Samuel D. Mobley of Chester County wrongly believed the noose over civil rights would continue for years to come: "The final chapter was written in that history [of the Red Shirt movement] when the last democratic convention of 1938 debarred the Negro from the rolls of the party. I feel like and believe that this provision will be in force for the next one hundred years."[15]

As soon as the Republicans lost the reins of the government, they quickly faced the truth of the situation: white Democrats had far more to offer — land that needed workers and political power. By aligning themselves with the politics of former masters and their children, they gained respect and lived in peace; but cast a ballot for a Republican and you would be labeled as a no-account — undeserving of respect, charity or good will and sometimes a job. Redemption, full redemption, would come later. Later a savior would come out of their own midst.

It might be argued that if the reform movement within the Republican Party had combined with the efforts of the 1875 Fusionists there might have been a complete change of course given a chance; but the July 1876 Hamburg Riot dashed those hopes forever. Too, it may be argued that had the conservatives continued the moderate course set by Hampton the state might have realized political progress and peace 90 years sooner. Hampton had set the stage for a Third Reconstruction, if you will, but it worked out no better that the two previous attempts. Assuming Hampton was put in the governor's office by the black vote (17,000, he said), that would have been a perfect time to mend and strengthen race relations rather than perpetuate "us or them" policies which eventually disenfranchised the black voter.

APPENDIX 1

The Making of South Carolina

Melodrama was a favorite form of entertainment in South Carolina from the mid–1800s to well into the twentieth century. Reconstruction and, especially, the Red Shirt Campaign were favorite subjects, not only in the South, but nationwide through motion pictures and other media. The main theme of melodramas dealing with Reconstruction centered on how the white man persevered during the evil black rule. These stage and movie dramas preached to the masses, showing the necessity of unity among whites in support of white supremacy. The theme often contained a story of a good, average man who was pushed to violence.

The Making of South Carolina, a historical pageant performed by the then all female student body of Winthrop College, was presented in Rock Hill on 6 May 1921.[1] The scene in Episode IX, entitled "The Red Shirts," begins when forty Red Shirt riders confront a small detail of United States Cavalry:

> The horseman in front carries a staff with a crosspiece near the top. On this is stretched an enormous yellow homespun shirt covered with red splotches. At the top of the shirt is fastened on each side of the staff a grinning Negro mask with kinky hair. Satan's appeal to the fallen angels: "Awake, arise, or be forever fallen," is emblazoned in large black letters on one side, and on the other: "None but the guilty need fear." The riders wear coarse gray trousers, high boots, black slouch hats, and shirts originally yellow but now stained as if with bloody bullet holes.

Henry Beaufort, leader of the cavalry, assured the Red Shirts they meant them no harm: "Men, we are here as soldiers to keep order and to prevent riots, but there are no riots when white men protect their property and their lives. We are men before we are soldiers. I fought for my convictions

176 Appendix 1

Top: The all-girl cast, a "symbolic group," of Winthrop Training School (now Winthrop University) in the performance of *The Making of South Carolina*. *Above:* Winthrop girls portraying mounted Red Shirts in the final scene of *The Making of South Carolina* (both courtesy of the Museum of Western York County, Sharon).

as a gentleman against gentlemen, but I will not strike a brave foe when he is down."

The troops ride away as the orchestra begins a medley of Southern music. But Beaufort removes his blue uniform coat revealing a yellow homespun shirt. The Red Shirt leader meets with the Union soldier and offers him turpentine, oil and Venetia red in which he quickly stains his shirt. Someone tosses him a slouch hat; he swings his horse into the company of Red Shirts and they ride into the distance.

APPENDIX 2

Asbury Coward

Among the 1854 graduating class of the Citadel were two Low Country young men who would leave an indelible mark on the up-country of South Carolina. Asbury Coward was born in 1835 on a Charleston rice plantation; his classmate and close friend, Micah Jenkins, was born the same year on Edisto Island. These two nineteen year olds shared a mutual dream: to found a military academy as a preparatory school for young boys.

Following his graduation Coward came to the small up-country town of Yorkville to study law under William Blackburn Wilson, a leading lawyer. Soon Coward realized that the confines of a law office did not agree with his more athletic nature. He began to view Yorkville as a prime location to fulfill his dream of a military academy and convinced Jenkins to join him in the venture. Since neither of these men were of legal age it became necessary for appointed guardians to make legal contracts. Attorney Wilson and physician James M. Lowry, both of Yorkville, stepped up to support the young advocates of education.

The Kings Mountain Military Academy was founded in January 1855 behind the doors of an old mansion, with a dozen students ranging from age 11 to age 16. Within five months the academy's reputation had grown so favorably that enrollment increased to 28 students; and by the end of the session it had swelled to 47. The fall session opened with 60 male students. The five-year curriculum included mathematics, Latin, French, German, grammar, English literature, history, chemistry, astronomy, geology, physiology and philosophy.

The rented mansion soon became too small for the growing enrollment and Coward hired a Columbia architect to design and supervise the construction of a new building. The contract was awarded to Richard

Hare, a 43-year-old stonemason from Ireland and a resident of Yorkville. As war drums began throbbing throughout the South, the Kings Mountain Military Academy was being conducted in the new, handsome building with nearly 140 students.

When South Carolina seceded from the Union the academy closed its doors while the two founders answered the call to duty. Micah Jenkins raised a volunteer company, the Jasper Light Infantry, mostly comprising the academy's graduates and the graduating class. This company, the first unit raised in Yorkville, formed the nucleus of the Fifth South Carolina Regiment. Under command of Colonel Jenkins the Jasper Guards, as the unit was also known, was sent to Sullivan's Island to occupy abandoned Fort Moultrie. Jenkins was killed in battle.

Asbury Coward entered the Confederate army as captain and attached to the adjutant general. He was soon assigned to the battlefield and commissioned major after the Battle of Malvern Hill in Virginia. In August 1861 he was commis-

Asbury Coward. Born on a Charleston rice plantation, Coward graduated from South Carolina's Citadel in 1854. At the age of nineteen he and his friend, Micah Jenkins, established the Kings Mountain Military Academy in Yorkville. During the Civil War he commanded the Fifth Regiment of South Carolina volunteers known as the Palmetto Sharpshooters. General Robert E. Lee said he was the best colonel in the Confederate armies. Coward fathered seventeen children and outlived all of them but one (courtesy of the Museum of Western York County, Sharon).

sioned colonel in the Fifth Regiment and assumed command of that unit in November 1862. Coward took part in several skirmishes and also saw action in some of the larger battles at Chickamauga, Lookout Mountain and Chattanooga and Knoxville. He was wounded at the battle near Chaffin's Farm, Virginia, and was with General Lee at the surrender at Appomattox.

After the war, Coward and his growing family returned to Yorkville. He had married Elsie Larimore Blum of Charleston, whose ancestors arrived in South Carolina in 1721. They were married on Christmas Day in Yorkville in 1856, eventually had 17 children and outlived all of them except for one.

The doors of the Kings Mountain Academy reopened during January 1866 with Coward alone at the helm and it remained so for twenty years. His friend, Micah Jenkins, had been killed by friendly fire. Coward's faithful bodyguard, Charles Bessear, returned to Yorkville and became cook for the academy. In 1882, the soldier-teacher became South Carolina's state superintendent of education and remained in that position for four years. The same year he stepped down from that position, he reluctantly but permanently closed the doors of the academy. In 1890 he returned to his alma mater, the Citadel, as its superintendent. He led the school into a bright future for 18 years, retiring in 1908. He was awarded a Carnegie pension that provided him with a comfortable retirement. He and his wife moved to Tennessee to live with one of their children but

Col. Micah Jenkins. When war broke out between the North and South, Jenkins and his partner, Asbury Coward, closed the doors of the Kings Mountain Military Academy in Yorkville. Sadly, at the Battle of the Wilderness Jenkins was killed by friendly fire (courtesy Culture & Heritage Museums).

Kings Mountain Military Academy. Established in an old mansion in 1855 near the town of Yorkville by Asbury Coward in partnership with his Citadel classmate and close friend Micah Jenkins, the school closed at the beginning of the Civil War and reopened in January 1866. Asbury was elected state superintendent of education in 1882, which caused the closing of the academy four years later. There were several unsuccessful attempts to reopen the school. Around 1900, Colonel W.G. Stephenson gave it a new start as the Kings Mountain Military Academy. This view of the campus' main building comes from a 1908 postcard. The school was permanently closed the following year (courtesy of Culture & Heritage Museums).

returned to Yorkville when he was 89 and Elsie was 87. The ends of their lives were brightened by their renewed friendship with the town's elite: the Brattons, Witherspoons, Wrights, Bells, Harts, Grists and a host of others. Asbury Coward died in 1925 and was buried in Rose Hill Cemetery.

APPENDIX 3

Lewis Mason Grist

The man who would become best known as the editor of the *Yorkville Enquirer* was born Lewis Mason Grist in 1831 in Spartanburg County, one of 8 children of John E. Grist and Elizabeth Lawrence Grist. His father was induced to come to Yorkville in 1833 by a Mr. Beatty and a Mr. Williams, who cited the town's need for a printer. On 15 June 1835 John Grist began editing and publishing the *Journal of the Times,* but this paper ceased to exist after two years. Grist continued his printing business and in 1840 introduced upper South Carolina to a new newspaper — the *Yorkville Compiler.* This paper did no better than its predecessor. Grist undoubtedly had ink in his blood, since in 1843 he began his third attempt at publishing a newspaper, the *Farmer's Miscellany.* As it was more successful than the others, Grist continued to publish this paper until 1851 when he sold it to his son, Lewis. The younger Grist continued printing the *Miscellany* until 1855, when, on 4 January, it was issued under a new name — the *Yorkville Enquirer.*

The *Enquirer* was the only newspaper in York County and by the beginning of the Civil War it had subscribers in nearly every county in the state, as well many readers in North Carolina. It was widely spoken of as the largest newspaper outside Charleston. Within months of South Carolina's secession, Lewis turned the paper's management over to his father and answered his state's call to duty. With the division in the Union fracturing along political party ideology, the *Enquirer* naturally became a proponent of the Democratic Party. The paper continued throughout the war, until the shortage of paper forced it to close in May 1865.

With Lewis Grist again at the helm, the paper resumed in August 1865 and steadily grew in subscribers. Throughout the Reconstruction Era the *Enquirer* boldly revealed its repugnance for the ideology of the Republican Party and rejoiced at the party's collapse following Wade Hampton's election to the governor's office.

In 1876 a competitive newspaper appeared in the county that eventually would become the *Rock Hill Herald*, the *Evening Herald* and finally, the *Herald*. This paper was the main choice of those living in Rock Hill and the eastern region of the county. Eventually the paper gained a large readership in western York County and many homes subscribed to both papers. Yet, there is no doubt that the *Yorkville Enquirer* remained dear to the hearts of the western towns and communities. In 1890 the whole operation of the *Yorkville Enquirer* was valued at about $10,000. That year the paper suffered a devastating fire in which many of its back issues were destroyed.

After the McClatchy corporation bought out the *Herald* and the *Yorkville Enquirer* (as well as every other paper in the county), Western York County readers saw a drastic change in the *Yorkville Enquirer* and, as some said, "It was not worth the wrapping of a fish." In 2007 the publishers, indifferent to the wishes of its readers, saw fit to change the *Yorkville Enquirer*'s name to the *Enquirer-Herald*. With one uncaring stroke of the pen a 150-year-old newspaper — the oldest in the state — was virtually brought to an end. By the end of the year the *Enquirer*'s office was moved to Rock Hill. One publisher asked, "What else can they do to piss off the people of Western York County?"

APPENDIX 4

General Evander McIver Law

Though General Evander McIver Law makes only two appearances in this work, he was a well-known figure in Yorkville. Law was born in 1836 in Darlington, South Carolina, where his grandfather and two great-grandfathers participated in the Revolutionary War under General Francis Marion. In January 1853 Evander Law was admitted into the South Carolina Military Academy (now the Citadel), and graduated in 1856. Two years after graduation he came to Yorkville, where he was employed by Micah Jenkins and Asbury Coward as professor of history at the Kings Mountain Military Academy.

While teaching at the academy, he met and married Jane Elizabeth Latta, the daughter of William Latta, a wealthy planter and railroad investor. Law remained in Yorkville until 1860, then moved to Alabama to establish a military high school in Tuskegee, with Robert Parks. When that state seceded from the Union, Law joined the Alabama militia as a captain. In April 1861 he was transferred to the army of the Confederate States of America as captain of the Fourth Alabama Infantry, the "Alabama Zouaves," a unit he had helped recruit from his former students.

His ascent of the chain of command was remarkable. Within a month he was promoted to the rank of lieutenant colonel and colonel in October 1861 at the first Battle of Bull Run. He participated in nearly all the major battles in Virginia and proved himself to be one of General Lee's more valuable officers. When Matthew Butler was wounded at the Battle of Bentonville, Law led the division until Butler returned to active duty. General Law received an arm wound at the first Battle of Manassas, 21 July 1861, and suffered a fractured skull and injured left eye at Cold Harbor in January

1864. While at the Siege of Petersburg he was transferred to Wade Hampton's Calvary, stationed in South Carolina. As Sherman bore down on Columbia, he was one of the commanders responsible for the evacuation of the city.

Following the war, Law resumed his duties at the Kings Mountain Military Academy until it closed in 1882, at which time he went to Alabama and became something of a jack-of-all-trades — teacher, writer, agriculturalist and journalist. He moved to Florida in 1893 and took a position as professor at Southern Florida Military Institute, which he held until 1903. In 1905 he tried his hand at being an editor of the *Bartow Courier Informant* until 1915 when he died. From 1912 to his death he served on the Bartow Board of Education. He was the last surviving Confederate major general.

Appendix 5

Isaac Donnom Witherspoon, Jr.

Isaac Donnom Witherspoon, Jr., the son of Isaac Donnom Witherspoon, Sr., and Ann T. Reid, was born 8 February 1833 in Yorkville, South Carolina, and died there on 24 March 1901. He was described as a large, tall man with dark hair and dark eyes. Donnom was loved and respected by nearly everyone, black and white. His character must have been superb, since he was said to have been intelligent, cultured, honest, courteous, noble, modest, sympathetic, kind, generous, pious and true. He graduated from South Carolina College (now the University of South Carolina) in 1854. He married a cousin, Jeannette Amelia Reese of West Point, Georgia, a daughter of George R. and Mary Witherspoon Reese. The following year he was admitted to the bar in Columbia and began practicing law with his father. The future was bright for the young couple, but Jeannette died in childbirth in August 1856. It may have been that Donnom wanted to get away from the scene of his personal tragedy, but for whatever reason, he moved to Montgomery, Alabama.

Again death interrupted his life. Two years after leaving Yorkville Isaac Witherspoon, Sr., died and Donnom returned to his home to act as administrator of his father's estate and establish a partnership with Colonel W.B. Wilson, who had been his father's associate. Two years later Donnom married Margaret Elizabeth Wright (born 1838), the daughter of James Leslie Wright and Martha J. Spratt Wright of Yorkville. "Mag," as she was called, had lost her mother when she was five and subsequently went to live with her uncle, Colonel William Wright, a wealthy merchant and president of the Kings Mountain Railroad.

Wright was a savvy investor in local concerns and businesses at large, as well as a heavy investor in railroads and banks. Among his investments in banks were the Bank of Newberry, the North Carolina State Bank, the Bank of Chester, the People's Bank of Charleston, the Southwestern Railroad Bank in Louisville, and banks in Camden and Hamburg. By January 1850, Wright had earned more than $28,000 in dividends alone.

Mag Wright was a graduate of Limestone College and was described as a woman of magnificent character — staunch, true and loyal. When Mag and Donnom were married in 1860, her guardian built a large house next to his and gave it to them as a wedding gift. The still-standing five bedroom, two-story house had a wrap-around porch, fifteen-foot ceilings and inlaid parquet floors. The home was decorated in the decorum of the day and furnished with stylish Empire furniture. Witherspoon's personal bed was constructed of Honduran mahogany and had four large octagon-shaped posts rising eight feet and supporting a frame for decorative netting. (The bed and matching bureau are now housed in the Museum of Western York County in Sharon, South Carolina.) In the parlor was a large, square piano with massive rosewood legs, as well as mahogany and marble-top tables, and chairs with needlepoint cushions. The fireplace mantel supported a long, gilt mirror and was flanked by a painted fire screen.

I. Donnom Witherspoon. An attorney from Yorkville and a Confederate veteran, Witherspoon was appointed judge of the Sixth District, which included Chester, Fairfield, Lancaster and York counties (courtesy of the Museum of Western York County, Sharon).

The main sitting room was dominated by a mahogany horsehair sofa, matching chairs, walnut and mahogany bookcases, marble-top tables and a gilt mirror over the mantel. In the dining room, twenty-four guests could sit at a large, mahogany table that stood on a fully carved pedestal with large claw feet extending outward. This pedestal opened as the table was extended. Accompanying the dining table were a large sideboard and a serving buffet. The Witherspoons' guests might be served using sets of English and French china, as the Witherspoons had a large assortment of serving dishes, fruit bowls, and ice cream and custard dishes.

In August 1861 Donnom enlisted in the Confederate army as a second lieutenant of Company A, Twelfth South Carolina Regiment. At the time of his enlistment Mag was five months pregnant with their first child. His letters show his tender concern for her health, fearing he may lose his second wife as he had his first. Isaac Donnom Witherspoon III was born in December while his father was stationed on the South Carolina coast. Due to some health problems Donnom was transferred to the Treasury Department, commissioned a captain and stationed in Columbia as commissary officer. The Museum of Western York County archives dozens of letters he wrote as commissary officer detailing the rations given to soldiers stationed in Columbia, hospital patients, prisoners and free blacks. These communiqués to his commander in Charleston report the ever-changing inventories of foodstuffs as well as his difficulty in locating and obtaining supplies from the surrounding counties.

After the war Donnom resumed his law practice, and sometimes he had the dubious honor of defending his friends and neighbors charged with "Ku Kluxing." As a Democrat, he supported Wade Hampton's bid for governor in 1876 and opposed Senator Hannibal White, a black Republican from York County. Witherspoon served in the South Carolina senate from 1876 to 1881, serving as president pro tem for several terms. During this period he practiced law in partnership with Charles E. Spencer and continued until 1882, when he was elected to the Sixth Circuit bench to replace retiring Judge Mackey. Donnom Witherspoon wore the judicial robes until his retirement in 1898, at which time he renewed his partnership with Spencer along with C.W.F. Spencer. The partnership continued until Donnom's death in 1901.

Appendix 6

Diary of Dr. James Rufus Bratton

The original papers from which these recollections by James Rufus Bratton, M.D., are taken are in the possession of United States congressman John M. Spratt. Transcription copies are housed in the York County Library at Rock Hill and the History Center in York. Bratton was stationed at the Winder military hospital in Georgia when he began these memoirs on 14 August 1863, and perhaps feeling his death was imminent he addressed them "For my children in future life":

> ...I volunteered my Service as Asst. Surgeon to Colo. Jenkins of the 5th Regiment — S Car Volunteers & was willingly and Cheerfully accepted — This Regiment had three companies from York — Captain Seabrooks — Capt. Jackson & Captain Glenn. It left Yorkville on Saturday 13th April 1861 went to Columbia, quartered in the Columbia Fair Grounds for two days & then went to the Race Course in Charleston where we stayed three days more & then were ordered to Sullivan's Island — Here quartered in the homes of Citizens & the Moultrie house we stayed & performed military duty in drilling &c until the 27th of May. During this time much sickness as Diarrhea and Dysentery existed among the troops & but one death only occurred during our stay there — This was Caleb Mason who was left in my charge on the Island when the Regiment was ordered to Virginia with a weeks furlough at home — I remained with him a few days, when growing better he insisted that he should be taken home but the fatigue on the Cars proved to be to heavy for him & I was forced to stop at Hunts Hotel with him where in two days he died — I then went on home stayed a week with your Mother & the three boys & started for Columbia again to be mustered into Same by Colo. Bee afterwards Genl. Bee & killed at the first Manassas battle Being taken sick with Dysentery I returned home and stayed until I recovered which was about a week after the Regiment had left here for Richmond (about the 7th June) In company with MR Barron (now DR) I joined the Regiment at Richmond encamped near the Reservoir where this Camp Winder Hospital is now situated & from which I now write this short history of myself & my works for your future pleasure,

gratification and instruction—The Regiment left Richmond about the 16th June & went by R. road to Manassas Junction thence 1½ miles above to a large field on the R. road, where we Encamped in tents & established a hospital in tents for the sick, of which there were many soon with measles & Typhoid fever—DR A[Andrew] W[allace] Thomson as Surgeon & myself as Asst-Surgeon to the Regiment worked well together doing all that we could for the comfort and relief of the patients—At this place we fared well in plenty to Eat, the anxiety of mind and Separation from Your Mother & You were the only causes of my troubles—These however I soon learned to bear with patience & fortitude. This camp was in Prince William County & was called Camp Walker in honor of Genl. Walker then of the Confederate army. Here we remained until the 17th July when we were ordered to prepare three days rations & march to a point just a short distance this side of Centreville, and take position in a cluster of woods near the Road so as to cover the retreat of Genl Bonham, who would leave Fairfax that night—All through the night the heavy lumbering of the Artillery waggons [sic] could be heard passing along the road to Mitchell's Ford as I and DR Thomson lay in the ambulance not far from the Regiment. At daybreak Genl Beauragard aide came to us in a hurry and told us to get back to McClanes ford as soon as possible as the Enemy was in our rear but a short distance—The Regiment & us with the ambulance made good time back to McClanes ford which we reached about 8 O'clock in the morning & began throwing up temporary breastworks against the Expected attack of the Enemy, Had we remained 20 minutes longer in the woods we would have been Surrounded & cut to pieces as the Yankee prisoners said who was taken in the fight of that day July 18th. The Enemy did not attack us at McClanes ford, but at Blackburns ford when they were met by the Georgia, La. & Va troops under

James Rufus Bratton, MD. Born in 1821, Dr. Bratton served in the Confederate army as a surgeon in Virginia under General Lee. On President Jefferson Davis' flight to Mississippi Davis spent the night in Bratton's Yorkville home. During the Ku Klux Klan era Bratton was accused of being a high official in the Klan; he fled to Canada to escape capture by federal agents (courtesy of the Museum of Western York County, Sharon).

Genl Longstreet & driven back with heavy loss, our loss about sixty killed, wounded & missing.

Our Regiment was not immediately Engaged though under fire of The Shells during the fight which began at 11 O'clock & lasted until 5 P.M. The wounded were carried to McClanes barn a Stone building at which the Yankees frequently shot though the hospital Yellow Flag was flying from its top — I assisted in dressing the wounds of men from other Regiments that Evening, some of whom died as soon as they were brought-in.

After dressing the wounded & whilst going from the Hospital across the field with DR. T to our Regiment several shots from the Rifled cannon called "Long Tom" were fired at us — one of which struck in four feet of my head after I had thrown myself on the ground to avoid the shell. Fortunately it did not burst — To Escape the Shells & the sight of the Enemy we were compelled to roll our bodies into a branch which ran through the field with high banks — This movement shielded us from their view & their shells — here we remained for a few minutes when we made our escape afterwards across the field in double quick time to our Regiment still at its post at the ford — here we remained until the fight on Sunday July 21st when we had another battle in which our Regiment had hot work late in the afternoon about 5 O'clock in Charging over a large broken field upon the Yankee batteries, which the enemy ran off with & thereby saved their batteries. Our Regiment lost _____ Killed & about thirty wounded DR T & myself were all that night (Sunday) to near day break busy in amputating limbs and dressing wounds. It was a gloomy weary day. My anxiety for myself though in rear of the Regiment exposed the whole time to flying & bursting shells & for Napoleon[1] who was on the field made me deeply sad & how thankful I was, when the battle was over that we should both meet again unhurt. I shall never forget the scene nor my feeling on that night when I went to the Camp & found Napoleon unhurt. Next morning by daylight I was ordered to take a squad of men with me, proceed to the battle ground & collect the balance of the wounded under a white flag — but the enemy had gone, leaving much of their camp equipage & provisions — The few of our wounded left on the field during the night was dressed & sent back to the Hospital The dead were collected on the center of the field & wrapped in their blankets with their hats over their faces were buried there — This was a solemn scene long to be remembered — This was on Monday a very wet day; we remained at our post until Wednesday (24th) when we were ordered forward nearer The Enemy; to our next Camp Called "Camp Pettus" — here we remained drilling every day until 12th August when the whole Brigade moved to Germantown beyond Centreville & left me in Chg of the Sick of the whole Brigade near about 400 men, with none to assist me but Barron & Meek then assistants — For the first week I had the hardest work of the Campaign — Here I remained for three weeks when the sick were sent back to the different hospitals of their respective Regiments & I took my sick to Makeley's church on Braddock Road. Here I attended the sick & sent away all that were able, to Richmond & others places & remained until the 15th of Octr, when I was ordered to rejoin my Regiment at Germantown & afterwards at the Camp near Fairfax C. House—In a few days we were ordered to fall back to our Entrenchments around Centreville, where we remained during the winter, Whilst at Germantown & Fairfax our Regiment whilst on Picket had frequent skirmishing with the Enemy—but with no loss to us—During the winter Centreville was the muddiest filthiest hole I ever Saw, & here I & Napoleon were attacked with Pneumonia & lay in the tent all the time—Meek, Barron, Bona & Myself slept together & so crowded were we that in a cold night when one turned all had to turn together to keep the cover on him—We with Dr T & his Brother the Major & their two Boys Bill & Dennis—& our two Frank & Sam made our mess—Frank afterwards was put in jail at Williamsburg for stabbing Dr Thomson's boy & Sam died with Pneumonia at Centreville & was buried there under an apple tree—Many a Sad thought ran through my weary mind whilst here & I was glad when we left on 8th March for Yorktown by Richmond; we reached Yorktown down the River by Boats thence by land on or about the 26th April. Here we lay on the side of Warrick Creek behind our fortifications for two weeks under the daily shelling of the Enemy.

 Having remained with the Regiment for more than two weeks over the Expiration of my time I volunteered (12 months) with the Consent of Col Jenkins and Genl Anderson Commg Brigade I left the Regiment for Richmond with the view to get a position in a hospital, where I would not be so much Exposed to the weather as I had become subject to Rheumatism. I stood my Examinations before the Army Med Board for Asst Surgeon, passed favorably & was ordered by the Surgeon Genl to report to DR A.G. Lane Chief Surgeon of this Hospital. On May 3rd 1862 I was placed on duty at the 1st Division—The rest of the buildings were called barracks and were occupied by Soldiers, many of whom were sick with Fever Typhoid—measles Diarrhea &c—I was ordered in a few days to organize more Hospitals out of the barracks buildings—DR Lane organized The second division, whilst I organized the 3rd, 4th & 5th Divisions—repaired the buildings with men detailed for the purpose—arranged the wards & their furniture, bedding &c—appointed the officers, cooks, ward masters, nurses & attendants for the three hospitals & then was placed by DR Lane in Charge of the 4th Division May 24th 1862. During this Year there were treated in this Hospital 4488 patients—many of whom were the wounded sent in from the battle fields around Richmond—I performed a number of amputations this year nearly all of whom got well—In this year DRS J.J. OBannon of Barnwell So Car & Frank Spencer of Maryland was with me—whose society & assistance I enjoyed very much. The Surgeon GenL after promising DR Lane that I should be promoted to the Surgery finally refused to do So, unless I stood my Exam—for full Surgeon before the Army Med. Board, Still sitting in Richmond—I was examined the 2nd January 1863 & received my appointment as full Surgeon on the 6th of Same month and continued on duty in the 4th Division—The result of my examination was Satisfactory to me since it made me independent of the Surgeon GenL & any one else. I stood upon my own merits, and by these was willing to rise or fall—This is the course I would advise You to adopt in life—arise with all Your

Energy — Put on all your efforts both of body & mind, regardless of apparent obstacles and difficulties and with the determination to succeed, and with a consciousness of the rectitude of Your course, guided by an all wise Providence let Your Motto ever be "Upwards & Onwards."

I have still Charge of this Hospital at this time Sept. 16th 1863 & will continue unless this winter climate affects my health, leaving me with a cough — Up to this date this Hospital has treated 2271 cases more wounded men this year than last, from Chancellorsville and Gettysburg. The wounded from Chancellorsville were badly wounded & I performed a number of amputations both of legs & arms & tied the Femoral Artery at its middle third — with success — the brachial & the Occipital Arteries with success — One amputation died — a case from No Carolina — Your Mother with Andral[2] then large enough to talk & run about & Moultrie nursing at her breast with Mahala & Nancy as nurses visited me in Richmond in September 1862 & I boarded them at Mr. Johnsons near the Hospital — We had a pleasant time together. They came on the last of August and Stayed until the 6th of Octr — 1862 — In January 1863 I went home on furlough stayed thirty days & returned to duty on the 3rd of August 1863 I also visited home & although I was not well still the pleasure of Your Mothers Company and you four boys Louis, Jonnie, Andral & Moultrie gave me much consolation & comfort — and I often wished that such times could last longer or even always (To be continued).

I continued in Chge of 4th Division until Octr 12th 1863 when GenL Bragg of the Tennessee Army having asked for more Surgeons for his army, twenty Surgeons from Richmond was sent by order of Secry of War to The Army of Tennessee — I reported to the Med Director S.H. Strait of that Army who being then at Marietta Geo. ordered me to La Grange Geo to take Charge of a Division there — Here I found the Hospital in need of much improvement both in facilities for preparing food and other Comforts for the Sick and their bedding &c — All of this however I was Enabled to supply in a few weeks. DR Williams (a nice old Gentleman from Va. who was on duty with me at Winder Hospital & who was sent with myself to La Grange) and I messed with a DR Jones & his family & DR Amman from Baltimore for two months (Novr & Decr) when we discerned that they were ____mmate rascals in stealing the candles & Sugar of the mess — we dissolved our association with such men and determined never again to be associated with any men north of the Potomac unless we knew them well beforehand — At La Grange DR W. and myself boarded with a Mrs. Gay & her Mother Mrs. Ware from the 1st Jany 1864 until the 12th May 1864 — With them we were living Comfortably and I regretted leaving very much — We paid $100 per month for board — La Grange was a beautiful and Comfortable little Town with fine residences and well cultivated gardens of flowers and vegetables a sum index of wealth, intelligence and refinement. On the 12th May 1864 I was ordered by Surgeon Strait Med. Director to proceed to Madison Geo and take Charge of all the Hospitals (named The Asylum, Blacke and Strait Hospital) as Surgeon of the Post. This promotion was as sudden as it was unexpected as I did not seek it — I found all the Hospitals here containing only 700 beds — I extended the Capacity immediately to 1050 and added another Hospital which I called "Rebecca Hospital" in honour of Your Mother and all other good women like her — This was the Baptist College and the Boarding house connected with it — It was a favorite with the Ladies of the Town and they paid great attention to the sick and wounded who were sent there — Madison was also just such a place as La Grange — The Ladies were very generous & Kind though the men seemed very fond of money and asked highest prices for all their property: Sugar was selling then for $10 per LB One old Baptist Elder asked me $10 for a Split bottom Chair — which prices of course I would not pay — I made many pleasant acquaintances there among them, COL Walkers family, WM Wade, Col. Reese, and Burney family (whose daughter Julia very handsome and intelligent often gave me some sweet music) — also the family of Mr. Holderman refuges from Kentuck and Col Clarke & wife — The CoL was wounded in the arm and I attended him and saved his arm — also attended to his wife during her sickness — I boarded at MR Thomassons a very pleasant house for $125 per month and promised myself much pleasures in the Expected visit of Your Mother with Andral & Moultrie to me at Madison in August or Septr but the Yankee army having destroyed the Railroad between Madison and Atlanta thereby cutting the Hospital from communication with the Med. Director — having burnt also the public buildings at Covington a Town twenty miles from Madison also a place called Social Circle, and threatened eny [sic] moment to attack Madison. Notwithstanding their expected attack I determined to remain with the sick and wounded of my Hospital at all hazards and not forsake my post of duty. Here I remained until the Evening of the 23Rd July when I received an order from DR Strait Med. Director instructing me to remove my Hospital from Madison to Augusta Geo. on account of the Yankee Raiders who threatened eny moment to come into the Town.

I obeyed the order reluctantly and sent out an order to all the Hospitals to get ready all their stores for Shiping to Augusta — At one O'clock that night (Saturday) we left Madison in the train for Augusta — with our Hospital Stores &c. all were unwilling to leave but the order had to be obeyed — When the Citizens heard I was going to move the Hospital they became much more alarmed than before and began immediately to pack up and take out with them all their valuables into the Country — It was a trying scene to witness the ladies in the Streets asking what they must do and the waggons loaded with furniture &c going at a rapid pace in all directions.

When I looked upon these scenes the question would often present itself to me why are these things permitted to be so imposed upon us by the Yankees; I prayed that the day of retribution would soon come when justice long withheld should be meted out to these ruthless invaders of our Country — we arrived in Augusta with the Hospitals on Sunday 4 O'clock P.M. when I was telegraphed by DR Strait from Macon to reopen my Hospitals in Milledgeville Geo. where I arrived on the night of the 28th July and the Hospital at Oglethorpe University — The buildings of which are admirably adapted for hospital purposes — I am boarding now at a private house with DR W.R. Lewis (who I forgot to mention began duty with me at Madison July 6th at $120 per month — The board is very high considering the quality but we must remember these are war times & war prices —(To be continued).

I was Engaged with the Hospitals as Post Surgeon when GenL Sherman & Stoneman entered it on the 19th Novr 1864 with their army on their way to Savannah. I was taken prisoner and remained so for 5 or 6 days with permission to visit the Hospitals but not to leave the lines —

After Sherman passed through and the army of GenL Hood followed there being no regular army of the west behind, I made application for transfer from Georgia to the Armies then in South Carolina — which was granted. I left Milledgeville about the last of March, passed through Washington Ga, Abbeville, Newberry & Union & by Sister Elizabeth Walker at Pacolet, where I got a carriage & horse and came directly on home with the matron of the Hospital Mrs. Campbell — This route was made nearly on foot except a few miles of Rail Road in Geo & S.C. Arriving at home about the 9th of April I met Soldiers coming from Va. who Stated that GenL Lee had surrendered his Army — I then concluded to remain a few days at home to learn all the particulars of the Surrender, during these days President Davis and his Aids & Cabinet came into Town on their retreat to the Trans Mississippi army. President Davis with his aids COL Taylor and Lubbuck stayed at my house all night. The citizens gathered around the house to see and offer their tokens of respect & Sympathy for him and the cause for which he contended. President Davis appeared to be somewhat fatigued in body and depressed in Spirits, though easily aroused with his native fire. He caressed and spoke kindly to my 4 boys, Louis, John, Andral & Moultrie — and when he left me in the morning & bade us good bye he observed, "do not expect anything just or right from the abolition Yankee — They will never grant You Your rights." What became of him afterwards history will tell You — In a day or so more GenL Sherman in No Ca and this ended the contest...."

Chapter Notes

Introduction

1. South Carolina governor Daniel Henry Chamberlain's declination of an invitation to the New England Society in Charleston, 1875.
2. Edmund L. Drago, *Hurrah for Hampton* (Fayetteville: University of Arkansas Press, 1998), 10.
3. Ibid., 9. "Waving of the bloody shirt" was equivalent to the more modern "Remember Pearl Harbor" or "Remember 9–11."
4. Walter Brian Cisco, *Wade Hampton* (Washington, DC: Brassey's, 2004), 225–226.
5. "Red Shirt Revolution," *Yorkville* (SC) *Enquirer*, 26 September 1911.
6. Clark Robinson Starnes, *My Reminiscences of the Civil War*, dictated 30 January 1921 to his son, William Clark Starnes, for the Ann White Chapter of the United Daughters of the Confederacy, Rock Hill, South Carolina.
7. "York County Red Shirts," *Yorkville Enquirer*, 1 September 1911.
8. Drago, *Hurrah for Hampton*, 9.
9. *The Encyclopedia of South Carolina* (New York: Somerset, 1993), 49.

Chapter One

1. Archie Vernon Huff, Jr., *Greenville: The History of the City and County in the South Carolina Piedmont* (Columbia: University of South Carolina Press, 1995), 18–19, 24. Captain John Jefferys of Union County, who served in the Indian War of 1776, reported he helped bury Anthony Hampton (Draper Collection, 23 vv 254–8, State Historical Society, Wisconsin).
2. Ibid., 44.
3. Manly Wade Wellman, *Giant in Gray* (New York: Scribner's, 1949), 15.
4. Walter Edgar, *South Carolina: A History* (Columbia: University of South Carolina Press, 1998), 271.
5. Wellman, *Giant in Gray*, 15.
6. Edgar, *South Carolina*, 276.
7. Wellman, *Giant in Gray*, 27.
8. Ibid., 34.
9. Ibid., 28.
10. Ibid., 32.
11. Ibid., 32.
12. Ibid., 47.
13. Ibid., 50.

Chapter Two

1. "Temper of the South," *New York World*, reprinted in the *Yorkville Enquirer*, 31 August 1865.
2. "The Admirable Conduct of the South," *Washington Intelligencer*, reprinted in the *Yorkville Enquirer*, 31 August 1865.
3. Some 845 persons in South Carolina, 650 of whom had property valued in excess of $20,000, were granted a "Special Presidential Pardon" upon application (John S. Reynolds, *Reconstruction in South Carolina, 1865–1877* (Columbia: State, 1905), 14–15).
4. "I, ___, do solemnly swear (or affirm), in the presence of Almighty God, that I will henceforth faithfully support and defend the Constitution of the United States and the Union of the States there under, and that I will in like manner abide by and faithfully support all laws and proclamations which have been fade during the existing rebellion with reference to the emancipation of slaves. So help me God."
5. Reynolds, *Reconstruction in South Carolina*, 13–14.
6. Archie Vernon Huff, Jr., *Greenville: The History of the City and County in the South Carolina Piedmont* (Columbia: University of South Carolina Press, 1995), 154.
7. "Public Meeting," *Yorkville Enquirer*, 17 August 1865.

8. Ibid. York County Democratic groups with special interests formed at least two other tickets: the "Soldier's Ticket" and the "People's Ticket."
9. Reynolds, *Reconstruction in South Carolina*, 17. Under the Constitution as it then existed, Congress was to meet on the first Monday in December *after* it was elected. This was changed in 1933 by the adoption of the Twentieth Amendment, which stipulated that Congress was to meet on 3 January following the year of election and would not expire until 3 January two years later.
10. "Garrison for Yorkville," *Yorkville Enquirer*, 28 September 1865.
11. James Lawrence Orr was appointed Minister to Russia in March 1872. He died in St. Petersburg, Russia, on 5 May 1873.
12. A second section of that amendment gave Congress the power to enforce the article by "appropriate legislation" and set forth a powerful precedent. While the first eleven amendments to the Constitution limited the powers of the federal government, the Thirteenth Amendment made way for the next six, which restricted the powers of the states and expanded those of the federal government.
13. Willis Mason West and Ruth West, *The American People* (Norwood, Massachusetts: Norwood, 1948), 456fn.
14. It is interesting to note that at this time (1865) state conventions in Wisconsin, Connecticut and Minnesota denied voting rights to their black citizens. During 1867 and 1868 Minnesota, Michigan, Ohio and Kansas by popular vote rejected giving suffrage to the black man (West & West, *The American People*, 456 fn).
15. Thomas Keneally, *American Scoundrel* (New York: Doubleday, 2002), 107–108.
16. Ibid., 115.
17. Ibid., 121.
18. Ibid., 122–125.
19. Ibid., 125, 128–129.
20. Ibid., 130.
21. Keneally, *American Scoundrel*, 334–346.
22. Ibid., 317–322.
23. Ibid., 323–324.
24. Ibid., 325.
25. Ibid., 333.
26. "South Carolina Redeemed," *Yorkville Enquirer*, 23 November 1865.
27. Reynolds, *Reconstruction in South Carolina*, 48.
28. Eric McKitrick, *Andrew Jackson and Reconstruction*, New York: Oxford University Press, 1960, 12.
29. Ibid., 14.
30. Reynolds, *Reconstruction in South Carolina*, 32.
31. The *Yorkville Enquirer* reported that 1,641 votes were cast in the election held in York County on 13 November 1866. Robert H. Glenn was elected sheriff, defeating E.A. Crawford, David G. Wallace, E.M. Kirkpatrick and John J. Wylie. J.N. McElwee defeated J.C. Chambers and S.C. Youngblood to win a seat in the South Carolina legislature.
32. "The Past Year," *Yorkville Enquirer*, 3 January 1867.
33. E.R. Craven, "The Log Cabin of Neshaminy and Princeton University," *Journal of the Presbyterian Historical Society* (1902): 203.
34. Reynolds, *Reconstruction in South Carolina*, 50; Samuel Eliot Morison and Henry Steele Commager, *The Growth of the American Republic*, New York: Oxford University Press, 1937, 487–488; McKitrick, *Andrew Jackson*, 482n.
35. Morison and Commager, *American Republic*, 488–489.
36. Ibid.
37. Appointed to the Boards of Registration for York County were P.J. O'Connell, F.M. Walker, E.E. McCaffrey, Hugh Simpson, H.A.D. Neely, Leroy Crook, Matthew Williams, J.A.J. Graham.
38. "The Union League," *Yorkville Enquirer*, 23 October 1867.
39. William Bigger, "The Black and Tan Republicans of the South" (Florence, SC: Francis Marion University, 2003).
40. Jerry L. West, "Return of the Republicans, 1932: A Crucial Year" (Sharon, SC: Broad River Notebook, 2000).
41. Ibid.
42. "Union Republican Convention," *Yorkville Enquirer*, August 1867.
43. "Registration Fun," *Yorkville Enquirer*, 22 August 1867.
44. "Registration in York District," *Yorkville Enquirer*, 22 August 1867.
45. Ibid.
46. Ibid.
47. James M. McPherson, *Ordeal by Fire: The Civil War and Reconstruction* (Boston: McGraw-Hill, 1982), 598.
48. Ibid., 597–598. While Southerners across the region constantly decried "Black Rule," only South Carolina could correctly lay claim to these situations. Only in South Carolina did blacks have the majority of both houses.
49. "The Conservative Convention," *Yorkville Enquirer*, 14 November 1867.
50. Military Order No. 98, issued by General E.R.S. Canby on 16 October 1867, ordered the election.
51. "The Convention Election," *Yorkville Enquirer*, 28 November 1867.

52. "Election Incidents," *Yorkville Enquirer*, 28 November 1867.
53. In obedience to General Canby's General Order No. 160, issued 28 December 1867.
54. William E. Rose later replaced Major Thomas B. Lee as superintendent of the state penitentiary after Lee had been falsely accused of cruelty to black prisoners.
55. Reynolds, *Reconstruction in South Carolina*, 78.
56. "To the Citizens of York District," *Yorkville Enquirer*, 2 April 1868. Because an election was determined by a majority of registered voters rather than those voting, an election could be declared invalid due to voter participation.
57. "The Conservative Mass Meeting," *Yorkville Enquirer*, 9 April 1868.
58. "A New Garrison," *Yorkville Enquirer*, 9 April 1868.
59. Edgar, *South Carolina*, 397–398.
60. "The Result of the Election," *Yorkville Enquirer*, 23 April 1868.
61. "The Late Election," *Yorkville Enquirer*, 23 April 1868.
62. "Colored Conservatives," *Yorkville Enquirer*, 23 April 1868.
63. "Conservative Clubs," *Yorkville Enquirer*, 21 May 1868.
64. "A Happy Family," *Yorkville Enquirer*, 11 May 1868.
65. Ibid.
66. Ibid.
67. Bruce Catton, *Bruce Catton's Civil War* (New York: Fairfax, 1984), 292–293, 304.
68. "The Mass Meeting," *Yorkville Enquirer*, 31 August 1868.
69. Formerly the South Carolina Sixth Regimental Band.
70. "The Mass Meeting," *Yorkville Enquirer*, 31 August 1868.
71. Ibid.
72. "The Mass Meeting," *Yorkville Enquirer*, 24 September 1868.
73. Alfred B. Williams, "Prostrate State Stirs with New-Found Hope," *The State* (28 November 1926).
74. "The Clark's Fork Meeting," *Yorkville Enquirer*, 15 October 1868; "Colored Democratic Club," *Yorkville Enquirer*, 1 October 1868.
75. "The Clark's Fork Meeting," *Yorkville Enquirer*, 15 October 1868.
76. "The Compromise of Debts," *Yorkville Enquirer*, 8 September 1868.
77. Ibid.
78. Several decades earlier the county had been divided into two regiments for raising militia.
79. "The Republican Meeting," *Yorkville Enquirer*, 15 October 1868.
80. "Soldiers in Yorkville," *Yorkville Enquirer*, 22 October 1868.
81. "Voting," *Yorkville Enquirer*, 22 October 1868.
82. "The Election," *Yorkville Enquirer*, 22 October 1868.
83. "Tuesday Next," *Yorkville Enquirer*, 22 October 1868.
84. "Every Vote Counts," *Yorkville Enquirer*, 22 October 1868.

Chapter Three

1. "Murders and Outrages," *Yorkville* (SC) *Enquirer*, 12 November 1868.
2. Jerry L. West, *The Reconstruction Ku Klux Klan in York County, South Carolina, 1865–1877* (Jefferson, NC: McFarland, 2002), 47.
3. Walter Brian Cisco, *Wade Hampton: Confederate Warrior, Conservative Statesman* (Washington, DC: Brassey's, 2004), 204–205).
4. Walter Edgar, *South Carolina: A History* (Columbia: University of South Carolina Press, 1998), 400.
5. Ibid., 399.
6. Ibid., 401.
7. West, *The Reconstruction Ku Klux Klan*, 116.
8. Edgar, *South Carolina*, 401.
9. Chamberlain had previously served as assistant to United States district attorney and chief prosecutor David T. Corbin, who prosecuted a number of men accused of being members of the Ku Klux Klan.
10. Hampton M. Jarrell, *Wade Hampton and the Negro* (Columbia: University of South Carolina Press, 1949), 42–43.
11. "Red Shirt Day," *Yorkville Enquirer*, 5 September 1911.
12. "Red Shirt Reunion," *Yorkville Enquirer*, 29 September 1911.
13. Ibid.
14. Allan D. Charles, *The Narrative History of Union County, South Carolina* (Greenville, SC: Press Printing, 1997), 234.
15. "Red Shirt Day," *Yorkville Enquirer*, 5 September 1911.
16. Papers of Senator I.D. Witherspoon, Museum of Western York County, Sharon, SC.
17. Ibid.
18. Ibid.
19. William Arthur Sheppard, *Red Shirts Remembered* (Atlanta: Ruralist, 1940), 36.
20. On 12 March 1889, Dr. Thomas McDow of Charleston, a ne'er-do-well drunk,

murdered Dawson. Before his death, Dawson had confronted McDow about stalking Dawson's pretty Swiss governess, Hellene Burdoron. McDow shot and killed the publisher and attempted to hide the body in his cellar, but he was captured the following day.

21. Sheppard, *Red Shirts Remembered*, 39.

22. John Hannibal White was a blacksmith by trade and served as a member of the 1868 Constitution convention. He was elected to the South Carolina House of Representatives in 1868 and to the Senate in 1872, serving until 1876. He died in the Freedman's Hospital in Washington, DC, 26 July 1878.

23. "Public Meeting," *Yorkville Enquirer*, 6 January 1876.

24. Although born and well known in South Carolina, Hampton had been only an occasional visitor to his home state; he lived on a Mississippi plantation that had yielded him $100,000 in 1860. One South Carolina newspaper reported that he and E.B.C. Cash were two men who had not consorted with Radicals.

25. Bertram Wyatt-Brown, *The Shaping of Southern Culture* (Chapel Hill: University of North Carolina Press, 2001), 278.

26. Papers of Governor D.H. Chamberlain, Columbia: SC Department of Archives & History, Box 11, Folder 15.

27. Sheppard, *Red Shirts Remembered*, 66, 67.

28. Ibid., 70–71.

29. Papers of Governor D.H. Chamberlain, Columbia: SC Department of Archives & History, Box 12, Folder 17.

30. Ibid., Folder 20.

31. Sheppard, *Red Shirts Remembered*, 80.

32. Jarrell, *Wade Hampton and the Negro*, 42.

33. Hampton had filed bankruptcy on 24 December 1868, confessing to more than $1,042,000, not including nearly $12,000 in bank interests and unknown amounts due to unknown creditors.

34. Sheppard, *Red Shirts Remembered*, 85, 88. Although Gary was ecstatic that Hampton wanted to run on the Straight-Out ticket, he would later become embittered when Hampton began working with African Americans and Fusionists.

35. Manley Wade Wellman, *Giant in Gray* (New York: Scribner's, 1949), 243–244.

36. A letter from President Grant to Governor Chamberlain dated 26 July 1876 (Papers of Governor D.H. Chamberlain, Columbia: SC Department of Archives & History, Box 13, Folder 28).

37. Hamburg was generally recognized as a seat of misrule and bad government ruled by Prince R. Rivers, an ex-slave of a Beaufort family. Rivers was a member of the legislature and major general of the militia. One of the first things Hampton did after the election, in order to establish a legal claim to the office of the governor, was to fire Aiken County trial justice Rivers.

38. Sheppard, *Red Shirts Remembered*, 89–90.

39. Ibid., 90.

40. Ibid., 92.

41. Ibid., reprinted in Manly Wade Wellman, *Giant in Gray* (New York: Scribner's, 1949), 244; Walter Brian Cisco, *Wade Hampton* (Washington, DC: Brassey's, 2004), 218.

42. "Red Shirt Revolution," *Yorkville Enquirer*, 26 September 1911.

43. Sheppard, *Red Shirts Remembered*, 146.

44. Cisco, *Wade Hampton*, 218.

45. Edmund L. Drago, *Hurrah for Hampton* (Fayetteville: University of Arkansas Press, 1998), 7–8.

46. *The State*, "Radicals Close Ranks for '76 Campaign" (12 September 1926).

47. Alfred B. Williams, "Radicals Close Ranks for '76 Campaign," *The State* (12 September 1926).

48. Ibid.

49. James Conner was one of Wade Hampton's field officers, serving as a major in the Hampton Infantry.

50. Sheppard, *Red Shirts Remembered*, 94.

51. Alrutheus Ambush Taylor, *The Negro in South Carolina During the Reconstruction* (New York: AMS, 1971), 240.

52. Ibid., 241.

53. Barry Goode, "Another Presidential Race Too Close to Call," *San Francisco Chronicle*, 13 November 2000.

54. Sheppard, *Red Shirts Remembered*, 94–97.

55. Ibid., 99–108.

56. Ibid., 108. Judge Mackey, as well as Thompson Cooke, had joined the ranks of the Scalawags shortly after the end of the Civil War.

57. Benjamin Chad Simpson, *Heroes or Hoodlums: The White Southern Republicans in Reconstruction South Carolina* (Charleston, SC: College of Charleston, 1997), 191.

58. W.W. Dixon, *American Life Histories: Manuscripts from Federal Writer's Project, 1936–1940*, Project 1655, Dr. Samuel B. Latham, 96 years old.

59. Sheppard, *Red Shirts Remembered*, 114–116.

60. Ibid., 120.

61. Cisco, *Wade Hampton*, 220.

62. Alrutheus Ambush Taylor, *The Negro in South Carolina During the Reconstruction* (New York: AMS, 1971), 239–240.

63. "Red Shirt Day," *Yorkville Enquirer*, 5 September 1911.
64. Jarrell, *Wade Hampton and the Negro*, 3.
65. Ibid., 68.
66. Ibid., 69.
67. Drago, *Hurrah for Hampton*, 10.
68. "Latest Wave of the Bloody Shirt," *Yorkville Enquirer*, 12 October 1876.
69. 4 September 1876, Papers of Governor D.H. Chamberlain, Columbia: SC Department of Archives and History, Box 14, Folder 25.
70. "Letter from Chester," *Yorkville Enquirer*, 15 March 1877.
71. Robertson, who had served as a "special agent" in York County, was placed before Governor Hampton for appointment as county treasurer. Though he was nominated by a number of people, W.C. Beaty of western York County wrote Hampton that he hoped the governor would not give him the appointment as he had been a resident of York County for only a few years and was hardly known by anyone west of the town of York (Papers of Governor Hampton, Columbia: South Carolina Department of Archives and History, Box 2, Folder 3). Robertson was appointed county treasurer on 28 May 1876 (Appointment of County Officers, Columbia: South Carolina Department of Archives and History, 198).
72. Wellman, *Giant in Gray*, 258.
73. Taylor, *The Negro in South Carolina During the Reconstruction*, 242.
74. Drago, *Hurrah for Hampton*, 31.
75. *Greenville Enterprise and Mountaineer*, 19 October 1876, quoted by Drago, *Hurrah for Hampton*, 31.
76. This group probably took its name from a post Civil War song entitled "Josiphus Orange Blossom," made popular by Christy's, a well-known blackface minstrel (Charles Earle Funk, Jr., *Horsefeathers and Other Curious Words* (New York: HarperCollins, 1958), reprinted in *2107 Curious Word Origins, Sayings & Expressions* (New York: Galahad, 1993), 877).
77. Wellman, *Giant in Gray* (New York: Scribner's, 1940), 258–259.
78. J.B. Grimball papers, E.B. Munro to his mother, 9 November 1876.
79. *Yorkville Enquirer*, 12 October 1876.
80. Alfred B. Williams, *Hampton and His Red Shirts* (Charleston: Walker, Evans, Cogswell, 1935), 224.

Chapter Four

1. Walter Brian Cisco, *Wade Hampton* (Washington, DC: Brassey's, 2004), 229.
2. Ibid., 229–230.
3. "Letter from Chester," *Yorkville Enquirer*, 21 September 1876.
4. "Republican State Convention," *Yorkville Enquirer*, 21 September 1876.
5. Chamberlain was embarrassed to be on the same ticket with Dunn, who had opposed his nomination, and Elliott, who had been outspoken about the governor not being trustworthy.
6. Cisco, *Wade Hampton*, 230.
7. Manly Wade Wellman, *Giant in Gray* (New York: Scribner's, 1949), 262.
8. "Meeting at Hickory Grove," *Yorkville Enquirer*, 21 September 1876.
9. The principle component of the 1868 constitution, the Democrats believed, was to levy taxes so heavily that land would go up for public auction by the sheriff and it would fall into other ownership ("Red Shirt Day," *Yorkville Enquirer*, 5 September 1911).
10. John Monk, "2000 Election Drama Mirrors Mess of 1876," *The State* (12 November 2000).
11. Papers of Governor D.H. Chamberlain, Columbia: SC Department of Archives and History, Box 14, Folder 34.
12. After the 1876 election Aiken County continued to be overwhelmingly Democratic; but in 1932, the county Republican Party placed its first woman to seek the office of state senator. Clara Harrigal switched to the Republican Party a short time before the political wrestling match between Republicans Hambright and Joe Tolbert; and when Hambright gained control of the state party, she "gained considerable authority." Harrigal was the daughter of Joseph Geiger Harrigal, an Aiken County Confederate veteran who claimed to have voted 36 times in the election of 1876 (*Yorkville Enquirer*, "Miss Clara for Senator," 11 October 1932).
13. Alfred B. Williams, "Prostrate State Stirs with New-Found Hope," *The State* (28 November 1926).
14. After Hampton took office these rifles were collected and issued to the state militia.
15. Alrutheus Ambush Taylor, *The Negro in South Carolina During the Reconstruction* (New York: AMS, 1971), 244–245.
16. Wellman, *Giant in Gray*, 263.
17. "Discussion Near Blairsville," *Yorkville Enquirer*, 28 September 1876. George Tilman was a brother of Benjamin "Pitchfork" Tilman, who would later become governor of South Carolina.
18. Ibid.
19. Ibid.
20. Ibid.
21. Ibid.

22. Ibid.
23. Ibid.
24. Ibid.
25. Ibid.
26. Papers of Governor D.H. Chamberlain, Columbia: SC Department of Archives and History, Box 14, Folder 39.
27. Ibid. About a dozen ex–Confederates had heard about the secret shipment of arms and had confiscated them for use by the Red Shirts.
28. William Arthur Sheppard, *Red Shirts Remembered* (Atlanta: Ruralist, 1940), 147.
29. "Proclamation," *Yorkville Enquirer*, 12 October 1876.
30. Papers of Governor D.H. Chamberlain, Columbia: South Carolina Department of Archives and History, Box 14, Folder 6.
31. "Latest Wave of the Bloody Shirt," *Yorkville Enquirer*, 12 October 1876.
32. Sheppard, *Red Shirts Remembered*, 147–148.
33. Ibid.
34. Ibid.
35. Papers of Governor D.H. Chamberlain, Columbia: South Carolina Department of Archives and History, Box 14, Folder 12.
36. Ibid., Folder 15.
37. Shortly after Hampton's nomination, James B. Bynum, editor of the *Benefactor*, purchased the other Rock Hill newspaper, the *Grange*, which was owned by Dr. T.C. Robertson, and placed them under one banner, the *Hampton Herald* ("A Look Back: Evolution of a Newspaper," *Rock Hill [SC] Herald*, 17 April 1997).
38. Perhaps the reason the North Carolina delegation came to the Rock Hill rally was due to Captain John Wilson Marshall, a Confederate veteran (b. 1841) who had organized and commanded Marshall's Cavalry, a Red Shirt organization composed of men from Fort Mill in York County and lower Mecklenburg County, North Carolina. In August 1911, Marshall's Red Shirts were reorganized in preparation for a county reunion that was scheduled for 4 September and a state event on 27–28 September. J.W. Marshall, living in Rock Hill at the time, was elected captain. Other officers elected were as follows: first lieutenant, S.H. Eppts, Sr.; second lieutenant, B.M. Faris; first sergeant, W.H. Crook; second sergeant, J.L. Kimbrell; and color bearer, W.R. Warren ("Fort Mill Red Shirts," *Yorkville Enquirer*, 1 September 1911).
39. "The Meeting at Rock Hill," *Yorkville Enquirer*, 12 October 1876. There is no mention of a club known as the Catawba Rifles; but in 1880, a black man testified at a trial that the reason the home of Captain Allen Jones was set afire by Parks Cooper and John Campbell was because it was believed it contained weapons belonging to the Catawba Rifles.
40. Red Shirts present for the parade came from Lancaster, Chester, Smith's Turnout, Fort Mill, Shiloh, Rock Hill (black), Rock Hill (white), India Hook, Ebenezer and Fishing Creek. Also, the Rock Hill Saber Club and the Chester Saber Club were present.
41. Alfred B. Williams, *Hampton and His Red Shirts* (Charleston: Walker, Evans, Cogswell, 1935), 275.
42. "Death of Union League," *Yorkville Enquirer*, 10 October 1924. Assisting Coward with the column for Hampton's welcome were D.C. McKinney, W.B. Smith, J.W. Colcock, W.W. Gaffney, G.J. Steele and William Smith Wilkerson. The column numbered about 600 and was composed of York County men from Bullock's Creek, King's Mountain, McConnellsville, Clay Hill, Bethel, Rock Hill, Hickory Grove, Cherokee, Ebenezer and Yorkville.
43. It may have been at this parade that eleven-year-old James N. Russell had come up with the Blairsville and Bullocks Creek contingent riding a mule and using an old quilt as a saddle. About two hundred men from that area were led by a Captain Thompson. With them was a black man who said he was a Democrat but who, after spending some time in York and drinking, began talking like a Republican. The black man was beside Russell when the captain leaned over and slapped him with the side of his saber, knocking the man off his mount.
44. Williams, *Hampton and His Red Shirts*, 279.
45. Alfred B. Williams, "Radicals Close Ranks for '76 Campaign," *The State* (12 September 1926).
46. John A. Leland, *A Voice from South Carolina* (Charleston: Walker, Evans & Cogswell, 1879), 164–165.
47. May 1876 (Papers of Governor D.H. Chamberlain, Columbia: SC Department of Archives and History, Box 12, Folder 20).
48. Letter to Chamberlain, Papers of Governor D.H. Chamberlain, Columbia: SC Department of Archives and History, Box 14, Folder 16.
49. Ibid., Box 14, Folder 18.
50. Wellman, *Giant in Gray*, 264.
51. *Charleston (SC) News and Courier*, 31 October 1876; Cisco, *Wade Hampton*, 239–240.
52. Cisco, *Wade Hampton*, 242–244.

Chapter Five

1. Advertisement, *Yorkville Enquirer*, 2 November 1876.
2. "The Meeting Last Saturday," *Yorkville Enquirer*, 9 November 1876.
3. "Making of York County," *Yorkville Enquirer*, 21 October 1924.
4. "Views and Interviews," *Yorkville Enquirer*, 4 December 1926.
5. "In the Days of Old," *Yorkville Enquirer*, 19 December 1922.
6. Ibid.
7. Ibid.
8. Ibid.
9. Years later, when Benjamin Tilman was governor of the state and was attending a Red Shirts reunion in Anderson, he dismissed Hampton as being gullible by believing that 16,000 blacks had voted for him in 1876. Typical of Tilman, at the reunion he took the low road and believed it was the high road, glorifying the violence and threats of the Red Shirt campaign and the Hamburg Massacre (Bruce E. Baker, *What Reconstruction Meant* (Charlottesville: University of Virginia Press, 2007), 61).
10. Manly Wade Wellman, *Giant in Gray* (New York: Scribner's, 1949), 268.
11. Walter Brian Cisco, *Wade Hampton* (Washington, DC: Brassey's, 2004), 246.
12. Wellman, *Giant in Gray* (New York: Scribner's, 1940), 268–269.
13. Ibid., 269–270.
14. Cisco, *Wade Hampton*, 247–248.
15. Ibid., 247.
16. There were reports that the Democrats brought in thousands of white men from Georgia to vote in Laurens and Edgefield counties, where they illegally voted for Hampton (John Monk, "2000 Election Drama Mirrors Mess of 1876," *The State* (12 November 2000)).
17. Alrutheus Ambush Taylor, *The Negro in South Carolina During the Reconstruction* (New York: AMS, 1971), 253.
18. Trials of those suspected of Klan activities in the Western District of South Carolina began in Columbia on 27 November 1871. Seated at this session of the U.S. circuit court were circuit judge Hugh L. Bond of Baltimore and district judge George S. Bryan of Charleston District. Bond had not wanted Bryan to share the bench because he had previously hampered convictions in Greenville during August and September 1871. Bond was a Democrat, a former slave holder, and was viewed by the Radicals as too sectional in his thinking. Bryan took his seat with Bond at Wade Hampton's urging, believing Bond would promote justice and to keep the Radicals from having free rein over the court system.
19. Benjamin Harper Massey Papers, 1854–1910, Columbia, South Caroliana Library.
20. Wellman, *Giant in Gray*, 275.
21. "South Carolina Affairs," *Yorkville Enquirer*, 30 November 1876.
22. Cisco, *Wade Hampton*, 249.
23. "The South Carolina Legislature," *Yorkville Enquirer*, 7 December 1876.
24. Ibid. In the Republican calculation for a quorum, they did not recognize any elected official from the contested counties of Laurens and Edgefield.
25. Mackey was the nephew of Judge Thomas J. Mackey who had deserted the Republican Party and had become an avid worker for the opposition.
26. During the 1876 campaign, Thomas Hamilton, a prominent planter, had reminded the men of his race that their welfare depended on the prosperity of the white man.
27. Carolina Hall was located in the Southern Life Insurance Building three blocks from the State House.
28. Wellman, *Giant in Gray*, 276.
29. Ibid., 276–277.
30. "South Carolina News," *Yorkville Enquirer*, 7 December 1876. The same issue reported that Walter R. Jones, a black private secretary to Governor Chamberlain and the probate judge elect of Richland County, had died on 29 November.
31. "The South Carolina News," *Yorkville Enquirer*, 7 December 1876.
32. Ibid.
33. William Arthur Sheppard, *Red Shirts Remembered* (Atlanta: Ruralist, 1940), 172–173.
34. Thomas was identified by the *Charleston (SC) News and Courier* as "the mulatto chairman of the committee of privileges and elections" and had led both houses in opening prayers.
35. "The South Carolina Legislature," *Yorkville Enquirer*, 7 December 1876.
36. Ibid.
37. Cisco, *Wade Hampton*, 252.
38. "The Wallace House," *Yorkville Enquirer*, 14 February 1913. Mr. Henry Massey of Rock Hill found this letter among his father's personal items and gave it to be published in the local newspaper.
39. Hampton M. Jarrell, *Wade Hampton and the Negro* (Columbia: University of South Carolina Press, 1950), 107; Sheppard, *Red Shirts Remembered*, 74; "The State Legislature," *Yorkville Enquirer*, 7 December 1876.
40. Wellman, *Giant in Gray*, 283.
41. Sheppard, *Red Shirts Remembered*, 174–175.

42. Alfred B. Williams, *Hampton and His Red Shirts* (Charleston, SC: Walker, Evans & Cogswell, 1935), 415–416.
43. Sheppard, *Red Shirts Remembered*, 176.
44. Cisco, *Wade Hampton*, 253–254.
45. Sheppard, *Red Shirts*, 177.
46. Ibid., 177–178.
47. Sheppard, *Red Shirts Remembered*, 178. Wellman states in his *Giant in Gray* that Hampton spoke from one of the State House windows.
48. "The South Carolina Legislature," *Yorkville Enquirer*, 7 December 1876.
49. Wellman, *Giant in Gray*, 284.
50. "The South Carolina Legislature," *Yorkville Enquirer*, 14 December 1876.
51. Sheppard, *Red Shirts Remembered*, 181–182.

Chapter Six

1. Diary of Rutherford B. Hayes, Volume III, Chapter 34, p. 38, 21 December 1876. Some histories have credited this remark to Hampton, written in a letter Mackey later delivered to Hayes. While Hayes' diary does not personally credit Hampton, it may be understood that Roberts was speaking for the men collectively.
2. Manly Wade Wellman, *Giant in Gray* (New York: Scribner's, 1949), 285.
3. Ibid.
4. Benjamin Harper Massey Papers, 1854–1910, Columbia: South Caroliniana Library. This letter was written on 12 December 1876.
5. Hampton M. Jarrell, *Wade Hampton and the Negro* (Columbia: University of South Carolina Press, 1949), 112.
6. "The South Carolina Legislature," *Yorkville Enquirer*, 14 December 1876.
7. "South Carolina News," *Yorkville Enquirer*, 4 January 1877.
8. Jarrell, *Wade Hampton and the Negro*, 115.
9. William Arthur Sheppard, *Red Shirts Remembered* (Atlanta: Ruralist, 1940), 194.
10. Sheppard, *Red Shirts Remembered*, 186; "South Carolina Affairs," *Yorkville Enquirer*, 30 November 1876.
11. Jarrell, *Wade Hampton and the Negro*, 116.
12. Ibid., 115fn.
13. "Will Not Be Senator," *Yorkville Enquirer*, 14 December 1876.
14. Ibid.
15. Walter Brian Cisco, *Wade Hampton* (Washington, DC: Brassey's, 2004), 256. Hampton received 92,261 votes to Chamberlain's 91,127. Hampton's running mate, W.D. Simpson, was elected as lieutenant governor over R.H. Gleaves by a vote of 91,689 to 91,150.
16. Wellman, *Giant in Gray*, 285.
17. Ibid., 286.
18. Sheppard, *Red Shirts Remembered*, 183.
19. Wellman, *Giant in Gray*, 286–287.
20. Walter Edgar, *South Carolina: A History* (Columbia: University of South Carolina Press, 1998), 405.
21. Cisco, *Wade Hampton*, 258–259.
22. Sheppard, *Red Shirts Remembered*, 188–192.
23. "South Carolina News," *Yorkville Enquirer*, 23 November 1876.
24. When Hampton reorganized the state militia, he included an all black infantry at Charleston at the same time Connecticut was refusing to incorporate a black unit in that state.
25. Sheppard, *Red Shirts Remembered*, 184; Wellman, *Giant in Gray*, 287.
26. Allen W. Trelease, *White Terror* (Baton Rouge: Louisiana State University Press, 1971), 352.
27. Ibid., 379.
28. Sheppard, *Red Shirts Remembered*, 194.
29. Jarrell, *Wade Hampton and the Negro*, 113.
30. Banks in Charlotte, NC, had $40,000 belonging to the state when Hampton gave them orders not to pay out any amount without his approval (*Charlotte* [NC] *Democrat*, 23 December 1876).
31. "The Legitimate State Government," *Yorkville Enquirer*, 4 January 1877.
32. "The Feeling in the State," *Yorkville Enquirer*, 11 January 1877.
33. "The Hampton Contribution," *Yorkville Enquirer*, 1 March 1877.
34. "South Carolina News," *Yorkville Enquirer*, 1 February 1877.
35. Cisco, *Wade Hampton*, 239. Government tabulations reported York County had submitted $4,767.25 by 2 March.
36. Edgar, *South Carolina*, 405.
37. "Republican Meeting," *Yorkville Enquirer*, 15 February 1877.
38. Clay Hill, in the mid–northern section of York County, centered around an African American church established in 1869. Today the church is known as Liberty Hill A.M.E. Zion.
39. Edgar, *South Carolina*, 406.
40. Cisco, *Wade Hampton*, 261.
41. Diary of Rutherford B. Hayes, Volume III, Chapter 34, p. 396, 1 December 1876.
42. Ibid. Prior to the Hayes-Mackey meeting, Hayes received a dispatch from C.P. Lessile giving his impression of Mackey: "I warn you

to beware of Tom Mackey.... He is a first class fraud." Hayes commented: "This is a specimen of the Southern complications" (Ibid.).
43. "Gov. Hampton to Gov. Hayes," *Yorkville Enquirer*, 4 January 1877.
44. Sheppard, *Red Shirts Remembered*, 186.
45. Ibid.
46. Ibid., 187.
47. Ibid., 188.
48. "The Hayes-Mackey Interview," *Yorkville Enquirer*, 11 January 1877.
49. "Letter from Chester," *Yorkville Enquirer*, 4 January 1877.
50. "Mere Mention," *Yorkville Enquirer*, 18 January 1877.
51. Sheppard, *Red Shirts Remembered*, 187.
52. "Wade Hampton," *Yorkville Enquirer*, 18 January 1877.
53. "Judge Mackey on the Situation," *Yorkville Enquirer*, 18 January 1877.
54. Jarrell, *Wade Hampton and the Negro*, 115. Others believed the writer was James M. King, who had overheard Hampton and Gary talking at Abbeville about a suggestion that South Carolina Democrats ought to cease their support of Tilden for president.
55. Sheppard, *Red Shirts Remembered*, 188–192.
56. "Grant on South Carolina," *Yorkville Enquirer*, 1 March 1877.
57. "Editorial Inklings," *Yorkville Enquirer*, 22 February 1877.
58. "More About Hayes' Southern Policy," *Yorkville Enquirer*, 1 March 1877.
59. Barry Goode, "Another Presidential Race Too Close to Call," *San Francisco Chronicle*, 13 November 2000.
60. Diary of Rutherford B. Hayes, Volume III, Chapter 35, p. 425, 14 March 1877.
61. Ibid.
62. Sheppard, *Red Shirts Remembered*, 195.
63. David T. Corbin had been seated in the United States Senate on 13 February on credentials signed by Chamberlain as governor of South Carolina.
64. Jarrell, *Wade Hampton and the Negro*, 113.
65. "Editorial Inklings," *Yorkville Enquirer*, 15 March 1877.
66. Cisco, *Wade Hampton*, 262.
67. Papers of Governor D.H. Chamberlain, Columbia: South Carolina Department of Archives and History, Box 16, Folder 40.
68. Papers of Governor D.H. Chamberlain, Columbia: South Carolina Department of Archives and History, Box 2, Folders 3 and 13 is found a letter from R.W. Shad, confirming Strain did not support Hampton during the campaign and election.
69. Letter to Governor Hampton from James L. Strain, 12 January 1877, Papers of Governor Hampton, Columbia: South Carolina Department of Archives and History, Box 2, Folder 31.
70. Letter to Governor Hampton from James L. Strain, 6 February 1877, Papers of Governor Hampton, Columbia: South Carolina Department of Archives and History, Box 3, Folder 8, and Box 2, Folder 31.
71. Ibid.
72. Ibid., Box 17, Folder 14. Letter dated 2 April 1877.
73. Letter from Benjamin F. Briggs to Governor Hampton 5 February 1877, Papers of Governor Hampton, Columbia: South Carolina Department of Archives and History, Box 3, Folder 6.
74. Ibid., Box 16, Folder 31. Letter dated 2 February 1877.
75. Ibid., Box 16, Folder 33. Note dated January 1877.
76. Diary of Rutherford B. Hayes, Volume III, Chapter 35, p. 425, 14 March 1877.
77. "The Attitude of the Administration," *Yorkville Enquirer*, 29 March 1877. The president would later explain he delayed his decision because he did not want to act until his constitutional advisors had been appointed and then, when they were appointed, they had to give immediate attention to vacancies in civil service.
78. Cisco, *Wade Hampton*, 262–263.
79. Jarrell, *Wade Hampton and the Negro*, 114.
80. "Chamberlain in Washington," *Yorkville Enquirer*, 5 April 1877.
81. Cisco, *Wade Hampton*, 263.
82. Several days after Hampton's stop at Enfield, a fire swept the town and destroyed nine stores and dwellings with an estimated value of $50,000.
83. "Governor Hampton's Visit to Washington," *Yorkville Enquirer*, 5 April 1877.
84. Ibid.
85. Cisco, *Wade Hampton*, 265.
86. Ibid.
87. Joseph T. Derry, *Story of the Confederate States* (Harrisonburg, VA: Sprinkle, 1996), 436; "Editorial Inklings," *Yorkville Enquirer*, 18 January 1877; Williams, *Hampton and His Red Shirts*, 109. The *Yorkville Enquirer* reported that Company D of the Eighteenth Regiment, numbering about 40 men under the command of Captain R.L. Morris, arrived in Yorkville 29 July 1876 from Columbia and that Company C of the same regiment, which had been in Yorkville since 1871 and under the command of Lieutenant Brenner, had left for Columbia on 1 August.

88. Diary of Rutherford B. Hayes, Volume III, Chapter 25, p. 430, 22 April 1877.
89. "Hampton's Return to Columbia," *Yorkville Enquirer*, 12 April 1877.
90. "The Evacuation of the State House," *Yorkville Enquirer*, 19 April 1877.
91. Manning was a young cousin of Hampton's who dropped out of school and joined the Charleston Light Dragoons in 1861. He served Hampton as orderly during the war. Wade Manning was described as having diverse interests that ran the spectrum from classical scholarship and poetry to skill as a marksman and fistfighter. Governor Hampton appointed him as his secretary soon after his inauguration.
92. "The Formal Surrenders," *Yorkville Enquirer*, 19 April 1877.
93. "The Evacuation of the State House," *Yorkville Enquirer*, 19 April 1877.
94. Chamberlain returned to South Carolina in the early 1890s as the "Receiver of the South Carolina Railroad." Here he remained for three or four years and enjoyed much appreciation from both Republicans and Democrats.
95. Quoted by Wellman, *Giant in Gray*, 295.

Epilogue

1. Alrutheus Ambush Taylor, *The Negro in South Carolina During the Reconstruction* (New York: AMS, 1971), 278.
2. Ibid., 280.
3. John A. Leland, *A Voice from South Carolina* (Charleston: Walker, Evans & Cogswell, 1879), 209–212.
4. Hampton M. Jarrell, *Wade Hampton and the Negro* (Columbia: University of South Carolina Press, 1949), 135–136.
5. Ibid., 136.
6. While many ex–Klan members were suspected of being members of the Red Shirts, we know of one York County man, Leonidas Lowry Smith, who had fled to Arkansas and returned when he was no longer sought by the federals.
7. Ibid., 136–137.
8. Ibid., 138.
9. Walter Edgar, *South Carolina: A History* (Columbia: University of South Carolina Press, 1998), 412.
10. Ernest McPherson Lander, Jr., *A History of South Carolina, 1865–1960* (Chapel Hill: University of North Carolina Press, 1960), 28. The "Eight Box Law" was a compromise between Hampton moderates and Gary extremists.
11. William Watts Ball, *The State That Forgot* (Indianapolis: Bobbs-Merrill, 1932), 169.
12. Lander, Jr., *A History of South Carolina*, 28.
13. Diary of Rutherford B. Hayes, Volume 3, Chapter 36, p. 509.
14. Journal of Rutherford B. Hayes, at the Soldier Home near Washington, Vol. 3, Chapter 36, 5 October 1878.
15. W.W. Dixon, *American Life Histories: Manuscripts from the Federal Writers' Project, 1936–1940*, Project 3613, interview with Samuel D. Mobley of Chester County, 74 years old.

Appendix 1

1. J.E. Walmsley, *The Making of South Carolina* (Rock Hill, SC: Record, 1921), 29–30.

Appendix 6

1. His brother, Napoleon Bratton.
2. Andral Bratton followed in his father's footsteps, becoming a physician. As a result of his serving western York County for many years, a number of male children were named for him.

Bibliography

Baker, Bruce E. *What Reconstruction Meant.* Charlottesville: University of Virginia Press, 2007.

Ball, William Watts. *The State That Forgot.* Indianapolis: Bobbs-Merrill, 1932.

Catton, Bruce. *Bruce Catton's Civil War.* New York: Fairfax, 1984.

Charles, Allan D. *The Narrative History of Union County, South Carolina.* Greenville: A Press, 1997.

Cisco, Walter Brian. *Wade Hampton.* Washington, D.C.: Brassey's, 2004.

Craven, E.R. "The Log Cabin of Neshaminy and Princeton University," *Journal of the Presbyterian Historical Society* (1902).

Derry, Joseph T. *Story of the Confederate States.* Harrisburg, VA: Sprinkle, 1996.

Drago, Edmund L. *Hurrah for Hampton.* Fayetteville: University of Arkansas Press, 1998.

Edgar, Walter. *South Carolina: A History.* Columbia: University of South Carolina Press, 1998.

The Encyclopedia of South Carolina. New York: Somerset, 1993.

Genovese, Eugene D. *Roll, Jordan, Roll: The World the Slaves Made.* New York: Random House, 1974.

Goode, Barry. "Another Presidential Race Too Close to Call." *San Francisco Chronicle,* 13 November 2000.

Huff, Archie Vernon, Jr. *Greenville: The History of the City and County in South Carolina Piedmont.* Columbia: University of South Carolina Press, 1995.

Hunter, William H. "Short Stories/Tall Tales." *Southern Partisan* (Spring 1985).

Jarrell, Hampton M. *Wade Hampton and the Negro.* Columbia: University of South Carolina Press, 1940.

Lander, Ernest McPherson, Jr. *A History of South Carolina, 1865–1960.* Chapel Hill: University of North Carolina Press, 1960.

Leland, John A. *A Voice in South Carolina.* Charleston, SC: Walkers, Evans, Cogswell, 1879.

McKitrick, Eric. *Andrew Jackson and Reconstruction.* New York: Oxford University Press, 1960 (reissued 1988).

McPherson, James M. *Ordeal by Fire: The Civil War and Reconstruction.* Boston: McGraw-Hill, 1982.

Monk, John. "2000 Election Drama Mirrors Mess of 1876." *The State* (12 November 2000).

Morison, Samuel Eliot, and Henry Steele Commager. *The Growth of the American Republic.* New York: Oxford University Press, 1937.

Reynolds, John S. *Reconstruction in South Carolina, 1865–1877.* Columbia, SC: State, 1905.

Sheppard, William Arthur. *Red Shirts Remembered.* Atlanta: Ruralist, 1940.

Simpson, Benjamin Chad. *Heroes or Hoodlums: The White Southern Republicans in Reconstruction South Carolina.* Charleston, SC: College of Charleston, 1997.

Stampp, Kenneth M. *The Era of Reconstruction.* New York: Random House, 1965.

Starnes, Clark Robinson. *My Reminiscences of the Civil War.* Dictated 30 January 1921 to his son, William Clark Starnes, for the Rock Hill, SC, Ann White Chapter of the United Daughters of the Confederacy.

The State. "Radicals Close Ranks for '76 Campaign" (12 September 1926).

Taylor, Alrutheus Ambush. *The Negro in South Carolina During the Reconstruction.* New York: AMS, 1971.

Trelease, Allen W. *White Terror.* Baton Rouge: Louisiana State University Press, 1971.

Walmsley, J.E. *The Making of South Carolina.* Rock Hill, SC: Record, 1921.

Wellman, Manley Wade. *Giant in Gray.* New York: Scribner's, 1949.

West, Jerry L. *The Reconstruction Ku Klux Klan in York County, South Carolina, 1865–1877.* Jefferson, NC: McFarland, 2002.

_____. "Return of the Republicans, 1932: A Crucial Year." Sharon, SC: Broad River Notebook, 2000.

West, Willis Mason, and Ruth West. *The American People.* Norwood, MA: Norwood, 1948.

Williams, Alfred B. "Prostrate State Stirs with New-Found Hope." *The State* (28 November 1926).

Wyatt-Brown, Bertram. *The Shaping of Southern Culture.* Chapel Hill: University of North Carolina Press, 2001.

Primary Sources

Diary of Dr. James Rufus Bratton, Historical Center, York, S.C.

Diary of Rutherford B. Hayes.

Benjamin Harper-Massey Papers, 1854–1919, South Caroliniana Library, Columbia, S.C.

Papers of Governor D.H. Chamberlain, South Carolina Department of Archives and History, Columbia, S.C.

Newspapers

Charleston (SC) *Courier and News*

Yorkville (SC) *Enquirer*

Index

Academy Grove (Aiken) 77
Adams, Capt. Doc 69
Adger & Company 95
Adickes, H.F. 104
Alabama: Montgomery 18, 186; Tuskegee 184
Aldrich, Robert 80, 127
All Black Democratic Clubs 48
Allen, W. Scott 124
Allendale Mounted Baseball Team 101
Allison, Dr. Robert T. 91
Amnesty Act 22, 24, 27
Anderson, Tom 168
Arlington Hook & Ladder Company 104
Army Appropriation Act 36
Army of Northern Virginia 18
Arraim, Frank 94
Ashley River 95
Avery, Maj. James W. 25

Babbitt, C.J. 164
Ball, Col. Beaufort W. 67
Ball, William Watts 8
Bank of Charleston 15, 17
Baritz, J.H.W. 30
Battle of Brandy Station 66
Battle of Bull Run 18
Battle of Gaines' Mill 18
Battle of Seven Days 18
Battle of Seven Pines 18
Battle of South Mountain 75
"the Bayonet House" (Republican) 120
Belknap, William W. 74
Bell, Thomas J. 93
Benjamin, Judah 18
Benner, Lt. 111

Bennett, Scripio 122
Bethany (York County) 110
Bethel (York County) 110
Birchard, Sardis 75
Bird, Daniel 131
Black, William 86
Black, William C. 24
"Black and Tan" 40, 41
"Black Codes" 27, 28, 32, 34, 93, 98
Blair, Frank P, Jr. 48, 50
Blair, Samuel 111, 112
Blairsville (York County) 19, 97, 110, 111, 112
Blease, Gov. Cole 58
Blum, Elsie Larimore 180
Board of Canvassers 81, 113–120, 122
Board of Registration 42, 47
Bond, Judge Hugh L. 116
Brabham, William 122
Bradley, Justice Joseph P. 150
Bratton, Andrel 19, 20
Bratton, Col. Dr. J. Rufus 19, 20, 189
Bratton, John 19
Bratton, Gen. John 79, 80, 149
Bratton, Louis 19
Bratton, Mary 19
Bratton, Moultrie 19
Breckenridge, Gen. John C. 19
Brian, Sheriff James 104
Brice, Charles S. 65, 66
Briggs, Benjamin 155
Broad River (York County) 19, 83, 145
Brooks, Sen. Preston 34, 66, 67
Brown, John D. 121, 123
Brown, Samuel 112
Buchanan, Pres. James 28, 30
Bullock's Creek (York County) 107

209

Burgess' Mill 44
Butler, A.P. 7
Butler, Harrison 70
Butler, John 70
Butler, Gen. Matthew C. 61, 66, 67, 70, 77, 80, 85, 112, 120, 141, 144, 156, 157, 184
Butler, Gov. Pierce Mason 67
Butler, R.J. 70
Butler, Robert 69
Butler, Thomas 69, 70
Butterworth, Sam 30

Cain, Richard H. "Daddy" 71, 112, 113
Cameron, James D. 117
Cameron, Sen. Simon 137
Cantey, Mary 12
Cardozo, Francis L. 43, 89
Carolina Hall 119, 121, 122, 123, 131, 136, 139, 162
Carolina Military Institute (NC) 161
Cartter, Chief Justice David K. 137
Cash, Gen. E.B.C. 67
Cavaliers 3, 4
Cave, Silas 122, 127
Chafee, Ada 7
Chamberlain, Gov. Daniel H. 3, 4, 57, 59, 60, 61, 63–66, 68, 70–73, 77, 78, 83, 84, 86, 88–90, 91, 94, 96, 100, 101, 102, 108, 117, 119, 120, 129, 124, 125, 131, 134–136, 139–144, 150, 151, 155–160, 163
Chambers, J.C. 97
Chandler, Zechariah 114
Charleston Hotel 109
Charleston Jockey Club 12
Charlotte Cornet Band 102
Chase, Chief Justice Salmon 37
Cherokee (York County) 110
Chester Brass Band 50
Chester Rifle Club 65, 161
Chester Sabre Club 102
the Citadel 32, 78, 103, 170, 178–181, 184
Civil Rights Act of 1875 169
Civil War 3, 4, 8, 9, 17, 23, 31, 33, 48, 60, 62, 66, 75, 83, 170, 182
Clark's Fork Creek (York County) 51
Clay Hill (York County) 110
Clendenin, Robert 20

Clover (York County) 51, 59
The Clover Herald 40
Coate's Tavern (York County) 110
Coker, Simon 94
Collins, Zion 108
Colombia 31
Confederacy 2, 18, 98
Congaree River 12, 145
Congressional Investigating Committee 137, 138, 151
Conner, James 72, 80, 95, 159
Conservatives 4
Consolidation Act 60
Cook, Jim 70
Cooke, Judge 91, 96, 146, 147, 149
Cooke, Thompson 109
Cooper River 95
Corbin, David T. 70, 94, 141, 153, 168
Cothran, James S. 65, 90
Coward, Col. Asbury 8, 58, 59, 81, 103, 106, 110, 178–181, 184
Coyle, John F. 78, 79
Credit Mobilier 74
Crittenden, Stephen S. 122
Crofts, G.W. 70
Crosby, Dave 111
Cuba 32
Cureton, Capt. J.J. 134

Daniels, Henry 119
Darcey, Thomas 95
Davidson, Samuel 154
Davie, Rev. Francis 84
Davie, Flora 85
Davies, Nelson 92, 93
Davis, Justice David 150
Davis, Pres. Jefferson 3, 18, 19, 20, 21, 62, 108
Dawson, Francis W. 61, 63, 65
De Cregh, Caroline 32
Delaney, Martin R. 85, 108, 140
Delarge, Robert 42, 43
Democrat Executive Committee 61, 72, 89, 147
Democrat State Committee 55, 61–64
Democratic Clubs 39, 47, 49, 63, 86, 97
Democratic Rifle Clubs 107
Democratic National Convention 78
Democrats 4, 5, 6, 22, 27, 28, 33, 34,

36, 37, 48, 52, 55–57, 61, 66, 68, 70, 78, 83, 85, 86, 91, 93, 96, 101, 108, 123, 167
Dennis, J.B. 117–119, 121, 124
Domeriquy, Senora 32
Drakeford, Massey & Company 127
Duffy, Bridget 29, 30
Dunn, T.C. 89

Early, Gen. Jubal 146
Ebenezer (York County) 110
Edinburgh, Scotland 43
Edwards, C.E. 64
Edwards, Frank 93
Elliot, Robert B. 72, 88, 89
Epps, Martha 12
Evarts, William M. 153, 154, 156
Evins, Col. John H. 89, 92, 99, 106

Ferriter 122
Fifteenth Amendment 160, 169
Fifth Avenue Hotel 114
"First Baptist Church Sewing Circle" 101
Fisk, Jim 74
Fitzsimmons, Ann 12
Fitzsimmons, Christopher 12
Florida 5, 71, 114, 140, 150, 152
Flud, Harriet 12
Fort Mill (York County) 108, 116, 127, 134, 155
Fort Moultrie 65, 179
Fort Sumter 31
Fourteenth Amendment 35, 36, 99, 160, 169
Freedmen 35, 37, 42, 50
Freedmen Bureau 35, 37, 85
Freedmen's Bill 35, 37
Frémont, John C. 122
Furman University 87
"Fusionists" 61, 63, 65, 68, 71, 78, 79

Gains, Rubin 155
Garibaldi's Red Shirts 6
Gary, Gen. Martin W. 61, 63–70, 71, 77–80, 82, 85, 100, 112, 113, 118, 119–121, 131, 123, 141, 149, 169
Georgia, Augusta 69
Gettysburg, PA 29, 31
Getzen, Henry 69, 70

Gibson, John 124, 131
Gleaves, R.H. 89, 131, 133, 134
Glover, Arthur 124
Gordon, Sen. John B. 125, 133, 144, 159
Gould, Jay 74
Grant, Pres. Ulysses S. 6, 30, 32, 54, 56, 69, 73, 74, 76, 87, 89, 94, 101, 107, 115, 117, 125, 126, 134, 139, 144, 150–152
Gray 124, 125
Great Britain 23
Greeley, Horace 74
Green, C.S. 125
Greenville & Columbia Railroad 58, 60
Greenville Cornet Band 87
Grist, Elizabeth Lawrence 182
Grist, John E. 182
Grist, Lewis M. 41, 182
Guy, W.O. 111, 112

Hagood, Gen. Johnson 61, 67, 68, 80
Hambright, Carl 40
"Hambrighters" 40, 41
Hamburg Riot 7, 69, 70, 71, 72, 77, 85, 93, 100, 168, 174
Hamilton, S.P. 61
Hamilton, Thomas 119, 122, 128, 124, 126, 127, 139
Hampton, Ann 11
Hampton, Anthony 11, 12
Hampton, Christopher F. 15
Hampton, Edward 11
Hampton, Elizabeth 11
Hampton, Harriet 15
Hampton, John 11
Hampton, Mary 19, 21
Hampton, Preston 11, 17, 21
Hampton, Wade I 12
Hampton, Wade II 11, 12, 15, 16, 17
Hampton, Wade III 4, 57, 8, 9, 11, 13, 14, 15, 17, 18, 19, 21, 26, 49, 55, 61, 62, 66
Hampton Day 7, 102, 109
Hampton's Legion 18, 44, 184
Hare, Richard 178
Harlee, W.W. 79
Harrison, Richard 11
Hart, Maj. James F. 43–45, 63, 97, 99, 110, 142

Hart, John R. 45
Harvard Law School 75
Harvard University 85
Haskell, Alexander 71, 72, 82, 100, 101, 107, 115, 118, 123, 149, 153
Hayes, Lucy Webb 152, 153, 159
Hayes, Rutherford 75
Hayes, Pres. Rutherford Birchard 75, 114, 125, 126, 133, 138, 140, 144, 145, 147–152, 154, 156, 157, 159, 168–170
Hayes, Sophia Birchard 75
Hayne, H.F. 89
Hayne, Henry E. 134, 139
Haynes, Lt. 164
Henderson, D.S. 70
Henderson, Ed 140
Hendricks, Thomas A. 76, 79
Hiberian Hall 66
Hickory Grove (York County) 7, 91, 112
Hogue, James A. 7
Hoover, Pres. Herbert 40
"Hornet's Nest Rifles" 161
Hotchkiss, L. 108
Houmans Plantation 15, 16
Howard, Perry 40, 41
Hoyt, James A. 90, 149
Hubbard, Detective 123
"Hunkidories" 86, 87, 129, 130

Indian Affairs 74
Ingersoll, Col. Robert B. 76
Ivanhoe 3

Jackson, A.S. 122
Jackson, Andrew 7, 12, 35, 48
Jasper Guards 179
Jasper Light Infantry 179
Jenkins, Micah 178–180, 184
Jeter, T.B. 122
Johnson, Pres. Andrew 4, 522, 23, 25, 27, 28, 32, 33, 36–38
Johnston, Gen. Joseph 18, 19
Jones, A.O. 117, 119, 123
Jones, Col. Cadwalder 24–25

Keith, S.J. 125, 136
Kell, William 111, 112
Kennedy, James 89
Kennedy, John D. 79, 149

Kenyon College 75
Kershaw, Joseph B. 64, 65
Key, Francis Scott 29
Key, Gen. Philip Barton 29, 30
Keys, D.M. 156
Kimpton, Hiram 60
Kings Mountain Military Academy 31, 103, 178, 180, 181, 184, 185
Kings Mountain Railroad 186
"Kitchen Cabinet" 49
Ku Klux Klan 4, 6, 8, 32, 47, 55–58, 65, 71, 81–83, 86, 94, 96, 106, 141, 156, 168, 170, 171, 187, 189
Kuykendal, Cora Lee 104

Lamar, Sen. John 70, 133
Lathan, Rev. Robert 50, 51
Lathan, Dr. Samuel B. 78
Latta, Jane Elizabeth 184
Latta, William 184
Law, Gen. Evander McIver 43, 51, 184
Leaphart, S.L. 80
Leland, John A. 167
Lee, Gen. Robert E. 17, 18, 19, 23, 103, 179, 180, 184
"Lily Whites" 40
Limestone College 187
Lincoln, Pres. Abraham 4, 22, 23, 27, 31, 33, 77
Lipscomb, Col. James N. 67
"Live Oaks" 86, 87
London, England 43
London, J.R. 103
Louisiana 5, 14, 15, 71, 114, 140, 150–152, 160, 169
Lowry, Hattie 104
Lowry, Henry 86
Lowry, Dr. James M. 178
"Loyal Leaguers" 86

Mackey, Edward W.M. 119, 122, 128, 123–125, 130
Mackey, Judge Thomas J. 77, 78, 83, 90, 91, 96, 120, 138, 140, 145, 149, 154, 157, 161, 187
"Mackey House" (Republican) 121, 122, 123, 131, 133.134, 136, 137, 141
Maher, Judge John J. 70
Manning, John L. 65
Manning, Gov. Richard 80

Manning, Wade Hampton 140
Manning, Wade W. 164
Marble, Manton 90, 91
Marcy, William 28
Marion, Gen. Francis 184
Marshall, W.R. 119
Massey, Benjamin H. 116, 117, 127, 128, 134
May, W.S. 102
McAiley's Mill 89
McCary, George W. 157, 160
McCaw, Robert G. 43, 45
McConnellsville (York County) 42, 89
McCorkle, Col. W.H. 50
McDonald, Edward 86
McElwee, J. Newman 52
McFreely, William 149
McGowan, Gen. Samuel 61, 90, 141, 147
McIver, Henry 61
McKitrick, Eric 35
Mead, John W. 41, 46
Meade, Commander 31
Merrill, Col. Lewis 56, 106, 167
Mexican War 49, 78
Meyers, N.B. 124
Millwood Plantation 12, 13, 14, 18
Minor, James 55, 124
Mississippi 8, 14, 15, 17, 19, 21, 25, 59, 64, 71, 133
Mississippi Plan 71, 83, 101
"Mississippi Tiger Policy" 93
Mobley, Samuel D. 173
Moise, Captain E.W. 80, 105, 106
Moore, James 95
Morton, Sen. Oliver P. 6
Moses, Gov. Franklin 57–61, 64, 88, 101
Moses, Franklin J., Sr. 115
"Mother's Little Helpers" 101
Mount Holly (York County) 110
Myers, N.B. 122, 124, 127, 128

Nash, William Beverly 43, 137
National Democratic Convention 49, 50
National Republican Party 129, 167
Neagle, John L. 46
Netherlands 32
New England Society 3, 4, 73

New York City 31
Nicholls, Gov. Francis 151
Nichols, Joe M. 111
Nichols, John 111
Nix, Fred, Jr. 122
North Carolina 21, 30–32, 38; Cashiers 8, 13, 68, 115; Charlotte 12, 102, 161; Dan River 11; Flat Rock 13; Greensboro 18, 19, 31; "High Hamptons" 13, 21

O'Connor, M.P. 61
Ohio, Delaware 75
Oregon 114, 140, 152
Orr, Gov. James L. 26, 28, 30, 36, 123, 125, 139
Ould, Robert 30

Packard, Gov. Stephen 150, 153, 160
Panama 31
Paris, France 32
Parker, Gov. Francis W. 6
Parker, Niles G. 60
Parrish, Theodore 50, 51
Patterson, "Honest John" 58, 100, 108, 154, 160
Patterson's Green 90
Pelton, W.Y. 149
Pendleton Band 87
Perry, Gov. Benjamin F. 24, 25, 26, 28.65, 87, 100, 141
Perry, Commodore Matthew 67
Pickins, Gov. Andrew 18, 66
Pickins, Gov. Francis Wilkerson 67
Pierce, Pres. Franklin 28
Pinckneyville Ferry 19
Pool, J. Rufus 155
Porter, W.D. 26
Preston, Margaret 15
Preston, William 146
Price, Gen. Sterling 78
Pride, C.J. 108
Pride's Old Mill (York County) 110
Proclamation of Emancipation 49

Queen Isabella II 32

Radicals 4, 6, 9, 23, 26, 27, 33, 36, 37, 48, 61, 66, 70, 79, 82, 115, 120
Rainey, John L. 31

Index

Rainey, Joseph H. 169
Randall, Samuel 151
Ray, John 102
Reconstruction 4, 6, 9, 23, 28, 31, 33, 43, 57, 61, 74, 182
Reconstruction Acts 9, 36, 37, 39, 44, 48, 51, 98
Reed, George 127
Reedish, W.H. 120, 121
Reese, George R. 186
Reese, Jeannette Amelia 186
Reese, Mary Witherspoon 186
the Regulators 32
Reid, John C. 114
Republicans 4, 5, 22, 28, 32, 33, 34, 36, 40, 41, 42, 46, 49, 51, 55, 57, 59, 64, 66, 68, 70, 71, 72, 78, 80, 89, 91
Richardson, John S. 61, 139
Ridgely, Octavia 87
Rion, Col. James H. 79, 80, 89, 149
Rivers, Prince R. 69
Robert E. Lee Fire Company 87
Roberts, Col. 133
Robertson, Dr. T.C. 85
Robertson, Sen. Thomas J. 125, 134, 138, 147
Robinson, Lucius 76
Rogers, Col. W.K. 156, 159
Rock Hill (York County) 7, 40, 51, 85, 86, 90, 102, 108, 143
Rock Hill Rifle Club 103
Roosevelt, Franklin D. 85
Rose, William E. 46
Rose's Hotel 19
Ross, Rev. Robert A. 25, 51
Roundheads 3, 4
Ruger, Gen. Thomas H. 107, 12, 113, 117, 120, 121, 125, 126, 134, 136, 160, 164
"Rump Parliament" (Republican) 123
Rutherfordton 19

Sand Hills Plantation 17
Savannah River 69, 94
Sawyer, Claude E. 129
Saylor 137, 151
Schorb, John R. 104, 105
Scoggins, John Thomas 57
Scott, Gov. Robert 55, 56, 58–60, 167
Scott, Walter 3

Seller, W.W. 61
Seymour, Horatio 6, 49, 50
Sharon (York County) 51
Shaw, H.A. 124
Sheppard, John C. 65, 77, 78, 119, 124, 136, 139
Sheppard, William A. 145
Sherer, Hugh Hicklin 58
Sherman, Gen. W.T. 18, 19, 21, 107, 152, 160, 171
Sickles, Gen. Daniel E. 28, 29, 30–33, 38, 52
Sickles, Teresa 28, 29, 30
Simons, Thomas Y. 61
Simonton, Charles H. 79
Simpson, William D. 51, 54, 61, 80, 88, 90, 124, 131, 139, 140–142
Sims, R.M. 80, 102
Smalls, Robert 73
Smarr, J.M. 154
Smith, L.L. 7
Smith, Judge William 45
Smith, William B. 59
Smith's Ford (York County) 19
South Carolina 5, 6, 8, 9, 11, 12, 18, 21, 22, 24, 25, 27, 31, 32, 33, 35, 38, 42, 43, 68, 71; Abbeville 53, 55, 61, 90, 138, 140; Abbeville County 107, 127; Aiken 7, 70, 77; Aiken County 83, 94, 101; Allendale 101; Anderson County 8, 55, 87, 88, 145; Barnwell 80, 127; Barnwell County 61, 101, 122; Beaufort 53, 73, 109, 119, 122, 128; Blackstock 89; Cainhoy 108, 109; Carmel Hill 89; Catawba River 21; Charleston 3, 7, 11, 13, 32, 38, 42, 66, 68, 78, 79, 87, 95, 100, 103, 108, 109, 112, 115, 129, 150; Charleston County 61; Chester 53, 56, 65, 78, 84, 86, 89, 91, 102, 146; Chester County 42, 55, 61, 83, 144, 173; Chesterfield County 56, 61; Columbia 5, 12, 15, 19, 21, 39, 40, 43, 50, 52, 63, 68, 95, 103, 109, 115, 123, 125, 126; Cross Keys 11; Darlington 53; Darlington County 55, 125, 184; Edgefield 53, 131, 127; Edgefield County 32, 55, 61, 65, 67, 68, 70, 101, 107, 112, 115–118, 121, 134, 139, 140, 141; Ellenton 93, 94, 96, 107,

168; Fairfield County 56, 83; Georgetown 53, 109, 125, 170; Granitesville 7; Greenville 67, 87, 88, 108, 124; Greenville County 102, 103, 107, 122, 129, 145; Hamburg 69, 90, 93, 94; Hazelwood 89; Lancaster County 56, 78, 83, 89, 102; Laurens 53, 127, 141; Laurens County 11, 32, 55, 56, 61, 115–117, 121, 131, 134, 139; Lewis Turnout 89; Lexington 109; Lexington County 55, 145; Marion County 61, 79; Newberry 53; Newberry County 32, 55, 56, 125; Ninety-Six 40; Orangeburg 109, 120; Pinckneyville Ferry 19; Rich Hill 89; Richland County 15, 61; Rossville 89; Saluda River 144; Spartanburg 86; Spartanburg County 56, 107; Summerville 109; Sumter 80, 107, 121; Sumter County 61, 122, 139; Union 19, 52, 53, 86, 122, 133; Union County 19, 55, 56, 56, 61, 83, 88, 102; Walhalla 90; Williamston 8; Winnsboro 138; Yemassee 95; York County (District) 7, 19, 20, 21, 25, 31, 39, 47, 51, 55, 56, 83, 89, 107, 108, 142; Yorkville 7, 19, 21, 25, 45, 46, 47, 50, 51, 52, 53, 58, 78, 81, 86, 99, 101, 103, 110, 142, 143, 148, 155, 178–180, 184
South Carolina College 12, 15, 17, 78, 170, 186
South Carolina Democratic Convention 78
South Carolina Democrats 79–81
South Carolina Fifth Regiment "Palmetto Sharpshooters" 57, 78, 103, 179, 180, 189
South Carolina Second Regiment 164
South Carolina Third Battalion 57
South Carolina Twelfth Regiment 188
Southern Florida Military Institute 184
Spain 31, 32
Spanish-American War 67
Spencer, C.W.F. 188
Spencer, Charles E. 188
Stanton, Edwin M. 28, 30, 36, 37
Starnes, Clark R. 7, 131
The State That Forgot 8
Stephenson, Col. W.G. 181

Steven, Thaddeus 34, 35
Stewart, W.S. 108
Stone, William 70
Stoneman's Troops 19, 21
Stonewall Fire Company 102
"Straight-Outer" 61, 62, 64–66, 68, 71, 78–80, 110, 114, 137, 148
Strain, James L. 83, 84, 154, 155
Stuart's Cavalry 18
Stuckey, J.W. 80
Suffrage plan for African-Americans 62, 92, 115
Sumner, Sen. Charles 34, 66, 67
Sweargin, John 70
Sweetwater Sabre Club 7, 69

Tammany Democrats 31
Tammany Hall 8
Tennessee 36, 37, 156
Tenure of Office Act 36, 37
Texas 34
Thirteenth Amendment 4, 27, 33, 160
Thomas 125
Thomas, Col. W.H. 49, 50
Thompson, J.G. 165
Thomson, Dr. Andrew Wallace 189
Tilden, Samuel J. 50, 76, 78–80, 90, 91, 114, 125, 137, 138, 144, 147–151
Tillman, George D. 7, 97
Tirzah (York County) 110
Tolbert, John 89
Tolbert, Joseph "Tieless Joe" W. 40, 41
Toombs, Robert 90
Trinity Episcopal Church 12, 80, 172
Twelfth Amendment 114

Union Pacific Railroad 74
United States Eighth Infantry 53
United States Supreme Court 116
United States War Department 95
University of Glasgow 43

Vance, Gov. Zebulon 102
Vanderhost's Wharf 95
Virginia 17, 22; Appomattox 2; Richmond 8; Shenandoah Valley 8

Wagner, Jim 111
Wagner, John A. 67
Walker, John 65

Index

Walker, Gen. W.A. 102
Wallace, Alexander S. 92, 97–99, 105, 106
Wallace, W.A. 54
Wallace, Gen. William H. 61, 120, 122, 128, 130, 133, 134, 137, 141
"Wallace House" (Democrat) 121, 123–125, 131, 133, 134, 136, 137, 139, 141, 142, 44
Walnut Ridge Plantation 15
Walthall, Sen. Edward 133
War of 1812 12
Washington D.C. 52, 67, 91, 95, 129, 137–139, 141, 156–158, 160
Watson, John 7
Westbury, J.W. 121, 122
Wheeler, Gen. Joe 1
Wheeler, William A. 75, 125, 137, 138, 147
Wheeler house 140
Whipper, William J. 59, 61, 63, 64, 72, 88
"Whiskey Ring" 74
White, Fanny 8
White, Hannibal J. 46, 58, 63, 97, 98, 140, 143, 188
White, Sandy 155, 156
Whitesides" Mill 51
Wild Woods Plantation 15, 17, 66
Willard, A.J. 101, 115
Willard's Hotel 158

Williams, Alfred B. 71, 72
Williams, Sen. John 59
Williams, W.B. 121
Wilson, Col. William Blackburn 178, 186
Wilson's Chapel 97
Winthrop Training School (Winthrop University) 175
Witherspoon, Ann T. Reid 186
Witherspoon, Isaac Donnom, Jr. 97–99, 142, 186, 187, 188
Witherspoon, Isaac Donnom, Sr. 186
Witherspoon, Leslie 97
Wooldridge, George 30
Worth, Maj. W.S. 53
Wright, J.J. 115
Wright, Margaret 97, 186
Wright, Martha J. Spratt 186
Wright, W. 41
Wright, Col. William 97, 186
Wyatt, Col. D. 67

Yorkville 110, 155, 184, 186
Yorkville Colored Club 51
The Yorkville Enquirer 7, 33, 41–43, 47, 48, 51, 52, 93, 101, 110, 182
Yorkville Female Academy Institute 104
Yorkville Red Shirt Regiment 110
Youmans, LeRoy F. 89, 109